CAMBRIDGE STUDIES IN COMPARATIVE POLITICS

General Editor
PETER LANGE Duke University

Associate Editors
ROBERT H. BATES Harvard University
ELLEN COMISSO University of California, San Diego
PETER HALL Harvard University
JOEL MIGDAL University of Washington
HELEN MILNER Columbia University
RONALD ROGOWSKI University of California, Los Angeles
SIDNEY TARROW Cornell University

OTHER BOOKS IN THE SERIES

Series list continues on page after index.

POWER IN MOVEMENT

Social Movements and Contentious Politics

SECOND EDITION

Unlike political or economic institutions, social movements have an elusive power, but one that is no less real. From the French and American revolutions through the democratic and workers' movements of the nineteenth century to the post-Soviet, ethnic, and religious movements of today, movements exercise a fleeting but powerful influence on politics and society. This study surveys the history of the social movement, puts forward a theory of collective action to explain its surges and declines, and offers an interpretation of the power of movement that emphasizes its effects on personal lives, policy reforms, and political institutions. While covering cultural, organizational, and personal sources of movements' power, the book emphasizes the rise and fall of social movements as part of political struggle and as the outcome of changes in political opportunity structure, state strategy, and transnational diffusion.

Sidney Tarrow is Professor of Government at Cornell University. He is author of *Peasant Communism in Southern Italy* (1967), *Democracy and Disorder: Protest and Politics in Italy, 1965–1975* (1989), and *Struggle, Politics, and Reform: Collective Action, Social Movements and Cycles of Protest* (1989).

POWER IN MOVEMENT

Social Movements and Contentious Politics

SECOND EDITION

SIDNEY TARROW

CAMBRIDGE
UNIVERSITY PRESS

PUBLISHED BY THE PRESS SYNDICATE OF THE UNIVERSITY OF CAMBRIDGE
The Pitt Building, Trumpington Street, Cambridge CB2 1RP, United Kingdom

CAMBRIDGE UNIVERSITY PRESS
The Edinburgh Building, Cambridge CB2 2RU, UK http://www.cup.cam.ac.uk
40 West 20th Street, New York, NY 10011-4211, USA http://www.cup.org
10 Stamford Road, Oakleigh, Melbourne 3166, Australia

First published 1998

Printed in the United States of America

Typeset in Garamond 10½/12, Penta System [RF]

*A catalog record for this book is available from
the British Library*

Library of Congress Cataloging-in-Publication Data is available.

ISBN 0 521 62072 4 hardback
ISBN 0 521 62947 0 paperback

For Chuck,
a teacher

CONTENTS

FIGURES

PREFACE

Since the completion of the first edition of *Power in Movement* in 1993, more has happened in the field of contentious politics and social movements than in perhaps any five-year period since the late 1960s. The 1989 collapse of state socialism was already accomplished, but it was too soon for its lessons to be reflected in much scholarly work. Those largely peaceful movements led to states that have been far from stable; in some cases they led to violent and volatile movements and, in one case – the former Yugoslavia – produced a savage civil war. I have tried to absorb some of the lessons of those transformations into this edition of the book.

The events of 1989 and what followed also demonstrated something to which I alluded in the final chapter of the first edition, but still had very little purchase upon: the rapid diffusion of contention across national boundaries. I am still cautious about predicting a world of movement without borders, but particularly in western Europe, evidence is accumulating that European union may be triggering a new wave of movements that cross the boundaries of the nation-state. Even outside the West, transnational advocacy networks have grown up to resemble in some ways the national social movements that are the main subject of the book. These changes have become so insistent that they are accorded a separate chapter in this edition.

Students of social movements and contentious politics have not been inactive either since the publication of the first edition of *Power in Movement*. Both in Europe and North America – and, to an increasing extent, outside those areas – original research monographs and collective volumes have been appearing at a dizzying pace. Several new book series have been launched in this growing area of research, as well as a new journal – *Mobilization* – entirely dedicated to the study of contentious politics. Among the recent works that I have drawn on in this edition are Donatella della Porta's *Social Movements, Political Violence, and the*

State, Bert Klandermans's *The Social Psychology of Protest,* Hanspeter Kriesi and his collaborators' *The Politics of New Social Movements in Western Europe,* Alberto Melucci's *Challenging Codes*, and Charles Tilly's *Popular Contention in Great Britain.* A collective volume published in the Cambridge Studies in Comparative Politics, *Comparative Perspectives on Social Movements,* so closely matches the organization of Part II of this book that I owe a special debt to its editors, Doug McAdam, John D. McCarthy, and Mayer N. Zald.

Are we living in a "movement society"? I still don't claim to know the answer to this question, but a new conclusion raises the issues and spells out their implications more clearly than I was able to do five years ago. If this edition helps to illuminate the question of the movement society for scholars and students of social movements, it is in no small part due to my collaboration with David Meyer in a recent collective volume, *Towards a Movement Society: Lessons for a New Century.* I also wish to thank Mark Lichbach and Tom Rochon for their culturally sensitive and rationally sensible comments on a draft of this version of the book.

As the world has been producing new social movements and scholars have responded with new research, my own ideas have evolved too. Since the publication of the first edition of *Power in Movement,* I have tried to understand how social movement theory can be extended to the general study of contentious politics, to areas outside Western democracies, and to the comparative study of revolution. In this respect, I have profited richly from my participation in a closely knit research network of scholars working together on mapping contentious politics under the aegis of the Mellon Foundation and the Center for Advanced Study in the Behavioral Sciences. Thinking side by side with the other members of this project – both senior and junior – has helped me to synthesize my ideas. Especially my two co-workers in that project, "Mc" and "T2," have helped me to better clarify the conceptual relationship between social movements and contentious politics, and I thank them for it.

ACKNOWLEDGMENTS

L ike a social movement, a book is a collective action. Beneath the visible road signs of author and title, there lies a long collective history of scholarship and collaboration. This book has had a particularly long and collective intinerary, and many debts, institutional and personal, lie just under the surface of the road.

My curiosity about social movements began at the University of California at Berkeley. Berkeley in the 1960s was not only an incubator for social movement activity; it also provided a fertile and contentious environment for intellectual work. The study that resulted from my stay there, *Peasant Communism in Southern Italy*, owed an intellectual debt to four of my teachers there – David Apter, the late Reinhard Bendix, Ernst Haas, and Joseph LaPalombara.

Anyone interested in the history of social movements sooner or later comes to France. The colleagues who welcomed me in 1969 at the Centre d'Etudes sur la Vie Politique Française became willing friends and unwitting accomplices in shaping the thinking that appears in this book. I am particularly grateful to the late Annick Percheron, and to Guy Michelat, René Mouriaux, and Françoise Subileau, all of whom helped me organize a fruitful semester as a CNRS fellow in Paris in 1990, and to Danielle Tartakowsky of the University of Paris VII, who has generously shared with me her immense knowledge of historical contention in France.

Many of the ideas that have gone into this book came out of my research on the movements of the 1960s and early 1970s in Italy. The study that resulted, *Democracy and Disorder*, was the outcome of a productive year spent at the Center for Advanced Study in the Behavioral Sciences at Stanford in 1980–1 and of two subsequent research grants from the National Science Foundation.

Moving from systematic data analysis to historical and interpretive narrative was not easy for this author and I am grateful to the National Endowment for the Humanities for the interpretive research fellowship that helped me to do so.

A grant from the German Marshall Fund of the United States helped me examine the links between international politics and national movements. The NEH also sponsored four summer seminars for college teachers between 1985 and 1996 on histories of collective action, social movements, and revolutions, providing a venue in which many of the ideas in the study were developed. I wish to thank the forty-eight participants in those seminars for helping me to nurture many of the ideas that appear in this book. I have a particular debt to Doug Imig and David Meyer, who – from NEH participants – have became valued collaborators and friends.

Busy colleagues who take time to read other people's work are owed a special debt. For detailed and thoughtful comments on drafts of all or most of the chapters of the first edition of the book, I am grateful to Donatella della Porta, Mario Diani, Bill Gamson, Mary and Peter Katzenstein, Bert Klandermans, Hanspeter Kriesi, Doug McAdam, David Meyer, Frances Fox Piven, Dieter Rucht, Susan Tarrow, and Richard Valelly. Individual chapters or drafts of chapters were read and commented upon by Glenn Altschuler, Ron Aminzade, Ben Anderson, David Blatt, Stuart Blumin, Valerie Bunce, Ken Bush, Richard Cloward, Maria Cook, Seymour Drescher, Matthew Evangelista, Miriam Golden, Jeremy Hein, Lynn Hunt, Doug Imig, Margaret Keck, David Kertzer, David Laitin, John Markoff, Diarmuid Maguire, Pauline Maier, Gerry Marwell, John Meyer, George Mosse, Victor Nee, Pam Oliver, Chris Rootes, Bill Sewell, Marc Steinberg, Anne-Marie Szymanski, Sarah Tarrow, Marc Traugott, George Tsebelis, and Xueguang Zhou. Ben Anderson's work was the origin of the concept of "modularity" and he remains a sensitive and provocative critic. To these friends and colleagues I offer my thanks and my apologies if I was not able to assimilate all the wisdom they offered.

A number of Cornell associates contributed their skills to the project and added substantially to what value it may have. Anita Lee, Tomoko Owazawa, Andrea Pierce, and especially Sung Woo ran down ornery references, checked the spelling, and built the bibliographies for various chapters. Sarah Soule was able to shift from the role of student to that of collaborator, critic, and editor with grace and sensitivity. Eva Lotta Hedman convinced me that the relevance of the work was not limited to a corner of Europe and North America. The patience and good humor of Lynette Harvey, Carolyn Lynn, and Karel Sedlacek are also gratefully acknowledged.

I owe special thanks to three people for the role they played in this book's conception and completion. In over three decades of scholarly work, Charles Tilly has fashioned an approach to contention and social movements that shows that social research can both be theory-driven and within history; Peter Lange went beyond his role as general editor of the Cambridge Comparative Politics Series to encourage, cajole, poke, prod, and kibitz the author with a unique combination of theoretical rigor and political acumen; Mary Katzenstein was a source of thoughtful and encouraging advice without intruding her own discourse into the book's formation.

For more years than she may care to remember, Susan Tarrow has awakened to the sound of computer keys clacking in the next room, a racket that followed her from Ithaca to places as widespread as Elba, Florence, Oxford, twice to Paris, (a very wet) Quercy, and Sydney. The computer is indifferent to her suffering, but I will be eternally grateful for her forbearance and her love.

INTRODUCTION

International Herald Tribune, March 17, 1997. The lead story in today's *"Trib"* covers the refusal of the European Union to send troops to Albania to deal with the consequences of the collapse of a financial scheme that bankrupted hundreds of thousands of citizens. The riots produced by the scandal sent hordes of protesters and thugs into the streets, emptying the armories of guns and tanks as the Albanian armed forces collapsed, and with them the government's legitimacy. The *Trib*'s reporter notes the worrying parallel with the breakup of Yugoslavia in the early 1990s. He might also have recalled that the Albanian collapse was triggered by a peaceful movement in Serbia earlier in the year, when hundreds of thousands of protesters forced the government to restore the opposition's local election victories (see Chapter 6).

The same issue of the *Trib* features seven other stories relating to social movements, protests, and rebellions from around the world. Also on page 1 are a report on the armed rebellion in eastern Zaire and another on the peaceful march of Belgian, French, and Spanish workers to protest the recent closure of an auto plant in Belgium (see Chapter 11). Page 4 covers both a peaceful protest march of twenty thousand poor people in Thailand against a government development project and a violent clash between rival ethnic groups in Indonesia. Page 8 features brief reports of a gunfight between Algerian troops and the Islamic militants who have been locked in a savage civil war with the regime for the past five years, and on the Salvadoran elections, which promise to bring the Farabundo Marti National Front – a former guerrilla movement – into the government. Even the business pages cannot avoid contention: a story on page 15 describes the previous week's protest of German coal miners threatened with layoffs. One ordinary day's newspaper coverage: ten stories coming from places as different as Belgium and Borneo, indicating the continuing power of contentious politics and social movements.

1

CONTENTIOUS POLITICS AND SOCIAL MOVEMENTS

As the preceding examples suggest, ordinary people often erupt into the streets and try to exert power by contentious means against national states or opponents. In the past forty years, the American civil rights movement, the peace, environmental, and feminist movements, and revolts against authoritarianism in both Europe and the Third World have brought masses of people into the streets demanding change. They often succeeded, but even when they failed, their actions set in motion important political, cultural, and international changes.

Contentious politics occurs when ordinary people, often in league with more influential citizens, join forces in confrontations with elites, authorities, and opponents. Such confrontations go back to the dawn of history. But mounting, coordinating, and sustaining them against powerful opponents are the unique contribution of the social movement – an invention of the modern age and an accompaniment to the rise of the modern state. I argue in this book that contentious politics is triggered when changing political opportunities and constraints create incentives for social actors who lack resources on their own. They contend through known repertoires of contention and expand them by creating innovations at their margins. When backed by dense social networks and galvanized by culturally resonant, action-oriented symbols, contentious politics leads to sustained interaction with opponents. The result is the social movement.

How ordinary people take advantage of the incentives created by shifting opportunities and constraints; how they combine conventional and challenging repertoires of action; how they transform social networks and cultural frameworks into action, and with what outcomes; how these and other factors combine in major cycles of protest and sometimes in revolutions; and how the social movement is changing as we approach the twenty-first century – these are the main themes of this book.

These issues take on special importance given the vast spread and growing diversity of social movements today. First we witnessed the civil rights and the student movements; then ecology, feminism, and the peace movements, first in the United States and then in western Europe; struggles for human rights in authoritarian and semiauthoritarian systems; Islamic and Jewish religious extremism in the Middle East and Hindu militantism in India; and, more recently, antiimmigrant violence in western Europe, Christian fundamentalism in the United States, and ethnic nationalism in the Balkans and the former Soviet Union. Over the past four decades of the century, a wave of new forms of contention have spread from one region of the world to another.

Not all of these events warrant the term "social movement," which I reserve for those sequences of contentious politics that are based on underlying social networks and resonant collective action frames, and which develop the capacity to maintain sustained challenges against powerful opponents. But all are part of the broader universe of contentious politics, which can emerge, on the one hand, from within institutions, and can expand, on the other, into revolution. Placing the social movement and its particular dynamics historically and analytically within the universe of contention is a central goal of this study.

THE APPROACH OF THE STUDY

In this book, I do not attempt a history of either contentious politics or the social movement. Nor do I press a particular theoretical perspective on the reader or attack others – a practice that has added more heat than light to the subject. Instead, I offer a broad theoretical framework for understanding the place of social movements, cycles of contention, and revolutions within the more general category of contentious politics. Too often scholars have focused on particular theories or aspects of movement to the detriment of others. An example is how the subject of revolution has been treated until quite recently. It is mainly studied in relation to other revolutions, and almost never compared with the cycles of protest that it in some ways resembles or with social movements (but see Goldstone 1997). We need a broader framework with which to relate social movements to contentious politics and to politics in general.[1]

The irreducible act that lies at the base of all social movements, protests, and revolutions is *contentious collective action*. Collective action can take many forms – brief or sustained, institutionalized or disruptive, humdrum or dramatic. Most of it occurs within institutions, on the part of constituted groups acting in the name of goals that would hardly raise an eyebrow. Collective action becomes contentious when it is used by people who lack regular access to institutions, who act in the name of new or unaccepted claims, and who behave in ways that fundamentally challenge others or authorities.

Contentious collective action is the basis of social movements, not because movements are always violent or extreme, but because it is the main and often the only recourse that ordinary people possess against better-equipped opponents or powerful states. This does not mean that movements do nothing else but contend: they build organizations, elaborate ideologies, and socialize and mobilize constituencies, and their members engage in self-development and the construction of collective identities. Some movements are profoundly apolitical, and focus on their internal lives or those of their members. But even such movements, as sociologist Craig Calhoun reminds us, encounter authorities in conflictual ways, because it is these authorities who are responsible for law and order and for setting the norms for society (1994b: 21). Organizers use contention to exploit political opportunities, create collective identities, bring people together in organizations, and mobilize them against more powerful opponents. Much of the history of movement–state interaction can be read as a duet of strategy and counterstrategy between movement activists and power holders.

The theory of collective action is therefore where we must begin, but not without a word of caution: collective action is not an abstract category that can stand outside of history and apart from politics (Hardin 1982; 1995).[2] Contentious forms of collective action are different than market relations, lobbying, or representative politics because they bring ordinary people into confrontation with opponents, elites, or authorities. They have power because they challenge powerholders, produce solidarities, and have meaning within particular population groups, situations, and national cultures.

This means that we will have to embed the general formulations of collective action theory into the concrete record of history with the insights of sociology and political science and even anthropology. In particular, we will see that bringing people together in sustained interaction with opponents requires a *social* solution – aggregating people with different demands and identities and in different locations in concerted campaigns of collective action. This solution involves, first, mounting collective challenges; second, drawing on social networks, common purposes, and cultural frameworks; and, third, building solidarity through connective structures and collective identities to sustain collective action. These are the main processes of social movements.

THE BASIC PROPERTIES OF MOVEMENTS

With the emergence of the national social movement in the eighteenth century, early theorists focused on the three facets of movements that they feared the most: extremism, deprivation, and violence. Both the French Revolution and early nineteenth-century industrialism lent strength to this reaction. Led by sociologist Emile Durkheim (1951), nineteenth-century scholars saw social movements as the result of anomie and social disorganization – an image well captured in the phrase "the madding crowd" (see the review in McPhail 1991).

Whereas the late nineteenth and early twentieth centuries saw a "civilizing process" of many of these trends, the movements of the interwar period – fascism, nazism, stalinism – fit the image of violence and extremism fostered by the French and industrial revolutions. With the exacerbation of ethnic and nationalist tensions since the fall of communism in 1989–92, this negative view of social movements has been reinforced. We see it in the "ancestral hatreds" view of the Balkan conflicts of the 1990s, most of them uniformed by social movement theory.[3] We also see it in the wake of the militia movements in the United States in the 1990s and in antiimmigrant violence in Europe, both of which reevoke the horrors of the interwar years.

But these characteristics are polar cases of more fundamental characteristics of social movements. Extremism is an exaggerated form of the frames of meaning that are found in all social movements; deprivation is a particular source of the common purposes that all movements express; and violence is an exacerbation of collective challenges. Rather than seeing social movements as expressions of extremism, violence, and deprivation, they are better defined as *collective challenges, based on common purposes and social solidarities, in sustained interaction with elites, opponents, and authorities.*[4] This definition has four empirical properties: collective challenge, common purpose, social solidarity, and sustained interaction. Let us examine each of them briefly.

COLLECTIVE CHALLENGE

There are many forms of collective action – from voting and interest group affiliation to bingo tournaments and football matches. But these are not the forms of action most characteristic of social movements. Movements characteristically mount *contentious* challenges through disruptive direct action against elites, authorities, other groups, or cultural codes. Most often public in nature, disruption can also take the form of coordinated personal resistance or the collective affirmation of new values (Melucci 1996).

Collective challenges are most often marked by interrupting, obstructing, or rendering uncertain the activities of others. But, particularly in repressive systems, they can also be symbolized by slogans, forms of dress or music, or by renaming familiar objects with new or different symbols. Even in liberal democratic states, people identify with movements by words, forms of dress or address, and private behavior that signify their collective purpose.[5]

Contention is not limited to social movements, though it is their most characteristic way of interacting with other actors. Interest groups sometimes engage in direct challenges, as do political parties, voluntary associations, and ordinary citizens who have nothing in common but a temporary coincidence of claims against others. Nor are contentious challenges the only form of action we see in movements. Movements – especially organized ones – engage in a variety of other actions ranging from providing "selective incentives" to members, building consensus among current or prospective supporters, lobbying and negotiating with authorities, to challenging cultural codes through new religious or personal practices. In recent decades, just as interest groups and others have increasingly engaged in contentious politics, movement leaders have become skilled at combining contention with participation in institutions.

But despite their growing expertise in lobbying, legal challenges, and public relations, the most characteristic actions of social movements continue to be contentious challenges. This is not because movement leaders are psychologically prone to violence but because they lack the stable resources – money, organization, access to the state – that interest groups and parties control. In appealing to new constituencies and asserting their claims, contention may be the only resource movements control. Movements use collective challenge to become the focal points of supporters, gain the attention of opponents and third parties, and create constituencies to represent.

COMMON PURPOSE

Many reasons have been proposed for why people affiliate with movements, ranging from the juvenile desire to flout authority all the way to the vicious instincts of the mob. Some movements are marked by a spirit of play and carnival whereas others reveal the grim frenzy of the mob; however, a more basic – if more prosaic – reason why people band together in movements is to mount common claims against opponents, authorities, or elites. Not all such conflicts arise out of class interest, but common or overlapping interests and values are at the basis of their common actions.

Both the theory of "fun and games" and that of mob frenzy ignore the considerable risks and costs involved in acting collectively against well-armed authorities. The rebel slaves who challenged the Roman Empire risked certain death when they were defeated; the dissenters who launched the Reformation against the Catholic Church took similar risks. Nor could the black college students who sat in at segregated lunch counters in the American South expect much fun at the hands of the thugs who awaited them with baseball bats and abuse. People do not risk their skins or sacrifice their time to social movement activity unless they have good reason to do so.

SOLIDARITY AND COLLECTIVE IDENTITY

The most common denominator of social movements is thus "interest," but interest is no more than an objective category imposed by the observer. It is participants' recognition of their common interests that translates the potential for a movement into action. By mobilizing consensus, movement entrepreneurs play an important role in stimulating such consensus. But leaders can only create a social movement when they tap more deep-rooted feelings of solidarity or identity. This is almost certainly why nationalism and ethnicity or religion have been more reliable bases of movement organization than the categorical imperative of social class (Anderson 1990; Smith 1996).[6]

Is an isolated incident of contention – for instance, a riot or a mob – a social movement? Usually not, because participants in these forms of contention typically have no more than temporary solidarity and cannot sustain their challenges against opponents. But sometimes even riots reveal hints of a common purpose or solidarity. The ghetto riots all over America in the 1960s or in Los Angeles in 1992 were not movements in themselves, but the fact that they were triggered by police abuse indicates that they arose out of a widespread sense of injustice. Mobs, riots, and spontaneous assemblies are more an indication that a movement is in the process of formation than movements themselves.

SUSTAINING CONTENTIOUS POLITICS

Long before there were organized movements, there were many forms of contentious politics on the scene of history – from food riots and tax rebellions to religious wars and revolutions. It is only by sustaining collective action against antagonists that a contentious episode becomes a social movement. Common purposes, collective identities, and identifiable challenges help movements to do this; but unless they can maintain their challenge, they will either evaporate into the kind of individualistic resentment that James Scott calls "resistance" (1985), harden into intellectual or religious sects, or retreat into isolation. Sustaining collective action in interaction with powerful opponents marks the social movement off from the earlier forms of contention that preceded it in history and still accompany it today.

POLITICAL OPPORTUNITIES AS STRUCTURING CUES

Yet movements are seldom under the control of a single leader or organization; how can they sustain collective challenges in the face of personal fear or egotism, social disorganization, and state repression? This is the dilemma that has animated collective action theorists and social movement scholars over the past few decades. My strongest argument will be that changes in political opportunities and constraints create the most important incentives for initiating new phases of contention. These actions in turn create new opportunities both for the original insurgents and for latecomers, and eventually for opponents and power holders. The cycles of contention – and in rare cases, the revolutions – that ensue are based on the externalities that these actors gain and create. The outcomes of such waves of contention depend not on the justice of the cause or the persuasive power of any single movement, but on their breadth and on the reactions of elites and other groups.

AN OUTLINE OF THE BOOK

In the past twenty years, influenced by economic thought, political scientists and sociologists have begun their analyses of social movements from the puzzle that collective action is difficult to bring about. That puzzle is a puzzle – and not a sociological law – because, in so many situations and against so many odds, collective action *does* occur, often on the part of people with few resources and little permanent power (Lichbach 1995).

Examining the parameters of collective action is the first task of Chapter 1. But the chapter approaches two equally important problems: first, the dynamics of mobilization once it has begun; and, second, the reasons why movement outcomes are so varied and so often fail to achieve their stated goals. Although Chapter 1 outlines these theories in a general way, the evidence for them will be found in the movements and episodes analyzed in the remainder of the book.

In Part I of the book, I show how and where the national social movement developed in the eighteenth-century West, when the resources for turning collective action into social movements could first be brought together over sustained periods and across territorial space. The focus in Chapter 2 is on what I call, with Charles Tilly, the modern "repertoire" of collective action; then, in Chapter 3, I turn to the changes in society that supported that transformation;

and, in Chapter 4, to the relationship between state building and the crystallization of social movements. Once "modular collective action" was established, it was diffused through state expansion, print and association, and the diffusion of repertoires of contention across the globe. That is the argument of Chapters 2 to 4.

Even deep-seated claims remain inert unless they can be activated. Chapters 5 to 8 – the analytical core of the book – outline the main powers I see in movement. In Chapter 5, I turn to the changes in political opportunities and constraints that trigger episodes of contention. In Chapter 6, I outline the three main aspects of contentious politics that movements employ – violence, disruption, and conventional forms of action. In Chapter 7, I examine how symbolism and collective action "frames" mobilize supporters and help them to construct claims. In Chapter 8, I turn to the major forms of social solidarity that help to form movement organizations. These are the four main powers I see in movement.

In the third section of the book, I turn from these analytical aspects of contentious politics and social movements to their dynamics and outcomes.

From the late eighteenth century on, once the resources for sustained collective action became available to ordinary people and to those who claimed to represent them, contention could spread to entire societies, producing the periods of turbulence and realignment that I call "cycles of contention." As I show in Chapter 9, the importance of this change is that, once a cycle begins, the costs of collective action are lowered for other actors, and master frames and models of activism are diffused. The movements that arise in such contexts do not need to depend as much on internal resources as on the generalized opportunities in their societies, and elites respond less to single movements than to the general context of contention with which they must deal.

Such periods of generalized disorder sometimes result in immediate repression, sometimes in reform, often in both. But in political-institutional and personal-cultural terms, the effects of cycles go well beyond a movement's visible goals. They are found both in the changes that governments initiate and in the periods of demobilization that follow. They leave behind permanent expansions in participation, in popular culture, and in ideology, as I argue in Chapter 10.

This takes us to the contentious politics of the current epoch and to two important new issues: "globalization" and the possible rise of a "movement society." In the past few decades, a wave of democratization spread across the world, culminating in the dramatic changes in southern Europe in the 1970s, in Latin America in the 1980s, and in central and eastern Europe and Africa since 1989. In the 1990s, a new wave of "ugly" movements, rooted in ethnic and nationalist claims, in religious fanaticism, and racism broke out, bringing the world to a peak of turbulence and violence that it has not known for decades. Electronic communication and cheap international transportation have reinforced these connections, creating the possibility that the age of the national social movement may be ending. If national movements were linked to the rise of the modern state, the central question raised by these new waves of movement is whether they are creating a transational movement culture that threatens the structure and sovereignty of the national state. These questions I turn to in Chapter 11.

A final question will take us from the often violent transnational movements of the non-Western world to the more pacific civic movements associated with liberal democracies. Where protest and contention have become easy to mount and are largely legitimized, where police and power holders prefer to discuss tactics with movements rather than repress them, where the media or the courts often settle questions that were once fought over in the streets: in these conditions, will the social movement be absorbed and institutionalized into ordinary politics, as were the strike and the demonstration in the nineteenth century? Or will the sheer volume of contention submerge the routine processes of electoral and interest group participation in a turbulent sea of unruly politics?

Disruptive conflicts have surely broken out around the world in the 1990s, as they always do at the ends of wars and during the collapse of empires. But just as the election campaign and the strike were absorbed into institutional routines during the nineteenth century, many of the new forms of participation that have arisen since the 1960s are being domesticated at the end of the twentieth. The shape of the future will depend not on how violent or widespread contention has become but on how it is absorbed into − and transforms − the national state.

CONTENTIOUS POLITICS
AND SOCIAL MOVEMENTS

Contentious politics emerges in response to changes in political opportunities and constraints, with participants responding to a variety of incentives: material and ideological, partisan and group-based, long-standing and episodic. Building on these opportunities, and using known repertoires of action, people with limited resources can act contentiously – if only sporadically. When their actions are based on dense social networks and connective structures and draw on consensual and action-oriented cultural frames, they can sustain these actions in conflict with powerful opponents. In such cases – and *only* in such cases – we are in the presence of a social movement; when contention spreads across an entire society, as it sometimes does, we see a cycle of contention; when such a cycle is organized around opposed or multiple sovereignties, the outcome is a revolution. The solutions to the collective action problem depend on shared understandings, on dense social networks and connective structures, and on the use of culturally resonant forms of action. But above all, I believe, they are triggered by the ebb and flow of political struggle.

In this chapter, I lay out each of these factors as they will be used to describe, analyze, and raise questions about contentious politics and social movements in the rest of this book. Before doing so, however, it will be helpful to see how previous generations of activists and scholars conceived of the problem of collective action and its relation to grievances, resources, cultural frames, and politics.

MARX, LENIN, AND GRAMSCI

Many sociologists trace the lineage of the field of social movements to the negative reactions to the horrors of the French Revolution and the outrages of the crowd.[1] While writers like Tarde (1989) and Le Bon (1977) make a convenient polemical starting point for theorists who reject their ideas, their work was in fact an offshoot of crowd psychology. In this book, conflicts between challengers and authorities will be seen as a normal part of society and not as an aberration. This is why we will begin with the preeminent theorist who saw conflict inscribed in the structure of society – Karl Marx.

MARX AND CLASS CONFLICT

It would not have occurred to the earliest theorists of social movements, Marx and Engels, to ask what makes individuals engage in collective action. Or, rather, they would have posed the problem as an outcome of society's structural development rather than one of individual choice. But although they saw collective action rooted in social structure, Marx and Engels seriously underrated the resources needed to engage in it, its cultural dimensions, and the importance of politics.

Marx answered the question of how individuals get involved in collective action largely in historically determined terms: people will engage in collective action, he thought, when their social class comes into fully developed contradiction with its antagonists. In the case of the proletariat, this meant when capitalism forced it into large-scale factories where it lost the ownership of its tools but developed the resources to act collectively. Among these resources were class consciousness and trade unions. It was the rhythm of socialized production in the factory that would pound the proletariat into a class for itself and give rise to the unions that would give it shape. Although there are many more elegant (and more obscure) formulations of this thesis, Marx puts it most succinctly in *The Communist Manifesto*:

> The advance of industry, whose involuntary promoter is the bourgeoisie, replaces the isolation of the labourers, due to competition, by their revolutionary combination, due to association. . . . The real fruit of their battle lies, not in the immediate result, but in the ever-expanding union of the workers. (Tucker 1978: 481, 483)

Marx dealt summarily with a problem that has worried activists ever since: why members of a group who "should" revolt often fail to do so. Concerned with the problem that the workers' movement could not succeed without the cooperation of a significant proportion of its members, he developed a theory of "false" consciousness, by which he meant that, if workers failed to act as "History" dictated, it was because they remained cloaked in a shroud of ignorance woven by their class enemies. The theory was unsatisfactory because no one could say whose consciousness was false and whose was real. Marx thought the problem would resolve itself when capitalism's contradictions and the solidarity that came from years of toiling side by side with others like themselves opened the workers' eyes to their real interests.

We now know that, as capitalism developed, it produced divisions among the workers and mechanisms to integrate them into capitalist democracy. Through nationalism and protectionism, workers often allied themselves with capitalists, suggesting that much more than class conflict was necessary to produce collective action on their behalf. A form of consciousness had to be created that would transform Marx's trade union consciousness into revolutionary collective action. But who would create this consciousness? Marx had neither a clear-cut concept of leadership, nor one of working-class culture, and he seriously underspecified the political conditions in which to provide opportunities for revolutionary mobilization (1963b: 175).

LENIN AND RESOURCE MOBILIZATION

The first of these problems – that of leadership – was Lenin's major preoccupation. Learning from the western European experience that workers on their own will only act on behalf of narrow "trade union interests," he proposed creating an elite of professional revolutionaries (1929: 52–63). Substituting itself for Marx's proletariat, this "vanguard" would act as the self-appointed guardian of the workers' real interests. When it succeeded in gaining power, as it did in Russia in 1917, it transposed the equation, substituting party interest for that of the working class (and ultimately, in the form of stalinism, substituting the interests of the leader for that of the party). But in 1902 this was far in the future. To Lenin, it seemed that organization was the solution to the workers' collective action problem.

With the virtues of hindsight, we can see that Lenin's organizational amendments to Marx's theory were a response to the particular historical conditions of czarist Russia. In superimposing an intellectual vanguard on the young and unsophisticated Russian working class, he was adapting Marx's theory to the context of a highly repressive state and the backward society it ruled – both of which retarded the development of class consciousness and inhibited collective action.[2] The theory of the vanguard was an organizational response to a historical situation in which the working class was unable to produce a revolution on its own, but it was applied indiscriminately to the world Communist movement with little regard to social and political opportunities and constraints. Some of these problems were addressed by one of Lenin's successors.

GRAMSCI AND CULTURAL HEGEMONY

When the Russian Revolution of 1917 failed to spread to the West, marxists like Antonio Gramsci who had embraced leninism realized that, at least in *Western* conditions, organization would not be sufficient to raise a revolution. For Gramsci, it would be necessary to develop the workers' own consciousness, and he therefore conceived of the workers' movement as a collective intellectual, one of whose prime tasks was to create a working-class culture.

This change was subtle but important. Just as he thought Italy shared Russia's social conditions, Gramsci had accepted Lenin's injunction that the revolutionary party had to be a vanguard. But after being clapped into Mussolini's prisons, he added to Lenin's organizational solution two theorems: first, that a fundamental task of the party was to create a historic bloc of forces around the working class (Gramsci 1971: 168); and, second, that this could only occur if a cadre of "organic intellectuals" was developed from within the working class to complement the "traditional" intellectuals in the party (pp. 6–23).

Both innovations turned out to hinge on a strong belief in the power of culture.[3] Gramsci's solution to the cultural hegemony of the bourgeoisie was to produce consensus around the party among the workers, give them a capacity for taking autonomous initiatives, and build bridges between them and other social formations. The process would be a long and a slow one, requiring the party to operate within the "trenches and fortifications" of bourgeois society, proselytize among nonproletarian groups, and learn to deal with cultural institutions like the church.

But Gramsci's solution – as could be seen in the fate of the Italian Communist Party after World War II – posed a new dilemma. If the party as collective intellectual engaged in a long-term dialogue between workers and bourgeoisie, what would prevent the cultural power of the latter – what Gramsci called "the common sense of capitalist society" – from transforming the party, rather than vice versa?[4] Without a theory of political mobilization, Gramsci's solution to the collective action problem – like Marx and Lenin's – was indeterminate about the influence of politics. Gramsci did argue that the battle had to be fought within the trenches and fortifications of capitalist society (1971: 229–39), but he provided no guide to how that battle should be fought nor did he differentiate between countries in which the opportunities and constraints would be strong or weak.

Each of these marxist theorists emphasized a different element of collective action: Marx focused on the cleavages of capitalist society that created a mobilization potential (what students of social movements would later call "grievance theory"); Lenin created the movement organizations that were necessary to structure it and prevent its dispersion into narrow corporate claims (what would later be called "resource mobilization" by American scholars); and Gramsci centered on the need to build consensus around the party's goals (what has come to be called "framing" and "collective identity" formation). But none of them specified the *political* conditions in which resource-poor and exploited workers could be expected to mobilize on behalf of their interests – what we will call the problem of political opportunities and constraints.

SOCIAL SCIENTISTS, SOCIAL MOVEMENTS, AND COLLECTIVE ACTION

Though they are seldom made explicit, these three elements of marxist theory have strong parallels in recent theorizing about collective action and social movements. Without sharing Marx's fixation on class or his assurance that history would produce a single, overriding class conflict, collective behavior theorists of the 1950s and early 1960s focused on the grievances responsible for mobilization. Without sharing Lenin's belief in an elite vanguard, resource mobilization theorists of the late 1960s and 1970s concentrated on leadership and organization; and like Gramsci, framing and collective identity theorists of the 1980s and early 1990s focused on the sources of consensus in a movement without, however, always specifying the agents responsible for creating new historic blocs. Let us examine how these recent schools of thought emerged from recent Western history and social science and what they contribute to our understanding of contentious politics and social movements.

GRIEVANCES AND COLLECTIVE BEHAVIOR THEORY

Like the marxists, nonmarxist sociologists took a long time developing a politically connected view of social movements. For many years, in fact, they conceived of movements outside the normal institutions of society – as part of a construct that came to be called "collective behavior."[5] Collective behavior theory posited that movements were little more than the most well-organized and self-conscious part of an archipelago of "emergent" phenomena, ranging from fads and rumors, to collective enthusiasms, riots, movements, and revolutions.

In some versions of the theory (e.g., see Kornhauser 1959), society itself was seen to be disoriented and mobilization resulted from the urge to recompose it. This could be linked to Durkheim's theory of "anomie," in which individuals – unhinged from traditional roles and identities – sought new collective identities through personal reintegration in movements (Durkheim 1951; Hoffer 1951). In other versions (e.g., Gurr 1971), there was no overall vision of breakdown, but individual deprivation was at the center of analysis. The most sophisticated versions of the theory linked collective behavior to a functional view of society in which societal dysfunctions produced different forms of collective behavior – some of which took the form of political movements and interest groups (Smelser 1962; Turner and Killian 1972).

Unlike Marx, who had a mechanistic class theory to predict which collectivities could be expected to mobilize at what stages of capitalism, collective behavior theorists had no preferred social subject. Perhaps because they related movements to more spontaneous forms of expression, they tended to underspecify the mobilization process. And because they started from the assumption that collective behavior was outside the routines of everyday life, few of them specified its relationship to the political (But see Smelser 1962; chs. 9, 10.) This may be why few variants of collective behavior theory retained their popularity when a new social movement cycle hit in the 1960s.

RATIONAL CHOICE AND RESOURCE MOBILIZATION

The decade of the 1960s revitalized the study of social movements in both Europe and the United States. The collective behavior tradition had been deeply influenced by two horrendous real-world phenomena: stalinism and fascism. But in the 1960s, a new generation of scholars, many of them coming out of the movements of that decade, gave social movements a new and more positive image. For former movement activists and those who studied them, the older image of "true believers" searching for roots in an atomized society was difficult to reconcile with the determined young activists in the civil rights and anti–Vietnam War movements (Keniston 1968).

The study of collective action was also affected by trends in the academy, where economics was becoming the master social science. In the traces of microeconomics, the problem for collective action came to be not how classes struggle and states rule, but how collective action is even *possible* among individuals guided by narrow self-interest.

The most influential student of this dilemma was the American economist Mancur Olson (1965). Though Olson acknowledged the importance of nonmaterial incentives, his theory started and finished with the individual. For Olson, the problem of collective action was aggregative: how to involve as high a proportion of a group as possible on behalf of its collective good. Only in this way could the group convince its opponents of its own strength. In his book, *The Logic of Collective Action*, Olson posited that, in a large group, only its most important members have a sufficient interest in achieving its collective good to take on its leadership – not quite Lenin's "vanguard" but not far from it.

The only exceptions to this rule were the very small groups in which individual and collective goods are closely associated (Olson 1965: 43–6).[6] The larger the group, the more people will prefer to "free-ride" on the efforts of the individuals whose interest in the collective good is strong enough to pursue it.[7] To overcome this problem, Olson posited that would-be leaders must either impose constraints on their members or provide them with "selective incentives" to convince them that participation is worthwhile (p. 51).

Olson's work would have gone unnoticed during the pre-1960s period, when it was assumed that grievances are largely sufficient to explain collective action. But in the 1960s, it converged with dissatisfaction with the collective behavior approach (McAdam 1982: ch. 1) and with the growing conviction of social movement scholars that grievances alone cannot explain mobilization. Indeed, Olson argued that rational people guided by individual interest might well *avoid* taking action when they see that others are willing to take it for them.

Olson's reception into the study of contentious politics was slow and uneven. Ironically, during a decade in which contentious politics was buzzing and blooming, he chose to focus on explaining why it is unlikely to occur (Hirschman

1982)! Moreover, he seemed to limit the motivations for collective action to material and personal incentives. But what of the thousands of people who struck, marched, rioted, and demonstrated on behalf of interests other than their own in the 1960s? Finally, though he named his theory "*collective* action," Olson had little to say beyond the individual level of motivation and aggregation. How could his theory be reconciled with the movement cycle of the 1960s?

Two sociologists, John McCarthy and Mayer Zald, proposed an answer that focused on the resources that were increasingly available in advanced industrial societies (1973, 1977). McCarthy and Zald agreed with Olson that the collective action problem was real, but argued that the expanded personal resources, professionalization, and external financial support available to movements provided a solution – professional movement organizations.[8]

While the earlier generation of scholars had focused on the why of collective action, McCarthy and Zald's theory, "resource mobilization," focused on the means available to collective actors – on its how (Melucci 1988). This emphasis on means was a source of disappointment to critics looking for structural explanations of the origins of movements, but it lent a refreshing concreteness to the study of movements, which had previously been seen as the expression of ideological abstractions. For McCarthy and Zald, there was a rational answer to Olson's paradox of the free rider and it lay in organization.

By the early 1980s, their theory of resource mobilization had become a dominant background paradigm for sociologists studying social movements, but, paradoxically, it was more often criticized than embraced. Why was this? For one thing, McCarthy and Zald used the language of economics (e.g., they spoke of movement "entrepreneurs," "movement industries," movement "sectors"), leaving many who had come out of the movements of the 1960s cold. What, the critics asked, about ideology, commitment, values, the fight against injustice? For another, McCarthy and Zald's social movement organizations (SMOs) were often difficult to distinguish from interest groups; particularly European scholars wondered how their theory would survive in the rough-and-ready world of European contention. And for a third, their emphasis on the "solution" of professional movement organizations seemed to ignore the many grass-roots movements that were emerging in the 1960s and 1970s in both Europe and America (Evans and Boyte 1992).

By the 1980s, an alternative model, emphasizing informal participation and internal democracy, arose (Fantasia 1988; Rosenthal and Schwartz 1990). In the general disillusionment with marxism of the 1970s and 1980s, some found a new paradigmatic alternative in culture, which – in the apolitical atmosphere of the early 1990s – emerged as a countermodel to resource mobilization.

THE CULTURES OF CONTENTION

If the collective behavior paradigm's emphasis on grievances recalled Marx, and resource mobilization's focus on leadership was parallel to Lenin, the cultural aspect of recent social movement studies is resonant of Gramsci. Just as Gramsci added a cultural dimension to Lenin's concept of class hegemony, many recent writers have tried to shift the focus of research on social movements from structural factors to the "framing" of collective action. The earliest hint of a paradigm shift came from E. P. Thompson's enculturation of the concept of class (1966). Thompson did not want to throw class out the window, but only to substitute for the productivist marxism of his forebears a focus on class self-creation. This took him far from the factory floor – to factors like custom, grain seizures, and consumer mentalities (1971). In a field that had previously been obsessed with class conflict, Thompson also brought to the study of contention a sensitivity to interclass reciprocity, a factor that he labeled the "moral economy" (1971).[9]

A second influence came from anthropologist Clifford Geertz (1973), whose approach of "thick description" was especially influential among scholars disheartened by the quantitative turn that their disciplines seemed to be taking. Geertz urged a distinction between analysis and interpretation, basing his sympathy for the latter on the insights it seemed to provide on the meaning of behavior to those who take part in it.

A third influence came from social psychology: first Erving Goffman's concept of framing (1974), and then Bert Klanderman's concept of "consensus mobilization" (1988, 1997), and Gamson's idea of "ideological packages" (1988). From assuming grievances, scholars of social movements began to focus on how movements embed concrete grievances within emotion-laden "packages" (Gamson 1992a), or in "frames" capable of convincing participants that their cause is just and important (Snow, Rochford, Worden, and Benford 1986). Partly blending with these insights was the influence of French poststructuralism, and especially the concept of "discourse" imported from the work of historian-philosopher Michel Foucault (1972, 1980).

Without anyone's intending it, and long before the fall of marxism-leninism, structural approaches seemed to be giving way to culture as a metanarrative in social movement studies, a shift that was reinforced by the challenge of the "new" social movements of the 1970s and 1980s – some of which seemed to have substituted "life-space" demands for the old structural programs of the past (Habermas 1981).[10]

With this new emphasis on culture, the reaction against resource mobilization ripened into a substantially new paradigm. This was reinforced by the "identity" politics that had developed out of the 1960s – and especially by the women's, gay and lesbian, and minority rights movements (Gitlin 1995); and by the new wave of studies of nationalism, where social constructionism was diffused by Benedict Anderson's metaphor of "imagined" communities (1991). But to more systematic innovators, all movements construct meanings and meaning construction is a social movement's primary function (Eyerman and Jamison 1991).

But if this was the case, why do waves of movements emerge in some periods and not in others, and why are some more adept at manipulating cultural symbols than others? Without an answer to these questions, culturalism might prove just as mechanical a metanarrative as the structuralism its proponents wished to displace. To this dilemma political scientists and politically attuned sociologists proposed an answer: the variations in political structure and the workings of the political process.

THE CONDITIONS OF POLITICAL STRUGGLE

True to their traditions, and led by the rise of contentious politics in that country in the early part of the 1960s, American scholars were first to develop a more political approach to movements, one that eventually centered on several versions of the concept that came to be known as "political opportunity structure."[11] The foundation stone in this tradition was laid by Charles Tilly, in his 1978 classic, *From Mobilization to Revolution*.[12] In that book, Tilly put forward a "polity model" for the analysis of collective action from which he elaborated a set of conditions for mobilization, foremost among which were the opportunity–threat to challengers and facilitation–repression by authorities (1978: chs. 3, 4, 6). Both of these dimensions linked collective action to the state.

Tilly argued that the development of the national social movement was concomitant, and mutually interdependent, with the rise of consolidated national states (1984b). It followed that movements could be studied only in connection with politics, and would vary in their strategy, structure, and success in different kinds of states. This was an insight that students of social revolution, like Theda Skocpol (1979), were also exploring, and that comparativists in political science were quick to pick up on (Kitschelt 1986; Kriesi, Koopmans, Duyvendak, and Giugni 1995; Tarrow 1989a, 1989b).

Given his grounding in European social thought, Tilly's model was resolutely structural (i.e., it focused on conditions that cannot be molded to actors' purposes). Americanists' models were more sensitive to the workings of the political process. Political scientists like Michael Lipsky (1968) and Peter Eisinger (1973) focused on American urban politics: the former linking the urban movements of the 1960s to the use of protest as a political resource, and the latter correlating protest with various measures of local opportunity. In a similar vein, Frances Fox Piven and Richard Cloward turned their attention to the historical relations between welfare policies and social protest (1993). But it was a sociologist, Doug McAdam, who synthesized these approaches into a fully fledged "political process model" of social movement mobilization by tracing the development of the American civil rights movement to political, organizational, and consciousness change (1982).

Although opportunity–threat and facilitation–repression were parts of the original tillian synthesis, through the 1980s, political process theorists tended to narrow their attention to opportunities. Some scholars – in Eisinger's footsteps – studied how different political structures provide greater or lesser degrees of opportunity to insurgent groups (Amenta, Caruthers, and Zylan 1992; Kitschelt

1986); others looked at how particular movements exploit the opportunities provided by institutions (Costain 1992); others looked at how the opportunities for
a particular movement change over time (Jenkins and Perrow 1977); and still
others studied entire cycles of protest to understand how the triggering of a wave
of mobilization affected successor movements (McAdam 1995; Tarrow 1989a).
In a major comparative synthesis, Hanspeter Kriesi and his collaborators used
the concept of political opportunity to analyze the new social movements in four
western European countries (1995).

As these works progressed, lacunae and ambiguities appeared.[13] For example,
political process models were seldom systematically applied outside the liberal democracies of the West (but see Boudreau 1996; Brockett 1991, 1995; Schneider
1995). A second question – whether threat has a positive or a negative impact on
movement formation – only began to be explored in the 1990s, with a series of
works inspired by Donatella della Porta (1995, 1996; della Porta, Fillieule, and
Reiter 1998) on police behavior. Third, whereas some scholars (McAdam 1996;
Tarrow 1996b) worked from a limited list of dimensions of opportunity, as more
and more aspects of the links between politics and movement formation emerged,
the concept tended to stretch (see Gamson and Meyer's critique, 1996).[14]

Nevertheless, the political process-opportunities approach proposed an answer to the question that dogged previous approaches: why does contentious
politics seem to develop only in particular periods of history and why does it
sometimes produce robust social movements and sometimes flicker out into sectarianism or repression? And why do movements take different forms in different
political environments? Moreover, because it does not claim to explain every
aspect of contentious politics or social movements, it can become part of a synthesis with insights from other branches of social movement theory, as I propose
here.

TOWARD A SYNTHESIS

The most forceful argument of this study will be that people engage in contentious politics when patterns of political opportunities and constraints change and
then, by strategically employing a repertoire of collective action, create new opportunities, which are used by others in widening cycles of contention. When
their struggles revolve around broad cleavages in society, when they bring people
together around inherited cultural symbols, and when they can build on or construct dense social networks and connective structures, then these episodes of
contention result in sustained interactions with opponents – specifically, in social
movements.

POLITICAL OPPORTUNITIES AND CONSTRAINTS

By political opportunities, I mean consistent – but not necessarily formal, permanent, or national – dimensions of the political struggle that encourage people

to engage in contentious politics. By political constraints, I mean factors – like repression, but also like authorities' capacity to present a solid front to insurgents – that discourage contention. There is no simple formula for predicting when contentious politics will emerge, both because the specification of these variables varies in different historical and political circumstances, and because different factors may vary in opposing directions. As a result, the term "political opportunity structure" should not be understood as an invariant model inevitably producing social movements, but as a set of clues for when contentious politics will emerge, setting in motion a chain of causation that may ultimately lead to sustained interaction with authorities and thence to social movements.

The concept of political opportunity emphasizes resources *external* to the group. Unlike money or power, these can be taken advantage of by even weak or disorganized challengers but in no way "belong" to them. In Chapter 5, I argue that contentious politics emerges when ordinary citizens, sometimes encouraged by counter elites or leaders, respond to opportunities that lower the costs of collective action, reveal potential allies, show where elites and authorities are most vulnerable, and trigger social networks and collective identities into action around common themes.

Like Hanspeter Kriesi and his collaborators (1995), I argue in Chapter 5 that both state structures and political cleavages create relatively stable opportunities. The most obvious of these are forms of access to institutions and capacity for repression. *Changing* opportunities and constraints, however, provide the openings that lead resource-poor actors to engage in contentious politics. Whether contention ripens into social movements depends on how people act collectively, on how consensus is mobilized around common claims, and on the strength and location of mobilizing structures.

THE REPERTOIRE OF CONTENTION

People do not simply "act collectively." They petition, assemble, strike, march, occupy premises, obstruct traffic, set fires, and attack others with intent to do bodily harm. No less than in the case of religious rituals or civic celebrations, contentious politics is not born in organizers' heads but is culturally inscribed and socially communicated. The learned conventions of contention are part of a society's public culture.[15] Social movements are repositories of knowledge of particular routines in a society's history, which help them to overcome the deficits in resources and communication typically found among the poor and disorganized (Kertzer 1988: 104–108).

Because social movements seldom neither possess selective incentives or constraints over followers, nor are bound by institutional routines, leadership has a creative function in selecting forms of collective action. Leaders invent, adapt, and combine various forms of contention to gain support from people who might otherwise stay at home. Albert Hirschman had something like this in mind when he complained that Olson regarded collective action *only* as a cost – when to many it is a benefit (1982: 82–91). For people whose lives are mired in drudgery and desperation, the offer of an exciting, risky, and possibly beneficial campaign of collective action may be a gain.

Forms of contention are inherited or rare, habitual or unfamiliar, solitary or part of concerted campaigns. They can be linked to themes that are either inscribed in the culture or invented on the spot or – more commonly – blend elements of convention with new frames of meaning. Protest is a resource, according to political scientist Michael Lipsky (1968), and the forms of contention are themselves a collective incentive to mobilization and a challenge to opponents.

Particular groups have a particular history – and memory – of contentious forms. Workers know how to strike because generations of workers struck before them; Parisians build barricades because barricades are inscribed in the history of Parisian contention; peasants seize the land carrying the symbols that their fathers and grandfathers used in the past. Political scientists Stuart Hill and Donald Rothchild put it this way:

> Based on past periods of conflict with a particular group(s) or the government, individuals construct a prototype of a protest or riot that describes what to do in particular circumstances as well as explaining a rationale for this action. (1992: 192)

These forms I turn to in Chapter 6.

CONSENSUS MOBILIZATION AND IDENTITIES

The coordination of collective action depends on the trust and cooperation that are generated among participants by shared understandings and identities – or, to use a broader category, on the collective action *frames* that justify, dignify, and animate collective action. Ideology, as David Apter wrote in his classic essay in *Ideology and Discontent*, dignifies discontent, identifies a target for grievances, and forms an umbrella over the discrete grievances of overlapping groups (1964: ch. 1).

But "ideology" is a rather dry way of describing what moves people to action. In recent years, students of social movements have begun to use terms like cognitive frames, ideological packages, and cultural discourses to describe the shared meanings that inspire people to collective action.[16] Whatever the terminology, rather than regarding ideology as either a superimposed intellectual category or as the automatic result of grievances, these scholars agree that movements do passionate "framing work": shaping grievances into broader and more resonant claims (Snow and Benford 1988) and stimulating what William Gamson calls "hot cognitions" around them (1992a).

Framing not only relates to the generalization of a grievance, but defines the "us" and "them" in a movement's conflict structure. By drawing on inherited collective identities and shaping new ones, challengers delimit the boundaries of their prospective constituencies and define their enemies by real or imagined attributes and evils (Hardin 1995: ch. 4). As much as through the content of their ideological messages, they do this through the images they project of both enemies and allies. This means paying attention to the "costumes" collective actors don as they appear on the public stage as well as to the ideological framing of their claims. This we attempt to do in Chapter 7.

Although movement organizers actively engage in framing work, not all framing takes place under their control. In addition to building on inherited cultural understandings, they compete with the media, which transmit messages that movements must attempt to shape and influence. As sociologist Todd Gitlin found, much of the communication that helped shape the American New Left in the 1960s passed through the medium of the media, in the place of what would have had to be organizational efforts in earlier periods (1980).

States are also constantly framing issues, both in order to gain support for their policies and to contest the meanings placed in public space by movements. In the struggle over meanings in which movements are constantly engaged, it is rare that they do not suffer a disadvantage in competition with states, which not only control the means of repression but have at their disposal important instruments for meaning construction. The struggle between states and movements takes place not only in the streets but in contests over meaning (Melucci 1996; Rochon 1998).

MOBILIZING STRUCTURES

Although it is individuals who decide whether or not to take up collective action, it is in their face-to-face groups, their social networks, and the connective structures between them that it is most often activated and sustained. This has been made clear through recent research both in the laboratory[17] and in the real world of movement mobilization.

In the early collective behavior approach, there was a tendency to see isolated, deprived individuals as the main actors in collective action. But by the 1980s, scholars were finding that it is life within groups that transforms the potential for action into social movements (Hardin 1995: ch. 2). For example, Doug McAdam's work on the Freedom Summer campaign showed that – far more than their social background or ideologies – it was the social networks in which Freedom Summer applicants were embedded that played a key role in determining who would participate in this campaign and who would stay at home (1986, 1988).[18]

Institutions are particularly economical "host" settings in which movements can germinate. This was particularly true in estate societies like prerevolutionary France, where the provincial parliaments provided institutional spaces where liberal ideas could germinate (Egret 1977). But it is also true in America today. For instance, sociologist Aldon Morris showed that the origins of the civil rights movement were bound up with the role of the black churches (1984). And political scientist Mary Katzenstein found that the internal structures of the Catholic world were unwitting accomplices in the formation of networks of dissident women religious (1998; also see Levine 1990; Tarrow 1988).

The role of social networks and institutions in stimulating movement participation helps us to put Mancur Olson's thesis that large groups will not support collective action in perspective. For when we look at the morphology of movements, it becomes clear that they are only "large" in an arithmetic sense: they are really much more like an interlocking network of small groups, social networks, and the connections between them.[19] Collective action may arise only among the best-endowed or most courageous members of these groups, but the connections between them affect the likelihood that one actor's action will incite another. This gives a special importance to what I call "connective structures" in Chapter 8. [20]

To summarize what will have to be shown in detail in later chapters: contentious politics is produced when political opportunities broaden, when they demonstrate the potential for alliances, and when they reveal the opponents' vulnerability. Contention crystallizes into a social movement when it taps embedded social networks and connective structures and produces collective action frames and supportive identities able to sustain contention with powerful opponents. By mounting familiar forms of contention, movements become focal points that transform external opportunities into resources. Repertoires of contention, social networks, and cultural frames lower the costs of bringing people into collective action, induce confidence that they are not alone, and give broader meaning to their claims. Together, these factors trigger the dynamic processes that have made social movements historically central to political and social change.

THE DYNAMICS OF MOVEMENT

The power to trigger sequences of collective action is not the same as the power to control or sustain them. This dilemma has both an internal and an external dimension. Internally, a good part of the power of movements comes from the fact that they activate people over whom they have no control. This power is a virtue because it allows movements to mount collective action without possessing the resources that would be necessary to internalize a support base. But the autonomy of their supporters also disperses a movement's power, encourages factionalization, and leaves it open to defection, competition, and repression.

Externally, movements are affected by the fact that the same political opportunities that have created them and diffuse their influence also affect others — either complementary, competing, or hostile. Particularly if collective action succeeds, these opportunities produce broader cycles of contention that spread from movement activists to those they oppose, to ordinary interest groups and political parties, and, inevitably, to the state. As a result of this dynamic of diffusion and creation, movements succeed or fail as the result of forces outside their control. This takes us to the concept of the cycle of contention, which is dealt with in Chapter 9.

CYCLES OF CONTENTION

As opportunities widen and information spreads about the susceptibility of a polity to challenge, not only activists but ordinary people begin to test the limits of social control. Clashes between early challengers and authorities reveal the weak points of the latter and the strengths of the former, inviting even timid social actors to align themselves on one side or another. Once triggered by a situation of generally widening opportunities, information cascades outward and political learning accelerates. As Hill and Rothchild write,

> As protests and riots erupt among groups that have long histories of conflict, they stimulate other citizens in similar circumstances to reflect more often on their own background of grievance and mass action. (1992: 193)

During such periods, the opportunities created by early risers provide incentives for new movement organizations. Even conventional interest groups are tempted by unconventional collective action. Alliances are formed, often across a shifting boundary between challengers and members of the polity (Tilly 1978: ch. 2). New forms of contention are experimented with and diffused. Political information and uncertainty spread, and a dense and interactive "social movement sector" appears in which organizations cooperate and compete (Garner and Zald 1985).

The process of diffusion in cycles of contention is not merely one of "contagion," though a good deal of such contagion occurs. It also results from rational decisions to take advantage of opportunities that have been demonstrated by other groups' actions: it occurs when groups make gains that invite others to seek similar outcomes; when someone's ox is gored by demands made by insurgent groups; and when the predominance of an organization or institution is threatened and it responds by adopting collective action.

As the cycle widens, movements create opportunities for elites and opposition groups too. Alliances form between participants and challengers; oppositional elites make demands for changes that would have seemed foolhardy earlier; governmental forces respond either with reform, repression, or a combination of the two. The widening logic of collective action leads to outcomes in the sphere of institutional politics, where the challengers who began the cycle have less and less leverage over its outcomes.

At the extreme end of the spectrum, cycles of contention give rise to revolutions. Revolutions are not a single form of collective action; nor are they wholly made up of popular collective action. As in the cycles to which they are related, collective action in revolutions forces other groups and institutions to take part, providing the bases and frameworks for new social movements, unhinging old institutions and the networks that surround them, and creating new ones out of the forms of collective action with which insurgent groups begin the process.

The difference between movement cycles and revolutions is that, in the latter, multiple centers of sovereignty are created, turning the conflict between challengers and members of the polity into a struggle for power (Tilly 1993). This difference – which is substantial – has led to an entire industry of research on "great" revolutions, which are usually compared only with one another. This specialization on great revolutions is understandable, but it has squandered the possibility of comparing revolutions with lesser conflagrations, making it impossible to isolate those factors in the dynamic of a cycle which lead it down the path to revolutions and those which lead it to collapse, as I argue in Chapter 9 (also see Goldstone 1997).

OUTCOMES OF MOVEMENTS

These arguments about the interactions within a cycle of protest suggest that it will not be particularly fruitful to examine the outcomes of single social movements on their own. In general cycles of contention, policy elites respond not to the claims of any individual group or movement but to the degree of turbulence and to the demands made by elites and opinion groups, which only partially correspond to the demands of those they claim to represent. Regarding the outcomes of social movements, the important point is that, although movements usually conceive of themselves as outside of and opposed to institutions, acting collectively inserts them into complex policy networks, and thus within the reach of the state. If nothing else, movements try to enunciate demands in terms of frames of meaning comprehensible to a wider society; they use forms of collective action drawn from an existing repertoire; and they develop types of organization that often mimic the organizations of those they oppose.

We can begin to study social movements as isolated confrontations between single social actors and their opponents, but – particularly when we examine their outcomes – we quickly arrive at the more complex and less tractable networks of politics. It is through the political opportunities seized and created by challengers, movements, and their allies and enemies that major cycles of contention begin. They, in turn, create opportunities for elites and counterelites, and actions that begin in the streets are resolved in the halls of government or by the bayonets of the army. Movements – and particularly the waves of movement that are the main catalysts of social change – are part of national struggles for power. Let us begin by turning to how that struggle first produced national social movements in the modern history of the West.

PART I

THE BIRTH OF
THE MODERN
SOCIAL
MOVEMENT

2

MODULAR COLLECTIVE ACTION

In the mid-1780s, as the foundations of France's old regime were crumbling, a series of scandal trials began to appear in Paris.[1] In one of the most notorious, the Cléraux affair, a servant who had resisted the advances of her master was accused of robbing him and was hauled into court. Not only was the case decided in her favor (*pace* Dickens), but a wave of popular outrage against the courts and the lewd master surged across Paris. In a routine that had become familiar by the late eighteenth century, the master's house was sacked, his goods thrown into the street, and he himself barely saved from the fury of the crowd. A contemporary observer described the *émotion* in this way:

> What violences! What tumults! A furious multitude filled the streets, straining to tear down the Thibault house with an ax, then threatening to burn it; covering the family with curses and outrages; almost sacrificing them to their hatred. (Lusebrink 1983: 375–6)

The affair contributed to the atmosphere of corruption surrounding the Old Regime, but its forms and its rhetoric were familiar from the European past.

Sixty years later, in February 1848, Alexis de Tocqueville left his house for parliament amid the tumult of Paris in revolution. Along his route, as citizens quietly watched, men were systematically putting up barricades. "These barricades," he observed,

> were skillfully constructed by a small number of men who worked industriously – not like criminals fearful of being caught *in flagrante delicto*, but like good workmen who wanted to do their job expeditiously and well. Nowhere did I see the seething unrest I had witnessed in 1830, when the whole city reminded me of one vast, boiling cauldron. (Tocqueville 1987: 39)

Of "seething unrest" and "boiling cauldrons" Europe would see a great deal in the months following February 1848. But at midcentury, Frenchmen were calmly building barricades, knew where to put them up, and had learned to use them.[2] That regularity marked a fundamental change in the structure of popular politics since the attack on Master Thibault's house sixty years before.

The contrast was more than one of scale. The tearing down of houses was a routine that had long been used against tax gatherers, brothel keepers, and grain merchants.[3] But these focused on the sites of wrongdoing and were limited to direct attacks on its supposed perpetrators. The barricade, in contrast, was what I call "modular." Once its strategic advantages were known, it could be used for a variety of purposes, unify people with different aims, and be diffused to various types of confrontation with authorities.[4]

In the 1780s, people knew how to seize shipments of grain, attack tax gatherers, burn tax registers, and take revenge on wrongdoers and people who had violated community norms. But they were not yet familiar with acts like the mass demonstration, the strike, or the urban insurrection on behalf of common goals. By the end of the 1848 revolution, the petition, the public meeting, the demonstration, and the barricade were well-known routines, employed for a variety of purposes and by different combinations of social actors. Before examining the forms in this new repertoire and its relation to the birth of the national social movement, let us first look at the concept of the repertoire of contention and at how it developed in early modern Europe.

REPERTOIRES OF CONTENTION

In 1995, capping more than thirty years of work on collective action,[5] Charles Tilly published his major work, *Popular Contention in Great Britain, 1758–1834* (1995b). In it, Tilly defined the "repertoire of contention" as "the ways that people act together in pursuit of shared interests" (p. 41).[6] In another work, Tilly takes the theme further, writing that "the word *repertoire* helps describe what happens by identifying a limited set of routines that are learned, shared, and acted out through a relatively deliberate process of choice." The limits of that learning constrain the choices available for collective interaction and lay the foundation for future choices. People experiment with new forms in the search for tactical advantage, but they do so in small ways, at the edge of well-established routines (1992: 7).

The repertoire is at once a structural and a cultural concept, involving not only what people *do* when they are engaged in conflict with others but what they *know how to do* and what others *expect* them to do. Had sit-ins been tried by challengers in eighteenth-century France, their targets would not have known how to respond to them, any more than the victim of a *charivari* today would know what it meant. As Arthur Stinchcombe writes, "The elements of the repertoire are . . . simultaneously the skills of the population members and the cultural forms of the population" (1987: 1248).

The repertoire changes over time, but only glacially. Fundamental changes depend on major fluctuations in interests, opportunity, and organization. These, in turn, correlate roughly with changes in states and capitalism. Major shifts resulted from the national state's penetration of society to make war and extract taxes and from capitalism's creation of concentrations of people with the grievances and the resources to act collectively. Though structurally based, these changes in repertoires show up in the major political watersheds that I refer to in Chapter 9 as "cycles of contention."[7]

What differences separated the new repertoire from the eighteenth-century forms reflected in the Cléraux affair? "If we push back into the strange terrain of western Europe and North America before the middle of the nineteenth century," writes Tilly, "we soon discover another world" of collective action (1983: 463). The older repertoire was parochial, bifurcated, and particular:

> It was *parochial* because most often the interests and interaction involved were concentrated in a single community. It was *bifurcated* because when ordinary people addressed local issues and nearby objects they took impressively direct action to achieve their ends, but when it came to national issues and objects they recurrently addressed their demands to a local patron or authority. . . . [and it] was *particular* because the detailed routines of action varied greatly from group to group, issue to issue, locality to locality. (Tilly 1995b: 45)

Contention often exploded at public celebrations, drawing on rich, often irreverent symbolism, religious rituals, and popular culture. Participants often converged on the residences of wrongdoers and the sites of wrongdoing, commonly appearing as members or representatives of constituted corporate groups and communities (Tilly 1983: 464).

The new repertoire did not appear fully blown, nor did the old forms of collective action ever disappear. The most visible triumphs of the new forms came when demonstrations, strikes, rallies, public meetings, and similar forms of interaction came to prevail. As compared with their predecessors, the new forms had a cosmopolitan, modular, and autonomous character:

> They were *cosmopolitan* in often referring to interests and issues that spanned many localities or affected centers of power whose actions touched many localities. They were *modular* in being easily transferable from one setting or circumstance to another. . . . They were *autonomous* in beginning on the claimants' own initiative and establishing direct contact between claimants and nationally significant centers of power. (Tilly 1995b: 46)

In his 1983 article, Tilly summarized the differences between the old and the new repertoire in an illustration reproduced here as Figure 2.1.

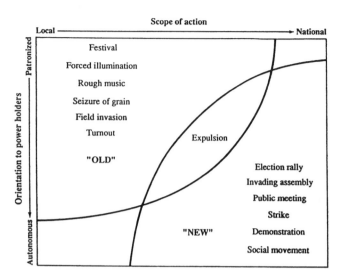

Figure 2.1. "Old" and "New" Repertoires in Western Europe and North America (SOURCE: Charles Tilly, "Speaking Your Mind without Elections, Surveys, or Social Movements," Public Opinion Quarterly 47. Published by the University of Chicago. Copyright 1983 by the Trustees of Columbia University.)

Implicit in the concept of a repertoire is that it is more or less general.[8] But the old and the new repertoires were not *equally* general. From the sixteenth to the eighteenth centuries, the forms of action used in attacks on millers and grain merchants, in *charivaris* and religious conflicts, were directly linked to the nature of their targets and the grievances of the actors who used them. Herein lies a key contrast with the modern repertoire: it was precisely the *lack* of generality of the older forms that impeded the rise of broader constellations of interest and action. It was the more general nature of the new forms that gave social movements a common cultural and behavioral foundation.[9] The question that emerges is, *What is the relationship between changes in the repertoire of contention and the birth of the social movement?* We will turn to that question after examining some traditional forms of contention typical of early modern Europe.

THE TRADITIONAL REPERTOIRE

For the great French historian Marc Bloch, collective action was a direct reflection of social structure. In writing of peasant revolts in feudal society, Bloch argued that "agrarian revolt seems as inseparable from the seignorial regime as the strike from the great capitalist enterprise" (1931: 175). He saw a general identity between the forms of collective action that people used and the substance of their claims, which resulted from the structure of their conflicts with others.

Bloch's axiom had two correlates: first, that the relationship between challenger and challenged is direct; and, second, that the forms of collective action are attached to the former's grievances and the power of the latter. But the same logic led to constraints on who could act alongside whom and on how widely a particular form of collective action could be used. If the agrarian revolt was aimed at the landlord, it followed that peasants who participated in it would associate only with those who share similar grievances against him in local village networks. The forms of action were rooted in the corporate structure of the feudal community.

Bloch was right for the estate societies he knew so well. In societies divided into orders, isolated by poor communication, and by lack of literacy, and organized into corporate and communal groups, forms of collective action were wedded to the conflicts that gave rise to them. When Protestants built a church in a Catholic district, the Catholic community would tear it down – or burn it with the parishioners inside (Davis 1973); when millers sold grain outside a district during a time of dearth, it would be seized and sold at a just price (Tilly 1975a); when authorities were responsible for the violent death of a local citizen, the funeral could turn into a funeral riot (Tamason 1980). The traditional repertoire was segmented, aimed directly at its targets, and grew out of the corporate structure of society.

Only when led by people who possessed organizational or institutional resources outside this corporate structure – for example, the church – or when they coincided with opportunities presented by religious wars or dynastic conflicts, such as the Reformation, did these episodes become part of broader confrontations, as in those studied by te Brake (1998). Then they could give rise to national or even international conflicts. More often, they flared up like scattered sparks that were rapidly exhausted or snuffed out. For the most part, as Tilly has recently argued, "local people and local issues, rather than nationally organized programs and parties, entered repeatedly into the day's collective confrontations" (1995a: 19).

Parochialism, direct action, and particularism combined in four of the most common types of popular revolt that fill the historical record until late in the eighteenth century. In conflicts over bread, belief, land, and death, ordinary people tried to correct immediate abuses or take revenge on those they opposed, using routines of collective action that were direct, local, and inspired by their claims.

DEMANDING BREAD

Probably the most common sources of contention in the course of history were the periodic food riots and grain seizures that accompanied dearth and price increases. Though the result of natural causes, famines almost always brought higher prices, hoarding, and speculation, providing protesters with concrete targets for their rage and desperation: merchants and middlemen, Jews and Protestants – more rarely, nobles and princes. As a result, providing the population with a steady and affordable source of grain became a major problem for centralizing states.[10]

For several centuries, even as national and international markets were replacing local grain sales, the forms of collective action triggered by dearth remained particularistic, direct, and dependent on inherited understandings. As E. P. Thompson wrote, "The records of the poor show . . . it is this miller, this dealer, those farmers hoarding grain, who provoke indignation and action" (1971: 98). Even during the revolution of 1789, the forms of food seizures changed little, although they were sometimes exploited by ambitious politicians for broader ends.

The most ancient form of food protest was what Tilly calls the "retributive action, in which a crowd attacked a person or the property of a person accused of withholding food or profiteering" (1975a: 386). Preventing a food shipment from leaving a locality was a second variant, which "acted out the belief that the locals should be fed, at a proper price, before any surplus left town" (p. 387). A third form, the price riot, was more characteristic of urban areas, and became more widespread with the growth of cities in the eighteenth century.

Grain seizures followed such a well-known routine that Thompson described them metaphorically as "collective bargaining by riot" (1971). They developed not so much out of raw hunger and outrage, as historians traditionally thought (Beloff 1963), but, rather, where people "believed others were unjustly depriving them of food to which they had a moral and political right" (Thompson 1966: 389). Although organized, these explosions seldom gained the common purpose or solidarity needed to mount a sustained campaign. Their limitations reflected the societies in which they arose. As Tilly writes, "small in scale, leaderless, and carried on by unarmed men, women and children, the food riot rarely consolidated into a larger rebellion" (1975a: 443). Broader political movements had to await the revolution of 1789, when "ordinary complaints about the incompetence and/or immorality of the local authorities and merchants now took on a political cast" (Tilly 1975a: 448).

ASSERTING BELIEF

Men and women in early modern Europe did not protest for bread alone. For most of known time, it is religion and religious conflict that have produced the most savage episodes of contention. In the centuries following the first millennium after Christ, waves of heretical sects developed within and against the Catholic Church. Some of these, local and based on the charisma of a single leader, were easily suppressed. But others, like the Cathars, who preached a dissident version of the Trinity, became briefly dominant in areas of southern France, where it took a crusade to uproot them. Later religious groups, like the Croquants and the Camisards, begin to resemble social movements (Bercé 1990; Tilly 1986: 174–8).

Existing forms of church organization provided both the targets and the models for the rebellions of these heretical sects. Collective actions mounted in the name of religion often savagely parodied their opponents' practices. In assaulting Catholics, French Protestants mimicked Catholic ritual and Catholics responded in kind.[11] The violence and cruelty of these conflicts certainly exceeded those of modern class conflict, but with hatred assuaged by blood and offending practices suppressed, no permanent new repertoires resulted.[12] It was only when religious fervor joined with peasant revolts, dynastic ambitions, or interstate conflict that rebels against religion gained access to the tools of the modern social movement.

With the appearance of the Protestant saint – the first social movement organizer – modern religious movements were born. As Michael Walzer has shown (1971: ch. 1), the saint was the forerunner of the modern movement militant. He not only believed deeply in his cause; he turned the mission of converting souls into a profession. The first "corresponding societies" were religious brotherhoods linked by couriers, secret codes, and rituals. But until then, religious movements ranged from physical attacks against Jews, Protestants, Catholics, and heretics to the sporadic local resistance of the Camisards.

CLAIMING LAND

Almost as common in early modern history as food riots and religious conflicts were peasant revolts. Traditional peasants depended on customary rights to land, water, or forage to survive and were most easily goaded into revolt when these were curtailed or abused. Rights were often claimed in the name of the peasant community, whose members would accuse landlords of breaking ancient conventions and usurping contracts. Even modern "struggles for the land" frequently hearkened back to usurpations more than a century old.[13]

The forms of land revolt often followed a ritual that took shape around the demands of the landless or land poor. Peasants brandishing pitchforks and scythes or carrying the cross or a statue of the Virgin would assemble in the town square, march to usurped land and "occupy" it. Such outbursts spread from village to village like wildfire without common agents or organizations. But once the occupation was over, local groups seldom found a way to organize around broader themes and almost never made common cause with the urban poor.[14] Apparent exceptions – like the Croquant movement of the late sixteenth century, which was organized by surprisingly modern-looking assemblies (Bercé 1990: ch. 2) – were not based on land, but were organized against marauding bands left over from the religious wars (Bercé 1990: 72–5). Such revolts were as easy to isolate and snuff out as they had been to spark.

MOBILIZING AROUND DEATH

It may be surprising to think of death as a source of collective action. But it is the reaction of the *living* – especially to violent death – that is the source of protest, rather than death itself. Death has the power to trigger violent emotions and brings people together with little in common but their grief and their solidarity. It provides legitimate occasions for public gatherings and is one of the few occasions on which officials will hesitate to charge into a crowd or ban public assemblies.

Death has always been connected to an institutionalized form of collective action – the funeral – that brings people together in ceremony and solidarity. In repressive systems that ban lawful assembly, funeral processions are often the only occasions on which protests can begin. When the death of a friend or relative is seen as an outrage, funerals can become the site for disruption. When a public figure offends the mores of the community, he can be symbolically killed in a mock funeral.

But the same reasoning tells us why death is seldom the source of a sustained social movement. For death's moment is brief and the ritual occasion offered by a funeral is soon over. It was only in the nineteenth century, in the context of movements formed for other purposes, that funerals begin to be the occasion for sustained mobilization against authorities (Tamason 1980: 15–31).[15]

Demanding bread, asserting belief, claiming land, mobilizing around death: in all four areas, contention was violent and direct, brief, specific, and parochial. With the exception of religious conflicts, where translocal institutions and common beliefs facilitated broader coalitions and greater coordination, the actors in these forms of contention seldom moved beyond local or sectoral interests or sustained them against authorities or elites.

It was not for lack of organization that pre-eighteenth-century Europeans failed to build social movements. Indeed, when they were aroused or had the opportunity to do so, they could organize powerfully, as the religious wars of the sixteenth and seventeenth centuries showed. Nor were food rioters or funeral marchers "apolitical": the former were not revolting at famine per se but against evidence that authorities were ignoring their inherited rights, while the latter had the political shrewdness to use a legitimate ceremony to air their grievances.

The major constraint on turning contention into social movements was the limitation of the forms and goals of collective action to people's immediate claims, to their direct targets, and to their local and corporate memberships. All this would change between the eighteenth and mid-nineteenth century. For this change the consolidation of national states, the expansion of roads and printed communications, and the growth of private associations were largely responsible.

THE MODULAR REPERTOIRE

Bloch's axiom embedding particular forms of collective action in specific social structures – perfectly applicable to the estate societies he studied – does not work nearly as well for the societies that had emerged in Europe and North America by the eighteenth century. In these places, a new repertoire developed that was cosmopolitan rather than parochial; autonomous rather than dependent on inherited rituals or occasions; and modular rather than particular. Centering around a few key routines of confrontation, it could be adapted to a number of different settings and its elements combined in campaigns of collective action. Once used and understood, it could be diffused to other actors and be employed on behalf of coalitions of challengers. The result was to make it possible for even scattered groups of people who did not know one another to combine in sustained challenges to authorities and create the modern social movement.

Of course, the inherited forms of the past – the *charivari*, the serenade, the illumination, the attack on enemies' houses – did not disappear with the invention of the new repertoire. But as new claims were diffused – together with information about how others had put them into practice – and people developed enhanced capacities for collective action, even these older forms were infused with more general meaning and combined with newer ones. Three examples from both sides of the Atlantic world of the eighteenth century will illustrate how the new repertoire came into use.

FROM EFFIGIES TO BOYCOTTS IN AMERICA

The American colonists brought with them from Europe an old repertoire of collective action. As the conflict with the mother country gathered force in the early 1760s, their first responses were traditional; when the British tried to impose a new and more onerous stamp duty in 1765, the instinctive reaction of Bostonians was to hang an effigy of the designated distributor on the future Liberty Tree. "In the evening a large crowd paraded the effigy, leveled a small building . . . reputed to be the future Stamp Office, then burned the effigy," writes historian Pauline Maier, "while a smaller contingent attacked the stampman's home" (1972: 54).

The agitation was infectious and spread rapidly through the colonies, using the forms inherited from the old country. Mock trials for stamps and stampmen were held, "funerals" were staged for liberty, and effigies were paraded in routines that strongly recalled traditional English practices (Maier 1972: 54–5). Serious rioting was a frequent accompaniment of these proceedings. But by September, with the news that the ministry of George Grenville had fallen in London, the wave of violence against the persons and policies of the stamp controversy quickly subsided (p. 61).

But the same period also saw a more organized, more general, and non-physical form of action appear – the boycott.[16] Colonial merchants first made "nonimportation" agreements against the Sugar Act in 1764, calling for reducing the import of luxury goods from England, above all of the mourning clothes and gloves traditionally worn at funerals. "These fledgling efforts," writes Maier, "were systematized in September 1765 [with the Stamp Act controversy] and thereafter nonimportation associations were organized in other commercial centers" (1972: 74). The boycott became a basic routine for the rebellious colonists, used over the next decade in response to virtually every effort of the British to impose stricter control. For Americans, "nonimportation could constitute an effective substitute for domestic violence," observes Maier; "opposition could retreat from the streets to the spinning wheel" (p. 75). If giving up mourning could contribute to the fall of a British minister, asked a writer in the *Boston Gazette*, "what may we not expect from a full and general Execution of this plan?" (p. 75).

Thenceforth, nonimportation and boycotting became the modular weapons of the American rebellion, employed most clamorously in the controversy over tea in Boston harbor.[17] The effectiveness of the tactic was not lost on Britain: in 1791, the English antislavery association used a boycott on the importation of sugar from the West Indies to put pressure on Parliament to abolish the slave trade (Drescher 1987: 78–9). From a parochial response to new taxes from the periphery of the British Empire, the boycott had migrated to its core. Other forms were evolving in Britain as well.

MASS PETITIONING IN ENGLAND[18]

The petition was an ancient form for individuals seeking redress from patrons or Parliament. As such, it was culturally acceptable, perfectly lawful, and scarcely contentious. But with the growth of the British economy in the early eighteenth century, petitioning spread to trades claiming injury from the expansion of the excise tax (Brewer 1989: 233). By the early 1780s, petitioning Parliament was still more of a "private" than a public act, "tied to the claims of specific injured parties or beneficiaries" (Drescher 1987: 76). When the first great petition against slavery was circulated in 1788, a representative of the Jamaican sugar lobby was incredulous: these abolitionists had neither been injured by slavery nor would they benefit personally from its end; what right had they to petition for its abolition (Drescher 1987: 76–7)?

During the two decades between 1770 and 1792, the petition was transformed from the tool of private interests seeking redress to a public act seeking justice in the name of general moral claims. And where earlier petitions were single acts launched by groups of petitioners, by the 1790s petitions were being regularly launched at public meetings and accompanied by boycotts, newspaper advertisements, and lobbying in extended movement campaigns.

Although Wilkes and others had used the petition for political purposes earlier – for example, it was a petition that preceded the outbreak of the Gordon riots of 1780 – it was the antislavery campaign launched in bustling Manchester that effected its transformation into a modular tool. Manchester's industrialists first used a petition to demand repeal of the government's revenue plans in the early 1780s. They then played a leading role in the petition campaign against a customs union with Ireland a few years later (Drescher 1987: 69). These were commercial issues, but they created the expertise that could "open the sluices of enthusiasm" for issues with broader policy or moral content (p. 69). Self-confident and wealthy – but electorally unrepresented – Manchester businessmen extrapolated the skills developed on behalf of their interests into a national moral campaign.

The antislavery campaign raised by a quantum leap the number of petitions and the numbers of signers who were coordinated in a single campaign. More important, the men of Manchester combined the petition with the use of Britain's dense network of provincial newspapers to advertise it in every major newspaper market, triggering a wave of petitions sent to Parliament from around the country (Drescher 1987: 70–2). In 1792, a new antislavery campaign quintupled the number of petitions, "the largest number ever submitted to the House on a single subject or in a single session," according to Drescher (p. 80).

By the 1790s, the use of mass petitions had spread: first to Radicals demanding the expansion of the suffrage and protesting the curtailment of free speech by a government frightened by Jacobinism (Goodwin 1979); then to advocates for electoral reform. Like the abolitionists, the Reform Societies used the provincial press to coordinate the efforts of different local associations, linking the signing of petitions with their lobbying efforts. By the 1830s, the decorous presentation of mass petitions had been combined by the Chartists with the collective use of public space to demonstrate the movement's strength. In presenting their "people's petitions" to Parliament, they brought thousands of people into the streets in April 1848.[19] From the plea of a dependent client to his patron, and from a lobby's claim of tax relief for its members, the petition had been transformed into a modular form of collective action to demand major changes in policy.

THE URBAN INSURRECTION IN FRANCE

Innovations in the repertoire were not limited to the Anglo-American world – although it was probably easier there to free them from traditional routines than on the continent. Even before the French Revolution, a repertoire of urban insurrection was forming in France. Though most forcefully implemented on July 14, 1789, in Paris, interestingly enough the model of the urban insurrection was provincial in origin.[20]

In June 1788, angered by the crown's attempt to replace the parlements with a new system of national courts, and exacerbated by the economic distress of local craftsmen, a disturbance began in the marketplace of Grenoble. What resulted was the "Day of the Tiles," probably the first fully secular urban insurrection in French history and a foretaste of what was to come at the Bastille a year later.

As in Boston, at first, the forms of action used by the Grenoblois were familiar, direct, and physical. They attacked buildings and officials at the marketplace and when troops were sent to quell the riot, they showered them with a rain of tiles from the rooftops above. But soon after, an urban leadership was formed, assembling illegally at the Château of Vizelle, and producing a major manifesto that put pressure on the king to call the Estates General.[21]

In the Grenoble events, we see a premonition of something that resembles the modern social movement. A variety of forms of collective action were employed in a sequence of contentious conflict with elites and authorities. Organization emerged at a meeting in which the claims of upper-class *parlementaires*, middle-class writers and clerks, artisans, glove makers, and women were merged under a broader umbrella of rights. In the words of some of the participants, the main demand was "the return of our magistrates, privileges and the reestablishment of the conditions which alone can make true laws" (Schama 1989: 279).

The concept of rights elaborated at Vizelle went much further than the particular claims of the participants. In addition to dignifying and uniting the claims of a broad coalition of social actors, it established the idea that an unauthorized assembly, acting in the name of "the laws and the people," could demand a contractual relationship with the state that went beyond parliamentary privileges or economic relief (Egret 1977: 177).

The boycott, the mass petition, the urban insurrection – these and other modern forms of collective action had already appeared when the French Revolution broke out in 1789. What they had in common was that they were cosmopolitan, modular, and autonomous of the claims and antagonisms of the actors who participated in them. They were facilitated by – and helped to create – movement networks that mounted and diffused contention in the name of general claims in sustained interaction with power holders. Together, modular repertoires, movement organizations, and broad collective action frames converged in the social movements that transformed popular politics in the nineteenth century, as we can see in the barricades that Tocqueville observed in 1848.

THE SOCIAL CONSTRUCTION OF THE BARRICADE

The most dramatic and feared expression of the new repertoire of the nineteenth century was the armed insurrection on behalf of popular sovereignty, symbolized by the barricade that became its main instrument (Traugott 1995). Barricades had first appeared in Paris when neighborhoods tried to protect themselves from intruders by stretching chains across the road. The term itself evolved after 1588, when these defenses were reinforced by filling barrels (*barriques*) with earth or paving stones.[22]

At the beginning, writes Traugott, barricades "were the collaborative creations of the members of small-scale communities, often directed against the representatives of constituted authorities" (1990: 3). By the 1830 revolution, they appear as offensive strongpoints in the streets of Paris, drawing friends and neighbors on a largely local basis. But by the February Days in the 1848 revolution, barricades have attracted "cosmopolitans" from other neighborhoods of Paris (Traugott 1990: 8–9). By the time of the 1871 Paris Commune, they were vulnerable to long-distance cannon, but still served a solidary and symbolic function (Gould 1995: 164).[23]

Like the demonstration and the strike, the barricade had an internal, as well as an external logic. As they faced off against hostile troops, the defenders came to know each other as comrades, developed a division of labor of fighters, builders, and suppliers, forming networks of comrades that would bring them together in future confrontations. As Traugott writes,

> from a vantage point atop a barricade, an entire generation of revolutionists was formed in the struggle against the Bourbon and Orleanist monarchies; matured in the struggles of the Second Republic; and saw its political aspirations crushed by the coup that ushered in the rule of Louis Napoleon. (1990: 3)

France was not far ahead of its neighbors; as insurrections spread across Europe in the spring of 1848, the barricade emerged as the quintessential modular form of revolutionary activity. From February 1847 to the middle of 1849, barricades appeared as far apart as Madrid and Lisbon, Messina and Milan, Berlin and Vienna (Godechot 1971; Soule and Tarrow 1991). In Vienna, they were raised to demand constitutional reform; in Sicily to demand independence from Naples; in Milan and Venice to end Austrian rule; and in the smaller Po Valley towns to demand unification with Piedmont. The barricades in the 1848 revolutions spread faster than a man could ride by coach from Paris to Milan. As Verdi wrote to Piave on his return to Italy, eager to take part in his country's revolution, "Guess whether I wanted to stay in Paris when I heard the news of Milan's Revolution? I left as promptly as possible, but I arrived only in time to see those fantastic barricades!"[24]

SMALL CHANGE AND HISTORICAL TRANSFORMATIONS

Events like those described in this chapter are the crucibles out of which new political cultures are born (Sewell 1990, 1996). Many of the future changes in the repertoire of contention first appeared in such great events as the taking of the Bastille or the February Days in Paris. But their foundations were developed in the interstices of the day-to-day practice of contention: like the mass petition that grew out of a prosaic business practice in Britain; the barricade that was first used to defend Parisian neighborhoods from thieves; and the urban insurrection that was first used to demand work in Grenoble, before becoming the instrument of revolution at the Bastille. From the point of view of the repertoire of popular politics, great events are often the culmination of structural changes that have been germinating unobtrusively in the body politic.[25]

The change from the traditional repertoire to the new one is a case in point. Where the old repertoire had been parochial, direct, and corporate-based, the new one was national, flexible, and based on autonomous forms of association created specifically for struggle. In the former, grain seizures, religious conflicts, land wars, and funeral processions were segmented both from one another and from elite politics. But with the latter, it was possible for workers, peasants, artisans, clerks, writers, lawyers, and aristocrats to march under the same banners and confront the same opponents. These changes made possible the coming of the national social movement.

This newly found power in movement had a profound impact on the structure of modern politics. For if, in the short run, people challenging authority brought down repression on their heads, over the longer run the new repertoire increased the leverage of ordinary people to challenge rulers and forced rulers to create means of social control more subtle than the cavalry charge or the cannonade. Over the years, parts of the new repertoire became components of conventional politics. The strike became an institution of collective bargaining; the demonstration was covered by a body of law that both regulated and distinguished it from criminal activity; and the sit-in and building occupation were treated with greater leniency than ordinary delinquency.

How did these changes come about and why did they begin when they did? Great national events, to be sure, had profound effects in providing models of collective action and collective consciousness for the future. But such events were episodic and usually limited to single countries; by the beginning of the nineteenth century, a new repertoire of contention was becoming internationally known and widely practiced. Though particular events left their mark on the changes we have identified, we must look beneath the surface of events for the causes of such powerful changes in popular politics.

3

PRINT AND ASSOCIATION

Social movements as we know them today began to appear in great numbers in the course of the eighteenth century. They drew their substance from structural changes that were associated with capitalism but preceded the industrial revolution. The major changes were the development of commercial print media and new models of association and socialization. These changes did not in themselves produce new grievances and conflicts but diffused ways of mounting claims that helped ordinary people to think of themselves as part of broader collectivities and on the same plane as their betters.

Printed books went back to the fifteenth century, but for a long time these were written in Latin, dealt mainly with religious subjects, and were inaccessible to ordinary people. This did not mean they were unimportant in spreading information – after all, the first political tracts were the religious books of the Protestant Reformation – but accessible publications had to await the spread of literacy and the lowering of the price of printed papers. Once that happened, popular newspapers and printed songs and pamphlets diffused images of ruler and aristocrat on the same sheets as bourgeois and plebeian, mechanic and tradesman, city dweller and rural notable.

New associational forms which escaped the tight corporate boundaries of estate societies first developed around church and commerce before being adopted by reading clubs, reform groups, and antislavery societies embodying moral purposes. Latent conflicts between people and their opponents were transposed into pamphlet wars, ribald songs, and scatological cartoons and prints. If the queen of France's body could be portrayed in print in a compromising position[1] and aristocrats and commoners could meet in the same coffee shops and reading clubs, how long would it be before the king's neck went under the guillotine and members of different classes joined in contentious collective action?

In the European past, corporate solidarities and face-to-face communications had often nurtured episodes of contention. Religious conflicts produced wars and revolutions, providing opportunities for peasant uprisings and tax revolts. But from the eighteenth century on, new forms of association, regular communications linking center and periphery, and the spread of print and literacy produced a secular change. Together, print and association made it possible for people in widely scattered towns and regions to know of one another's actions and join across wide social and geographic divides in national social movements.

A REVOLUTION IN PRINT[2]

In both Europe and America, the spread of literacy was a crucial determinant of the rise of popular politics.[3] Without the capacity to read, potential insurgents would have found it hard to learn of the actions of others with similar claims, except by word of mouth.[4] But John Markoff finds that, of the forms of contention accompanying the French Revolution, only tax revolts were especially characteristic of the literate countryside (1997: 383). Literacy per se was less responsible for the spread of social movements than the increasing ownership of books, as the readership of newspapers and pamphlets spread to social sectors that had formerly done little reading (Chartier 1991: 69).

Increased demand for reading matter was part outcome and part cause of changes in the production and diffusion of commercial printing (Chartier 1991: 70–6; Darnton 1989). Although a peasant who could sign his name to a parish register might or might not have the self-confidence to claim his rights, a man who had invested in expensive publishing equipment had a commercial incentive to produce news for a larger audience, and would find that audience only outside the circles of the rich. It was out of the audiences for the products of commercial print that invisible communities of discourse were formed.[5] In places like The Hague, Lausanne, and Philadelphia, men who specialized in the production of books, newspapers, pamphlets, and cartoons found both work and profit in printing.

By the middle of the eighteenth century, there began a "drive to tap new print markets, which differentiated the profit-seeking printer from the manuscript book dealer" and "worked against elitism and favoured democratic as well as heterodox trends."[6] After 1760, French booksellers began to open *cabinets de lecture*, which "enabled subscribers to read extensively while spending little and made prohibited titles discreetly available" (Chartier 1991: 70). If reading increased commerce, the converse was also true: in America, notes Gordon Wood, "the strongest motive behind people's learning to read and write, even more than the need to understand the scriptures, was the desire to do business" (1991: 313).

The francophone press that was established outside the borders of France typified the intersection of profit and politics in the print industry. On the one hand, clandestine publications intended for the French market allowed the small states on France's borders to enrich their coffers; on the other, printers and publishers had a free hand to produce books that were too subversive to be published in France. The "neutrality" of these entrepreneurs was as subversive as capitalism, and for the same reason – in the name of profit, they were indifferent to the claims of religious creeds or dynastic causes (Eisenstein 1986: 194).[7]

One of these new men was particularly notable. In 1774 a failed English excise worker named Thomas Paine stepped off a boat in Philadelphia with a letter of introduction from Benjamin Franklin to Robert Aiken, a well-known printer in the town. Paine's ideas were not particularly new or even radical.[8] What made his impact on history so great was not only his role in two revolutions – the American and the French – but his extraordinary talent as a publicist.[9]

Paine had arrived in a country that was literally covered in printed paper.[10] In addition to almost forty newspapers, there were broadsheets, speeches, extracts of sermons, and, above all, pamphlets. It was in the form of pamphlets that the democratic implications of print really appeared. "Highly flexible, easy to manufacture, and cheap, pamphlets were printed in the American colonies wherever there were printing presses, intellectual ambitions and political concerns" (Bailyn 1967: 4). By the time of Paine's arrival in the colonies, pamphlet wars were a familiar part of the political landscape.[11]

COMMUNITIES OF PRINT

The expansion of publishing for a mass market triggered a competitive capitalist cycle. Vying to involve new readers in their enterprises, editors and publishers created invisible communities of print. "By means of letters to the editor and other devices," writes Eisenstein, "the periodical press opened up a new kind of public forum" helping to create something like a public opinion well before the French Revolution (Eisenstein 1986: 196–7). Diderot's *Encyclopédie* was only the most successful of these, linking publishers and readers, intellectuals and lay people, metropole and provinces. Such journals as the English *Present State of the Republick of Letters* and Pierre Bayle's *Nouvelles de la République des Lettres* "extended lifelines to isolated subscribers, conveying a new sense of forward movement to their readership" (Eisenstein 1986: 196).

A new kind of social life developed around the reading and exchange of books and printed papers. In France, provincial cities like Besançon had public libraries and reading clubs. Even residents of small towns like Saint-Amour asked permission of the authorities "to rent a room where they could meet, read gazettes and newspapers and indulge in games of chance." In conservative Franche-Comté, the clergy promoted the distribution of religious publications to fight secularization (Vernus 1989: 127).

If the book was the first mass-produced commodity, newspapers were its most subversive extension – "a book sold on a colossal scale . . . a one-day bestseller," as Benedict Anderson writes (1991: 34–5). If a man could read about a great event on the same day as thousands of others he didn't know, he and they became part of the same invisible community of readers. And if a newspaper described the actions of rulers and dignitaries in the same language it used to discuss the doings of the merchants and traders who read it, the status of rulers and readers was leveled. Rather than emanating authoritatively from above, newspapers circulated horizontally; they "spoke polyphonically," writes Anderson of a later time and place, "in a hurly-burly of editorialists, cartoonists, news agencies, columnists . . . satirists, speech-makers, and advertisers, *amongst whom* government order-givers had to jostle elbow to elbow" (1991: 31, 34–5).

First created in capital cities, newspapers spread to the provinces to report on doings in the metropole. In England, writes Donald Read, "such provincial newspapers helped to build up knowledge outside London of parliamentary and London politics, filling their columns not so much with local news as with news and comment copied from the London press, especially from the lively journals of the Opposition" (1964: 19). By the 1760s, provincial readers were well schooled in opposition politics, and this helps to explain why they rose up in support of Wilkes in the 1770s and responded so rapidly to antislavery a decade later.

Competing with the capital city press was not easy, even in times of revolution. "From the first sittings of the National Assembly," wrote the *Journal de Normandie* in 1790, "we hoped to produce our paper every day, but we found out that it isn't possible to sustain competition with newspapers from the capital" (Marseille and Margairez 1989: 10). As a result, the provincial press became a vehicle for reporting on local news and expressing local attitudes about goings-on in the capital, rather than simply reprinting news from the center.

Revolutionary episodes provided the most fertile ground for the creation of new journals. The campaign for the Estates General in France loosed a torrent of publications, the catalog of the Bibliothèque Nationale listing 184 periodicals published in Paris alone in 1789 and 335 in 1790 (Popkin 1989: 150). The 1848 revolution had a similar effect, but on an international scale. It spawned some two hundred new journals in Paris, and a wave of new newspapers in German, many published as far away as the United States. In Italy, over one hundred journals were registered in Florence alone.[12]

While newspapers circulated the idea of movement, movements expanded the market for print as people tried to share – if only vicariously – in what was happening elsewhere. In their very mastheads, newspapers announced themselves as agents of movement. In Java in the early twentieth century, the founding of a journal called *The World on the Move* was followed by *Islam on the Move, Workers on the Move,* and *The People on the Move* (Anderson 1990: 32). Through print, people as far apart as Messina and Warsaw, St. Petersburg and Beijing could imagine themselves not only as Italians, Poles, Russians, and Chinese, but as Jacobins and *sans-culottes*, radicals and Communists, and their local enemies as feudatories and rentiers, aristocrats and capitalists.

The popular press did not so much make rebellion heroic as make it ordinary. If Philadelphians in 1773 could read in the New York papers that a rebellion was brewing up north, rebellion became thinkable in the Quaker colony (Ryerson 1978: 43–4). If Norwich's citizens could read how thousands in Manchester were signing petitions against slavery, it became intolerable to allow slavers to go unblamed in Norfolk (Drescher 1982). If a man could read in his national press about how insurgents in another country overthrew their ruler, then ruler overthrow became conceivable everywhere. As Anderson writes of the French Revolution, "once it had occurred, it entered the accumulating memory of print. . . . The experience was shaped by millions of printed words into a 'concept' on the printed page, and, in due course, into a model" (1991: 80).

ASSOCIATIONS AND MOVEMENT NETWORKS

People have always come together in groups, both religious and secular. But until the late eighteenth century, corporate and communal organizations predominated in European society. These, as William Sewell Jr. argues for the case of France, were aimed more at the defense of established and communal privileges than at the acquisition of new rights and benefits (1980, 1986). Rather than bringing people together on behalf of emergent or contingent interests, corporate and communal ties divided them into insulated pockets emphasizing corporate identities and differences. In any case, these corporate ties were limited to solid burghers, trade guilds, and clerics, leaving most of the population outside their protection.

Even when people did come together in groups around contentious purposes, their ties were most frequently founded on locality and personal proximity. The religious conflicts of the sixteenth and seventeenth centuries produced hundreds of militant groups across Europe, but few of them gave rise to durable associations, if only because – once established – their churches frowned on independent associations. In France, the Croquant movement, though organized through remarkably modern-seeming assemblies, was limited by local ties, its organizers never able to construct a broader movement (Bercé 1990). In England, the infamous "Gunpowder Plot," the origin of the modern Guy Fawkes Day, was organized by a network of Catholic friends and relatives, most of whom lived within easy reach of one other in the Midlands.[13] So out of touch were they with the communities around them that they imagined that blowing up Parliament would trigger a general rising against the Protestant regime.

Early in the eighteenth century, a new kind of association developed to help occupational groups protect themselves against state expansion and influence legislation in their favor. In England, where commerce was king, the expansion of the excise tax stimulated such groups as early as 1697 for the leather trades, 1717 for tanners, and the 1760s for glassmakers and brewers. "The levying of indirect taxes," writes John Brewer (1989: 233), "encouraged the emergence of organizations which transcended local and regional boundaries."

By the middle of the eighteenth century, a rich and varied associational life was developing in both Europe and North America. Government officials came to depend on them for information and they, in turn, cultivated contacts with ministers and members of Parliament to improve their chances of gaining favorable treatment (Brewer 1989: 232–34). But association would not remain for long within such narrow confines.

THE MODULARITY OF ASSOCIATION

England, where new forms of association grew out of earlier commercial and religious models, was ahead of the continent. The antislavery agitation of the 1780s first appeared among dissenting sects before spreading to Manchester's industrial interests (Drescher 1987: 61–3). The Yorkshire Association adopted the correspondence committees, which had been used earlier by commercial lobbies (Read 1964). O'Connell's Catholic Association adopted the subscription tactic of the lobbies, asking his members to contribute a penny a year for emancipation. The Catholics' success was not lost on the parliamentary reformers, who used subscriptions to finance the Political Unions that extracted the Reform Act from Parliament (Tilly 1982). By 1832, the special purpose association had become a modular form of social organization (Tilly 1995b: ch. 7).

England's American colonies were in advance of the metropole. The anti–Stamp Act movement was mounted by a network of local committees. With the hardening of British financial policy in the 1770s, a new wave of committees and associations rose. Association was no longer limited to merchants and traders; in 1772, the mechanics of Philadelphia formed a Patriotic Society, which Wood describes as the first organized nonreligious public pressure group in Pennsylvania's history (1991: 244). This was followed by similar moves in New York and Massachusetts in 1773, culminating in the formation of the Continental Association of 1774.[14] By the time the guns were fired at Lexington and Concord, a national web of associations, couriers, and spies was in place.[15]

As in England, religion was a cradle for associational development, but more so, due to the weakness of the established church before the revolution and the secular role of the churches in local communities (Moore 1994). Habits and forms of association learned in prayer meetings and to stamp out sabbath work were applied to moral crusades and then to civic and social movements. This can be seen in the militant evangelical protestantism of the Second Great Awakening. When historian Paul E. Johnson examined the social structure of the newly established city of Rochester, New York, he found that by 1830, it already possessed a rich network of religious associations (1978).

What was interesting in Rochester was not that a new town on the Erie Canal had a large number of churches. After all, churches had been the organizing matrices of New England society for two hundred years. What was remarkable was how easily special-purpose associations were formed *across* denominational lines for secular purposes.[16] Such coalitions would be instrumental in the moral crusades of the later nineteenth century. From the associational crucible of evangelical protestantism, such movements as antimasonry, sabbatarianism, temperance, evangelical revivalism, and its most revolutionary product – abolitionism – would come.[17] Women, a new social actor in American popular movements, first organized in church groups, before turning to temperance, abolitionism, and feminism (Cott 1977).

MOVEMENT NETWORKS

It was not so much these formal organizations, but the informal social networks that lay at their heart and the informal connective structures among them that were potential centers of collective action. This was even truer in France than in America, for legislation dating from the revolutionary Le Chapelier law restricted combination in that country. Under the Old Regime, guilds and corporations had been legal bodies, regulating trade and restricting practices, but workers' corporations and *compagnonnages* were illegal. With the liquidation of guilds by the revolution, workers' combinations remained but were outside the law. It was only in the 1830s, and then briefly, that they took legal form, and their repression after 1834 left the workers to organize in clandestine networks until 1848 (Sewell 1986).[18]

The same was true in rural areas like the Var. Like the English coffeehouses, the popular *chambrées* that developed in the Midi in the 1840s were places where a man could drink with his friends without being overheard by outsiders or paying the tax on alcohol. Never a formal system of association, but rather a set of similar informal groupings modeled on the social *cercles* of upper-status Frenchmen, they had enough in common to permit them to become centers of collective action when the opportunity arose. In such settings, republican newspapers could be read and a sense of solidarity developed, while the occasional traveler dropped by with news of what was happening in the wider world. At first tolerated by authorities, the *chambrées* came to be feared as potential sites for the instigation of collective action. "For the lower classes of Provence," concludes Maurice Agulhon, "to set themselves up as a *chambrée* was, just as much and perhaps even more than learning to read, to become accessible to whatever was new, to change and to independence" (1982: 150).

Sociable groupings like the *chambrées* help us to understand the subversive role that informal networks played in spreading new models of collective action. Painites, Radicals, and reformers in England; Whigs and patriots in the American colonies; liberals, republicans, and *montagnards* in France; *carbonari* and freemasons in Italy: they used the tools of association developed by commercial, religious, and reformist groups when they were legal but could relapse into informal networks in times of demobilization or repression.

Less easily infiltrated by the police than formal associations and less subject to factionalization, informal networks had advantages during a time when governments were becoming increasingly wary of combination. They could develop and reside within friendship and family networks, "lying low" during times of repression and emerging actively during times of stress or opportunity.[19] They were difficult to repress and control, for who could complain if a man wanted to drink with his friends in a private house or in back of a café?

COMMUNITIES OF PRINT AND ASSOCIATION

If print and association were complementary channels in the development of social movements, together they were an explosive combination. As Eisenstein notes of the reading clubs and corresponding societies of the late eighteenth century, they had no fixed memberships and, in the case of informal gatherings, no membership at all. But readers of the *Encyclopédie* and other similar periodicals were conscious of a common identity.[20] To subscribe to such a journal linked them to unknown others with similar views in invisible communities whose amplitude could only be imagined and could easily be exaggerated – as their publishers had ample reason to do.

By the time of the Revolution, the intersection between print and association was explicit. "To a greater extent than is often appreciated," writes Eisenstein, "the events of 1788–9 in France hinged on both a suspension of governmental controls over the printed word and on the freeing of associations." At the same time as the government was convoking the Estates General, it legalized Parisian clubs and freed a number of booksellers and printers from jail, resulting in what Lefebvre calls "an outpouring of pamphlets that astonished contemporaries."[21] What followed was the first deliberate public opinion campaign in history.

England's history was both more pacific and more advanced in joining print and association. By the late eighteenth century, reform associations were becoming skilled in using the press to advance their views. As a strategic directive from the London to the Sheffield Corresponding Society put it:

> if every [reform] society in the island will send forward a petition, we shall ultimately gain ground, for as much as it will force the members of the senate repeatedly to discuss the subject, and their deliberations, printed in the different newspapers, will most naturally awaken the public mind towards the object of our purpose. (Read 1964: 45)

The link between print and association was even more explicit in America. During the Stamp Act controversy, according to Pauline Maier, the Sons of Liberty in Connecticut "instructed local groups to 'publish their proceedings in the *New London Gazette.*'" Printers were active members of the Sons of Liberty in Boston, Rhode Island, and Pennsylvania. Long after the Sons were dissolved in

1766, "these papers and others like them . . . remained a forum for public discussion" (Maier 1972: 90–1).

DIFFUSION BY SOCIAL COALITION

Elites in the nineteenth century had a fixation on social class, first with respect to the French Revolution, which had to be either "bourgeois" or not based on class at all (Furet 1981); then with respect to the formation of the modern English working class; and finally with respect to the failure of socialism in America, which was supposedly based on the predominance of ethnicity over class in America's immigrant workers. In all three cases, class became the analytical pivot on which the outcomes of social movements were supposed to turn.

Karl Marx was the first to propagate the view that *the* social movement of the nineteenth century would be class-based. He thought that as capitalism produced a more and more socialized mode of production, the resulting homogeneity of the working class would counteract its tendency to compete for jobs. When intellectuals joined their efforts to those of the workers, they were "leaving" their class of origin as a sign of capitalism's coming collapse (Tucker 1978: 481). When different classes formed coalitions – as in the *Eighteenth Brumaire of Louis Bonaparte* – this was only the result of an intermediate stage of development that History would soon render archaic (in Tucker 1978: 604–5).

But the societies that produced the movements we have encountered in this and the last chapter were not yet the homogeneous industrial societies that Marx foresaw nor were they the estate societies that preceded them. How could they produce such powerful social movements as British abolition, American independence, and French revolution? The answer is that the loose ties created by print and association, by newspapers, pamphlets, and informal social networks, made possible a degree of coordinated collective action across groups and classes that the supposedly "strong ties" of social class seldom accomplished.

As an analytical building block, social class is an equivocal concept in explaining social movements, especially during periods of rapid social change. Consider the early English industrial workers: they were not easy to distinguish from their artisan and journeyman antecedents. When they cooperated with the latter groups in the popular movements of the late eighteenth and early nineteenth centuries, either the coincidence was thought to be accidental, like ships passing in the night, or a "declining" social formation – artisans and journeymen – were being absorbed into their "rising" successor.

The result of this predominant focus on class has been to obfuscate the important degree of *interclass* coalitions linked by print and associations among diverse and often divergent sectors of social movements. It was through the diffusion of information and the formation of coalitions within movement organizations that claims were coordinated and collective action co-occurred among social groups with different social interests and identities through which the metaphor of class was propagated. The diffusion of contention through both class and coalition has remained a central process in social movements up to the present day (Meyer and Rochon 1997).

WEAK TIES AND STRONG MOVEMENTS

This is not to say that the strong ties of homogeneous groups like "the working class" at the base of social movements are unimportant. In institutional settings like the factory or the mine, class was the basis of the primary solidarities at the base of militant social movements. The problem is that, when it came to forming broader movements, class homogeneity was rare and could inhibit solidarity; what movements needed to be successful were strong informal connective structures among heterogeneous and interdependent social groups and localities (Marwell and Oliver 1993). Class solidarity was a tool in mounting strikes, but it was much less important – and it could be even counterproductive – in the sustained interactions with authorities that were needed to build national social movements.

CONCLUSIONS

Primary associations and face-to-face contacts provide solidarity for social movements among people who know and trust one another. But print, association, and coalitional campaigns build connective structures among larger numbers of people and allow movements to be diffused to new publics. They thus permit the formation of loose, often contingent social coalitions, dealing with sympathetic or parallel issues, and giving shape to broad movement cycles.

Because of their narrower range, it was easy for historians to pinpoint the localities and the actors in earlier waves of collective action. Thus, geographer Andrew Charlesworth was able to characterize English riots from 1548 to 1900, accurately delimiting their social actors and geographical sites (1983). The reason for this is that most of these encounters involved a particular social category living in a limited territorial space and making a distinct set of claims on others. Their local or corporate ties gave them the confidence and the means of communication to attack others simultaneously or in a rapid series of assaults. But the same strength of local or corporate ties limited their capacity to spread elsewhere or to form coalitions with other social actors.

Sometime during the eighteenth century, we begin to see a broadening of claims, a wider geographic reach, and a more sustained capacity to mount collective action. Pauline Maier found it in the cross-class and intercolonial spread of tax resistance in America in the 1760s (1972: 69, 87). Seymour Drescher observed it in the antislavery agitation in England (1987: 80–1). Ted Margadant saw it in the urban and rural, middle- and lower-class interaction in the 1851 insurrection in France (1979: chs. 7–8). It was print and association – and especially the two in combination – that made possible such sustained campaigns of collective action on the part of broad coalitions making claims against elites and authorities: these created the national social movement.

But national movements would need more than the "push" provided by print and association; they also needed the pull of a common target and a pivot for their claims to focus around. These they found in contact with the expansion and consolidation of the national state and in reaction to its demands and incentives. The limits of national state development were found in Britain's overseas empire, while its greatest intensity was experienced in the prerevolutionary and Napoleonic states in France. At both extremes, social movements grew up around the armature of the national state, as we shall see in the next chapter.

4

STATE BUILDING AND
SOCIAL MOVEMENTS

National states are so central a focus for the mobilization of opinion today
that we often forget that this was not always so. During the centuries prior
to absolutism in western Europe, national states worthy of the name could hardly
be said to exist. "On the one hand," writes Norbert Elias in *State Formation and
Civilization*,

> kings were forced to delegate power over part of their territory to other
> individuals. The state of military, economic and transport arrangements at
> that time left them no choice. . . . On the other hand the vassals represent-
> ing the central power were restrained by no oath of allegiance or loyalty
> from asserting the independence of their area as soon as the relative power
> positions of the central ruler and his delegates shifted in favour of the latter.
> (1994: 276–7)

In such a system, contention was constant, largely territorially based, and changed
its contours according to whether the monarch was temporarily ascendant or
suffering a crisis.

From roughly the fifteenth century on, this pattern began to give way, as
the expansion of a money economy gave kings the power to hire mercenary
soldiers, build roads on which to deploy them, and hire civil servants to collect
taxes, administer rules, and overcome provincial nobles. Where they could establish a rough balance between the aristocracy and the rising burghers of the
towns, they developed a "royal mechanism," which led to the formation of absolutist states – as in France (Elias 1994: ch. 2). Where they were forced to share
power with their nobles and eventually with an assertive merchant class, the
result was constitutional or segmented monarchy – as in England or the Low
Countries. And where they failed altogether to gain territorial sovereignty, the

result was a set of loosely confederated states – as in Italy or the German-speaking lands until late in the modern era.

During all this time, contentious politics did not cease, but its character changed from the more or less constant struggle for territory among knights and their followers to alternating periods of war and relative peace, with outbursts of popular politics over land, religion, bread, and taxes. Between the fifteenth and the seventeenth century, popular contention developed among the triad of ordinary people, local rulers, and national claimants to power, particularly when wars and revolutions opened opportunities for ordinary people. "All across Europe," writes Wayne te Brake,

> revolutionary challenges in one part of a composite monarchy – rooted usually in opposition to princely taxation to finance war or, as in the sixteenth century, in the prince's aggressive claim to cultural (e.g., religious) sovereignty – opened up opportunities for popular political actors elsewhere. (1997: 12)

Viewed from the perspective of national politics and through the narrative historiographies that centered on them, these episodes were sideshows on the road to the establishment of parliamentary states. But each major episode of political change opened opportunities for ordinary people, either to ally with local rulers against national claimants or to connect their fates to princes against local oligarchies. They usually lost, but not before affecting the type of national state that eventually emerged. As te Brake concludes, "ordinary people could be so deeply involved in the eventual creation of parliamentary democracies precisely because they were an essential part of the political process from the very beginning of the modern era" (1997: 14).

And so they remain today. What changed was the form and consistency of their presence in contentious politics as the form of the state evolved, either centering around plebiscitory leaders, constitutional parliaments, or both. The major changes took place between the late eighteenth and the middle of the nineteenth centuries. This is not to say that national state building only began in the nineteenth century, but that state consolidation implying the creation of national forms of citizenship and identity dates from that period.[1]

Alexis de Tocqueville was the first to theorize about the implications of these changes for collective action. In his *Democracy in America* and *The Old Regime and the French Revolution*, he taught that differences in patterns of state building produced differences in the opportunity structures of social movements. Centralized states (i.e., France) aggrandized themselves by destroying intermediate bodies and reducing local autonomy. This discouraged institutional participation and meant that when confrontations did break out, they were violent and likely to lead to despotism.

In contrast, in weak states (i.e., the United States), in which civil society and local self-government were stronger, participation was regular and widespread, diffusing confrontation and allowing democracy to flourish. Tocqueville's under-lying message was that state building creates an opportunity structure for col-lective action of which ordinary people take advantage. Tocqueville's vision will provide a convenient starting point for examining the relationship between state building and the rise of national social movements.

CENTRALIZATION AND LOCALISM

Tocqueville began by asking why the French Revolution should have broken out in France – where the peasantry was far removed from feudalism – and not in more backward countries of Europe (1955: x). His answer was that, in France, state aggrandizement had denuded the aristocracy and other corporate groups of their positive functions, reducing them to parasitic weights on society. Because a society stripped of intermediate bodies lacked a buffer between state and society, Frenchmen became "self-seekers practicing a narrow individualism and caring nothing for the public good" (p. xiii). The result was jealous egalitarianism, sporadic and uncontrolled mobilization, and, ultimately, the revolution: "a grim, terrific force of nature, a newfangled monster, red of tooth and claw" (p. 3). No one would want to live in such a state, and, after a decade of terror and chaos, a despotism more absolute than the Old Regime ensued.[2] That despotism went the way of its predecessors, but for Tocqueville, it left its heritage in a Jacobin state that forced conflict upward into dangerous periodic confrontations.

So possessed was Tocqueville with the horrors of the French Revolution that he failed to notice that citizenship was being invented at the same time (cf. Schama 1989) and that intermediary bodies like the parlements played a key role in triggering its development. As for a whole school of institutionalists who followed him, centralization deprived citizens of the fiber in their civil society necessary to channel discontent into positive interactions and moderate the striv-ings of an acquisitive society.[3] In its absence, contention – and thus democracy – led straight to breakdown.

Where could such fiber be found? In both state and society, Jacksonian America showed Tocqueville a mirror image of the strong state and weak society that dismayed him in his native land. In the United States, no strong central state constrained associational life and flourishing civil politics. To be sure, Amer-ica had never had the traditional corporate bodies whose passage Tocqueville regretted in France. But it had a functional equivalent in the churches, interest groups, and local assemblies that provided Americans with self-help and a buffer against state expansion (Tocqueville 1954: ch. 16). With its weak state and flourishing associations, American democracy could avoid the pendulum between the extremes of anarchic egalitarianism and statist despotism that France was suffering.

But if Tocqueville's image of a France bereft of intermediate bodies exag-gerated both societal atomization and state strength, his glowing picture of Jacksonian America underestimated the relationship between state building and contention there. For one thing, the bucolic image he drew of antebellum America left the relationship between association and contentious politics in the shadows. For another, he mistook the non-European character of the early American state for the absence of a state *tout court*.[4]

To begin with the second point, although the nineteenth-century American state was not centralized, neither was it a *non*state. The Federalists had constructed what was for the late eighteenth century an effective state for their purposes, achieving fiscal consolidation, debt reduction, diplomatic maneuver, and westward expansion (Bright 1984: 121–2). The state that Tocqueville found in his travels was weak, but it had been weakened not by Americans' inherent love of freedom, but by a political stalemate between two expanding, sectionally based socioeconomic systems, North and South (pp. 121, 134). State weakness was a historical – and not a characterological – property of the American state. As Charles Bright observes, "the periods of greatest paralysis in federal policy corresponded with the periods when party mobilization was the fullest and the margins of electoral victory the slimmest" (p. 136).

What of American contention? Tocqueville saw this through the red lens of the Terror that had decimated his family and his class. Finding nothing of this kind in America, he saw few social movements.[5] But the United States in the late eighteenth and early nineteenth centuries was bursting with contention! The sabotage of British rule and the raising of a popular army in the 1770s; the local rebellions that followed the revolution and required troops for their suppression; popular opposition to and support of the 1812 war; the frontier mobilization that produced Jackson's presidency; the religious fervor of the Second Great Awakening that "burned over" wide swatches of newly settled territory: these episodes escaped the neat institutional pluralism that Tocqueville thought he saw in his travels through America.

The center of gravity of American social movements was still local in 1832 and this both fit the Tocquevillian paradigm and contrasted with the national insurrections he bemoaned in France. But as in other federal systems, localism did not mean an absence of social movement activity (Wisler and Giugni 1996). Even before industrialization, there was a lively urban workers' movement with a strong dose of Painite republicanism (Bridges 1986; Tarrow 1998b; Wilentz 1984). Already, regional and national movements were developing a capacity for collective action in a rough dialectic with the national struggle for power, and laying the groundwork for temperance and abolitionism, and, indirectly, for the first feminist movement in the world. The sectional conflict that had begun by paralyzing national policy making ended in the most cataclysmic episode of contention in the nation's history – one that would turn the American state into a modern Leviathan (Bensel 1990). Decentralized America might be, but it was hardly lacking in contention!

There were differences in state centralization, association, and collective action between centralized France and localized America. But in both countries, state building provided an opportunity structure for emerging movements, and movements of ordinary people helped to shape each future state. In both countries – and all over the West, for that matter – the expansion and consolidation of the national state prodded the social movement into existence, and ordinary people's struggles helped shape the modern state. In this chapter, we will examine how state building provided opportunities for contentious politics during the phase of state consolidation in Britain, France, and the United States.

STATE BUILDING AND CONTENTION

Even before the revolution of 1789, and in places more pacific than France, the national state was gaining unprecedented power to structure the relations among citizens and between them and their rulers. Expanding states made war and needed roads and postal networks, armies and munitions factories to do so. In order to finance such improvements, states could no longer rely on a surplus extracted from the peasantry, but depended on the growth of industry and commerce, which in turn required that law and order be maintained, food be supplied, associations be licensed, and citizens gain the skills necessary to staff the armies, pay the taxes, and turn the wheels of industry.

These efforts at state building were not intended to support mobilization – quite the contrary. But they provided means of communication through which opinion could be mobilized, created a class of men experienced in public affairs, and led to financial exactions on citizens who were not always disposed to pay them. In addition, states that took on the responsibility for maintaining order had to regulate relations between groups, and this meant creating a legal framework for association as well as providing more subtle mechanisms for social control than the truncheons of the army or the police. By these efforts, states not only penetrated society; they created a standard set of roles and identities that were the basis of modern citizenship. Within this matrix, citizens not only contested state expansion; they used the state as a fulcrum to advance their claims against others.

The most obvious example was in the extension of the suffrage and the legalization of public gatherings that it necessitated. Bourgeois states might not wish to see workers marching on the prefecture or peasants milling around the village square; but even under a restricted suffrage, the meeting and drinking that attended election campaigns provided umbrellas under which "undesirable" social actors and contentious forms of action found shelter. Even without elections, as Raymond Grew writes, all states, "as if by irresistible mandate, encouraged easier nationwide communication and a minimal universal education. . . . Once citizenship became a formal matter of birth or oaths registered by the state, it remained so even though specific criteria could be altered" (1984: 94).

Three basic policies – making war, collecting taxes, and providing food – were part of the campaign waged by expanding states to assure and expand their power. While they began as pressures on citizens and as efforts to penetrate the periphery, each produced new channels of communication, more organized networks of citizens, and unified cognitive frameworks within which ordinary people could mount claims and organize. In states as different as liberal monarchical Britain, absolutist France, and colonial America, these policies became arenas for the construction of movements, and movements – or the fear of them – shaped the national state.

WAR AND MOVEMENT IN BRITAIN

The most portentous changes were produced by war and colonization, not only because they required taxes and granted governments more power, but because they mobilized people in an organized way and provided opportunities for collective action. Mobilization to make war had been a limited affair until, in trying to realize their ambitions, rulers raised larger standing armies than their noblemen could lead or mercenaries could staff. The size of armies grew geometrically in the eighteenth century,[6] as did the financial and logistical requirements for putting them in the field. From multinational assemblies of mainly mercenary battalions, armies became national; [7] and national mobilization, though it came nowhere near twentieth-century levels, was great enough to cause severe social and financial dislocation – and sometimes revolution (Skocpol 1979).

In late eighteenth-century England, both the formation of the party system and opportunities for mobilization were advanced by the most aggressive activity of the British state: colonization and warmaking. Whereas the early years of the American war produced an increase in public support for the government, the later war years, with their disillusionment, financial strain, and fear of French invasion, brought attempts to mobilize opinion on a continuous basis. These were at first elite-led movements centering on London. But after failing to find a new basis for political organization in the 1760s (Brewer 1976: ch. 5), the government's opponents encouraged a broad-based and continuous attack on ministers on the basis of economic reform. It was in this context that Wilkes made his famous plea connecting the war to parliamentary reform: "The American war," he argued, "is in this truly critical era one of the strongest arguments for the regulation of our representation" (Christie 1982: 65).

Although London politics was the spark for this movement, much of the opposition came from sections of the country – like Yorkshire – whose trade was badly hit by colonial boycotts of English goods and then by the blockade of American ports. Clergyman Christopher Wyvill's Yorkshire Association began its activities with a platform combining a call for economic and parliamentary reform with an attempt to build a national network of county associations.[8] The association drew up a petition that gained nearly nine thousand signatures in Yorkshire and elected a committee of correspondence.

Forming a committee to manage a petition was nothing new in the England of 1779, as we have already seen. What *was* new was that the Yorkshire committee was designed to maintain a sustained pressure for reform (Read 1964: 13). Wyvill wanted to "keep a foot on machinery in Yorkshire for promoting his political program" (Christie 1982: 76). His example was followed in Middlesex, Westminster, and Gloucestershire, where his correspondents formed similar committees. No wonder the Tory government condemned the effort as an attempt to imitate the "seditious" American Continental Congress.

The Gordon riots of June 1780 produced a reaction against extraparliamentary association, and the Yorkshire and other branches of the movement petered out in the later years of the war (Read 1964: 14–16). The reaction was intensified when the Jacobin phase of the French Revolution appeared to threaten British institutions (Goodwin 1979). But while Jacobin and Painite agitators were suppressed, the movements for economic and parliamentary reform and the war that fostered them firmly established the future form of the social movement in England. "War made the state and the state made war," writes Charles Tilly (1975b: 42). But making war also created the space and incentives for social movements.

PROVISIONING FOOD IN FRANCE

Not only in wartime, but around more routine activities of national states, collective claims were organized. A traditional function of European states was to regulate the supply and the price of food – in part, to tax it but also to assure subsistence and public order. In the past, the battle had been fought mainly by city burgesses trying to gain control of their hinterlands. But as cities grew, states expanded, and markets internationalized, national states became responsible for guaranteeing food supply and were held responsible when it failed.

The provisioning of food was never wholly free of public control. For example, the insistence that the trading and weighing of food be done in a public place was not only a way of insuring its taxation but of assuring minimal standards of quality and price (Kaplan 1984: 27–31). At one time or another, communities, manors, churches, and states were all involved in the control of food supply. But "only states unequivocally acquired greater power to intervene in the food supply over the long run" (Tilly 1975a: 436) because it was states that were ultimately threatened by dearth and the popular contention it could foster.

As in much else, the connection between provisioning food and preventing disorder was most explicit under the French monarchy. According to an eighteenth-century administrator, the prerequisite for order "was to provide for the subsistence of the people, without which there is neither law nor force which can contain them."[9] Indeed, the obligation to assure subsistence came to be seen as a major responsibility of paternal kingship, for "what more solemn duty could a father have than to enable his children to enjoy their daily bread?" (Kaplan 1984: 24).

Though conflicts over food frequently occurred when people felt their right to subsistence was threatened, this situation was only generalized "when states began to assure the subsistence of those populations most dependent upon them and/or threatening to them." These included, most notably, the armed forces, state administrators, and the populations of capital cities (Tilly 1975a: 393). Since all three expanded rapidly in the eighteenth century, it is no accident that subsistence crises and food rebellions punctuated that century – most notably in the years before and after 1789. With the spread of physiocratic ideas, the proposal to free the price of grain came up against the prevailing paternalistic policy of assuring subsistence to the cities – and especially to Paris.

Provisioning Paris was seen as a special state responsibility, not only because of the city's enormous population, but because it was assumed (correctly, as it turned out) that Parisians were quite capable of overthrowing the government. The state thus made it its business to assure the amount of food supplied to Paris as well as the quality of the grain and flour that entered the capital.[10] The deepest conflicts in times of dearth arose between Parisian officials and the local communities that produced grain for the metropolis and competed for its supply. "The fiercest intercommunity struggle for subsistence," writes Kaplan, "opposed the local market town to the vulturous capital" (1984: 39).

Resistance took both physical and legal form. During grain shortages, while consumers were blocking the export of grain and demanding to pay a "just price" for bread, local officials might be barring Parisian suppliers from the local trade, causing long delays at the marketplace, requisitioning Paris-bound merchandise, and working out clandestine routes of supply and reserves (Kaplan 1984: 39). The result was recurring uprisings "affirming the intensely felt right of the community to its subsistence" (p. 39).

The 1789 revolution, though triggered by broader conflicts over taxation and parliamentary power, showed how deeply the national state had become involved in conflicts over food. The municipal insurrections that followed the news of the fall of the Bastille were in some places radicalized by the cry of "bread at two sous" (Lefebvre 1967: 125). Even the Jacobins, fearing to be outflanked on their left when they took power, found it convenient to set maximum prices on bread, sending revolutionary armies to scour the provinces for grain. From a set of local, parochial, and episodic conflicts over subsistence, food provision became a pivot for the spread of revolution. It would remain an important element in each revolutionary cycle up to 1848.

LEVYING TAXES IN AMERICA

The common denominator of all of the modern state's policies is its ability to raise revenue to support its other activities. The result is that fiscal problems, writes Gabriel Ardant,

> are to be found in the beginnings of great social changes, such as the liberation of the serfs of Western Europe, the subjugation of the peasants of

Eastern Europe, wars for independence (that of Portugal as well as that of the United States), revolutions, the creation of representative governments, etc. (1975: 167)

The growth of the modern state was most often contested by revolts against the growing burden of taxes. The hated *gabelle* in France and the *dazio* in Italy led to revolts that flared up for years. In France, the monarchy's tactic of selling the right to collect taxes to tax "farmers" increased people's resentment while making it easier for them to assault the collector. Tax revolts rose and fell, more commonly in peripheral than in core areas, but were by no means limited to the lower classes, as the history of the relations between the French monarchy and the provincial parlements shows.

But it was only in the late eighteenth century that tax revolts became sufficiently broad-based and well organized to feed into national movements. If the states of the late eighteenth century had a new fiscal problem, it was because their expanded ambitions required a degree of financial universalism that was contradicted by their dependence on their clerical and land holding elites. Both paid few or no taxes, regarding the military role of the nobility and the spiritual one of the clergy as sufficient service to the state. Rulers who toyed with equalizing the burden of taxes had to face the prospect of losing the support of one or the other of their major allies (Ardant 1975: 213).

England's difference from the continental powers was that basic reforms in its tax system were never attempted. This was in part because the expansion of global trade – much of it British and carried in British ships – produced large revenues from the excise tax, and in part because the effective center of the British state was a Parliament in which landed proprietors held a majority of seats (Ardant 1975: 207). Revenue collection thus weighed relatively lightly on the land, on which the wealth of the parliamentary elite depended[11] and heavily on trade – particularly on trade with the colonies. What Americans called "The French and Indian War" brought these pressures to a head, because it was immensely more expensive to wage than any previous British struggle, and because Parliament chose to make the colonists pay for it rather than raise taxes in Britain. This was justified by the argument that the war in North America had been fought for the benefit of the colonists and it was they who ought to pay for it (Ardant 1975: 204).

But such a fiscal strategy was foolhardy. For the American colonists lived an ocean away and had their own provincial governments, which depended on much the same mix of revenues as the mother country.[12] The new imperial fiscal policy was not only offensive and difficult to collect; it threatened the autonomy of the colonial political system that, in the absence of a large land army, was an instrument of indirect rule.[13] To enforce it, the British would have to retract the considerable autonomy that they had accorded the colonies.

There was a fundamental reason for Parliament's obduracy; in refusing to finance a war that had supposedly been fought for their benefit, the colonists were challenging nothing less than the expansion of the British state. Parliament was "inherent and inseparable from the supreme authority of the State," in Lord Dartmouth's words (Maier 1972: 233). If Parliament could be challenged on this issue, the state might face even greater challenges at home – or in Ireland. The first major colonial revolution in history was a response to state building, indicated its limits, and demonstrated the power of movement to shape it.

THE STATE AS TARGET AND MEDIATOR

Activities like making war, provisioning cities, and levying taxes stimulated new and more sustained episodes of collective action. As the activities of national states expanded and penetrated society, the targets of contention shifted from private and local actors to national centers of decision making. The national state not only centralized the targets of collective action; it involuntarily provided a fulcrum on which claims could be mounted against *non*state antagonists through the mediation of the state.

During much of the eighteenth century, as we learn from Charles Tilly's recent research on Britain, the targets of the prevailing forms of contention were millers and grain merchants, local gentry, members of the community, and peripheral agents of the state like tollgate managers or tax collectors. But from the late eighteenth century, with a brief inflection between 1789 and 1807, Tilly finds a decisive movement of collective challenges away from private and local targets and toward the use of public meetings with Parliament as their main target. By the 1830s, Parliament had become the object of approximately 30 percent of the contentious gatherings in southeast England (Tilly 1995a: 36).

State building not only made the national government a target for citizens' claims; it led to the broader cognitive and political framing of citizen actions. The standardization of taxation, of administrative regulations, and of census categories encouraged the formation of coalitions of groups that had previously been opposed or indifferent to one another. The classification of citizens into what started out as artificial groupings (e.g., payers of a certain tax, residents of particular cities, counties, or *départements*, soldiers conscripted in particular years) constructed new social identities or laid the bases for broader coalitions.[14]

We see this integrative effect most clearly in the effects of taxation on collective action. As taxes shifted from a congeries of disparate duties on different classes of citizens to simplified national imposts collected by a central bureaucracy, tax revolts could unite diverse social groups and localities. Conscription had a similar effect – especially when resistance to it was linked to ideological or religious objections. The Vendée Rebellion which followed the French Revolution was only the first in a series of such movements, ending, most recently, in opposition to the Vietnam War, in which the trigger for mobilization was resistance to the draft (Tilly 1964: ch. 13).

One result of these changes was a massive decline in the amount of violence attending contention (Tilly 1995a: 35). Another was the appearance of a number of forms of contention that were more integrated in the polity than earlier ones had been – like British industrial action, American religious movements, and French republicanism. A third was that state growth and consolidation had to take account of popular will but be prepared to suppress it when it got out of hand. The two most characteristic areas of state growth in the nineteenth century – the expansion of the suffrage and the growth of a professional police – were both linked to fear of popular contention.

BALLOTS AND NO BARRICADES IN AMERICA

The fundamental fact about American workers in the nineteenth century was that, as the result of a revolution for citizen rights that was won before an industrial working class existed, workers had the vote much earlier in their development than in Europe. This not only meant that workers' collective action was channeled by the ballot; it meant that in the future, workers' participation would be territorially oriented. And since the bulk of the working class was urban from a very early stage, workers' collective action was directed at urban politics, where lively political machines could make use of their votes and provide them with channels for upward mobility.

These institutional factors made the American working class different than the one that was appearing in western Europe at about the same time (cf. Aminzade 1993). In 1830, American workers shared with their English cousins an artisan republicanism, understood the coming of the industrial system in similar ways, and used the same language of master and slave (Bridges 1986: 158). But the fact that they voted in an already electoralized state "changed the arena in which the newly created working classes struggled to achieve their goals" (p. 161). As Amy Bridges concludes, "sheer numbers, the search for allies, geographical dispersion or concentration, and the rules of the electoral game all affected the political capacity of the working classes" (p. 161).

Thenceforth, the integration of the waves of immigrants who fed the American industrial machine was shared between the unions, which organized workers on an occupational basis, and the urban political machines, which sought their vote on territorial lines (Katznelson 1981: 45–72). "Class" as an organizing category was far from absent in the factory, but in elections, it had to contest for workers' loyalty with territory and ethnicity, both of which were combined with party by electoral politics. The long-term institutional trends created by the revolutionary settlement created – and shaped – political opportunities for the workers for generations to come.

REPRESSION AND CITIZENSHIP

Not all the long-term changes in state structure created opportunities for contention; many were deliberately designed to check them. For once the idea of combining consistently on behalf of collective claims was widely diffused, the fear of uprisings led national states to strengthen the police and pass legislation restricting the rights of assembly and association. It does not seem accidental, for instance, that the British created a professional police force after the Peterloo massacre, when uncontrolled troops had fired on unarmed workers.[15] A second major strengthening of police forces coincided with the increase in labor disputes, particularly when the mass strike was developed toward the end of the nineteenth century.[16] The rhythms of repression followed the pulse of popular politics.

In France, it was less strikes than the fear of insurrection that kept authorities plotting new strategies of order. After each wave of revolutionary agitation (1830, 1848, and 1870–1), new attempts were made to restrict collective action, both by limiting association and preparing the forces of order for urban warfare. Both were draconian on the surface but each adapted in the long run to the inexorable pressures of citizenship and civil society.

With respect to association, "French law and administrative practice forbade the discussion of politics within [bourgeois] associations," writes historian Carol Harrison, but this did not prevent thousands of Frenchmen from joining them (1996: 45). It did give the state the power to investigate associations that it thought dangerous. But at each opening of political opportunity, new or revised forms of association sprang up, evading the authorities with their ingenuity or apparent innocence.[17]

As for combating urban insurrection, the police won that battle. The barricades that had sprung up during the 1830 and 1848 revolutions corresponded to a temporary balance of technical power between urban insurgents and authorities. By June 1848, the Parisian barricades could no longer resist the determined firepower marshaled by the army, and most were blown apart (Gould 1995; Traugott 1995a). Under the Second Empire, the restructuring of Paris by Baron Haussmann spelled the doom of the barricade as a defensive weapon. For the tangled warren of streets in the old quarters of Paris, Haussmann substituted today's broad boulevards to facilitate the reduction of future barricades by cannon fire.

But the decline of the barricade had a latent effect, leading to the development of new tools of agitation by working-class militants – mainly the strike and the public demonstration. Both were far less threatening to republican order and therefore harder to repress. By the late nineteenth century, both a jurisprudence and the conventions of police practice led to the institutionalization of these newer forms, culminating in the development of the *service d'ordre*, by which demonstrators largely agreed to police themselves (Bruneteaux 1996). The characteristic tools of twentieth-century popular politics were born through a long-term dialectic between violent protests and equally violent state repression.

This lesson can be generalized: as movements learned to use the apparatuses of national communications and consolidated states, governments had to accept grudgingly forms of collective action whose legitimacy they had earlier resisted. The English leaders who had condemned petitions in favor of Wilkes as subversive, and who linked the Yorkshire Association to the Continental Congress, were eventually forced to accept mass petitions and political associations as legitimate. There was a reaction during the war with France, but, by the early 1800s, voluntary associations were so common in England that innkeepers routinely kept their funds and papers in locked boxes (Morris 1983: 95–118). By the 1830s, the private association for advancing group purposes was a familiar part of the political landscape (Tilly 1982).

We should not think of the progress of the social movement as smooth, not even in liberal Britain. For once revolution had broken out on the continent, even mild reform movements like the British one raised suspicions of sedition among frightened elites. Books and pamphlets were censored, radical associations banned, and even moderate ones lost membership. "The result of this confusion and the inexpedient policies that flowed from it," observe Malcolm Thomis and Peter Holt, "was often the creation of revolutionaries where none had previously been." Governments, they conclude, "helped to create and sustain that very danger to themselves that they supposedly wished to avoid" (1977: 2).

But by the second half of the nineteenth century, movements and their potential for disruption led national states to broaden the suffrage, accept the legitimacy of mass associations, and open new forms of participation to their citizens. In a very real sense, citizenship emerged through a rough dialectic between movements – actual and feared – and the national state. From the postrevolutionary American suffrage reforms to British factory legislation of the 1840s to the unemployment and health reforms of imperial Germany and the factory inspectors instituted in the French third Republic, state reforms were either direct responses to social movements or attempts to preempt their development. As Bright and Harding point out, "contentious processes both define the state vis-à-vis other social and economic institutions and continually remake the state itself" (1984: 4).

CONCLUSIONS

It is time to recapitulate what has been argued in this and the two preceding chapters. Contentious politics has characterized human society for as long as there has been social conflict – which is to say, from whenever human society can be said to have begun. But such actions usually expressed the claims of ordinary people directly, locally, and narrowly, responding to immediate grievances, attacking opponents, and almost never seeking allies among other groups or political elites. The result was a series of explosions – seldom organized and usually brief – punctuating periods of passivity.

Sometime in the course of the eighteenth century, a new and more general repertoire of collective action developed in western Europe and North America. Unlike the older forms, which expressed people's immediate grievances directly against antagonists, the new repertoire was national, autonomous, and modular:

that is, it could be used by a variety of social actors on behalf of a number of different claims and serve as a bridge among them to strengthen their hand and reflect broader and more proactive demands. Even inherited forms like the petition were gradually transformed from the tool of individuals seeking grace from superiors or groups lobbying power holders into a form of mass collective action.

The root causes of this change are difficult to tease out of a historical record that has been mainly collected by those whose job it was to repress rebellion. But as we saw in Chapter 3, two main kinds of resources helped to empower these early movements: print and association. Both were expressions of capitalism but both expanded beyond the interests of capitalists to fuel the spread of social movements. The commercial press not only spread information that could make potential activists aware of one another and of their common grievances; it also equalized their perception of their status with that of their superiors and made it thinkable to take action against them. The private association reflected existing solidarities, helped new ones to form, and linked local groups into movement networks that could contest the power of national states or international empires. Social coalitions, sometimes purposefully constructed but often contingent and provisional, concerted collective action against elites and opponents in the name of general programs.

Although the new movements often aimed at other groups in society, the framework for their actions was increasingly the opportunities for collective action provided by the national state. In making war, provisioning cities, and raising taxes, as well as by building roads and regulating associations, the state became both a target for claims and a place in which to fight out disputes with competing groups. Even where access was denied, the standardizing and unifying ambitions of expanding states created opportunities for less well endowed people to mimic and adapt the stratagems of elites.

We thus arrive at a historical situation in which contentious politics organizes on the boundaries of institutions and is never truly accepted by institutional elites. However, because of its historical relationship to the development of citizenship, it can never be fully suppressed without endangering democracy itself. What this means is that contentious politics forms around the armature of institutional politics, and rises and falls with the rhythm of changes in political opportunities and constraints, as we will see in Chapter 5.

PART II

FROM CONTENTION TO SOCIAL MOVEMENTS

5

POLITICAL
OPPORTUNITIES AND
CONSTRAINTS

When will ordinary people pour into the streets, risking life and limb to lay claim to their rights? The question has fascinated observers and frightened elites since the French and industrial revolutions. Outraged by the excesses of the mob and the dislocations of industrialization, early scholars saw contentious politics as the expression of the mentality of the crowd, of anomie and deprivation. But even a cursory look at modern history shows that outbreaks of contention cannot be derived from the deprivation people suffer or the disorganization of their societies. For these preconditions are far more enduring than the movements they support. What does vary widely from time to time and place to place are the levels and types of opportunities people experience, the constraints on their freedom of action, and the threats they perceive to their interests and values.

In this chapter, I argue that contention is more closely related to opportunities for – and limited by constraints upon – collective action than by the persistent social or economic factors that people experience. Contention increases when people gain the external resources to escape their compliance and find opportunities in which to use them. It also increases when they are threatened with costs they cannot bear or which outrage their sense of justice. When institutional access opens, rifts appear within elites, allies become available, and state capacity for repression declines, challengers find opportunities to advance their claims. When combined with high levels of perceived costs for inaction, opportunities produce episodes of contentious politics.

Of course, changing opportunities must be seen alongside more stable structural elements – like the strength or weakness of the state and the forms of repression it habitually employs (Kriesi et al. 1995). Moreover, external opportunities do not necessarily produce sustained social movements. That process requires challengers to employ known repertoires of contention, to frame their messages dynamically, and to access or construct unifying mobilizing structures (see Chapters 6, 7, and 8). But in revealing allies and exposing the weakness of enemies, opportunities communicate crucial information for movement formation.

Not only that: by communicating information about what they do, once formed, movements *create* opportunities – for their own supporters, for others, for parties and elites. They do this by diffusing collective action and displaying the possibility of coalitions, by creating political space for kindred movements and countermovements, and by producing incentives for elites and third parties to respond to. Challengers who seize political opportunities in response to openings in the polity are the catalysts for social movements and cycles of contention – and occasionally for revolutions and for democratic breakthroughs.

Threats are the logical antimony to opportunities, and few challengers would risk life or limb if they did not fear inaction. But threats can produce sullen resentment as easily as collective action; it is only when a threat is accompanied by perceived opportunities for action and seen as potentially irreversible if not stopped that challengers will risk what often turns out to be a heroic defeat (Golden 1997).[1]

WHY OPPORTUNITIES MATTER

Like much else in contemporary social movement theorizing, the concept of political opportunity dates from the last major upheaval in the West – the 1960s. In both western Europe and the United States, many were struck with how changes in modern society were expanding the incentives for contention. In western Europe, the dominant paradigm – founded on the work of Habermas and the Frankfurt school – focused on the urge to create new "life-spaces" produced by the capitalist welfare state; in the United States, it was increased affluence and the "postmaterial" orientations it fostered that were thought to trigger new social movements among those whose personal affluence is assured enough to think beyond material goods (Habermas 1981; Inglehart 1977, 1990).

Whereas the Frankfurt school's perspective brought to bear a cultural view of social movements, that of the advocates of "postmaterialism" drew on the individualistic paradigm that is often described as "rational choice." Both perspectives help to understand the "why" of mobilization; but neither could explain why people lend support to movements during certain periods of history and why some countries within the West – an area of widespread prosperity and relative cultural homogeneity – experienced more sustained contention in the 1960s than others. To answer those questions, it would be necessary to trace how underlying social structure and mobilization potential are transformed into action.[2] In such a transformation, the role of political opportunities and constraints is crucial. This can be illuminated by looking at the differences in working-class mobilization in different Western countries in the 1930s.

Other things being equal, workers are more likely to go on strike in boom times than in depression.[3] The logic of the connection is clear: prosperity increases employers' need for labor just as tight labor markets reduce competition for jobs. As workers learn this, they demand higher wages, shorter hours, or better working conditions. As a result, the strike rate follows the curve of the business cycle upward when a declining unemployment pool leaves employers prey to the pressure of the labor market and downward when the demand for labor declines.[4]

The depression of the 1930s saw the rise of a number of social movements in Europe and the United States. We would normally expect economic crisis and widespread unemployment to depress contention. But in some countries of the West, industrial workers struck, demonstrated, and occupied factories in response to sackings and reductions in pay, while in others they did not or allowed themselves to be repressed. Whereas workers in Britain languished through most of the Great Depression and German workers were brutally repressed by the Nazis, French and American workers reacted to the crisis with unprecedented levels of contention.

How can we explain the increase in industrial insurgency by hard-pressed workers in France and the United States, while in Germany and Britain workers accepted their lot? The answer, I propose, lies in the changes in the opportunities and constraints surrounding the different working classes. There were strike waves in France and the United States in the 1930s – and not in Germany or Britain – because the reform administrations that came to power in France in 1936 and America in 1933 were willing to innovate in political-economic relationships and reluctant to support the suppression of labor. It was the opening of political opportunities and the relaxation of labor repression opened by the French Popular Front and the American New Deal – and not the depth of workers' grievances or the extent of their resources – that encouraged labor insurgency in those countries.

Returning to the present, we can see that political opportunities are seized and transformed by a variety of challengers under many different conditions. Our first effort will be to classify the dimensions of opportunity that help shape movements, while our second will be to show how they intersect with three main dimensions of the state: state strength, prevailing strategies, and repressiveness. But before turning to these analytical tasks, let us see how the concept of changing opportunities and constraints can be used to understand a major watershed of contention in recent years, the rise of a democratization movement in the former Soviet Union.

LIBERALIZATION AND CONTENTION IN THE FORMER SOVIET UNION

In the late 1980s, contentious politics arose in the most unlikely place in the world – the highly centralized and police- and party-controlled former Soviet Union. Research by political scientist Mark Beissinger has documented this rise of contentious politics, which mainly took the form of peaceful demonstrations,

NUMBER OF PROTEST DEMONSTRATIONS

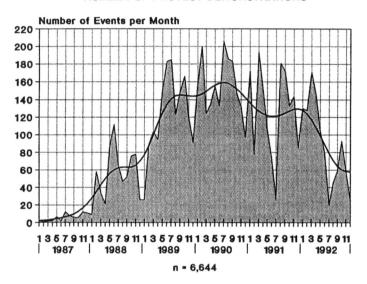

Figure 5.1. Protest Mobilization at Demonstrations in the former Soviet Union, 1987–1992 (SOURCE: Mark Beissinger, "Event Analysis in Transitional Societies: Protest Mobilization in the Former Soviet Union," in Dieter Rucht, Ruud Koopmans, and Friedhelm Neidhardt, eds., Acts of Dissent: The Study of Protest in Contemporary Democracies *{Berlin: Sigma, 1998}.)*

strikes, and protest marches, but sometimes took violent forms as well. Figure 5.1 shows what Beissinger found as the result of his employment of an event analysis for the last years of the Soviet Union.

How did so sudden a wave of political contention develop in so centralized and police-controlled a regime, after years of suppression and tightly controlled participation? As Tocqueville wrote, because people act on opportunities, "the most perilous moment for a bad government is one when it seeks to mend its ways" (1955: 176–7). Tocqueville was writing of the collapse of the French Old Regime; had he been present two hundred years later, he might well have applied his theory to the Soviet Union. Here, as in France in the 1780s, an international power mired in corruption and torpor and unable to compete with a more dynamic market-oriented society (Bunce 1984–5; cf. Skocpol 1979) sought to reform itself from within. Incoming party secretary Mikhael Gorbachev was convinced that his country could not survive as a world power without reforming itself. The late 1980s "engendered a process of liberalization that sparked an explosion of organized extra-state political activity" (Fish 1995: 32).

As was inevitable in a highly centralized system, liberalization began at the top, with a change in official policy on questions of association. A modest concept of socialist pluralism was proposed, which "amounted to de facto toleration of the formation of some small, non-state citizens' organizations" (Fish 1995: 32). But it did not take long for the opening of new possibilities for legitimate association to stimulate the formation of more independent groupings; for example, a group called "Memorial," which was dedicated to investigating the crimes of stalinism, and another called "Citizen's Dignity," dedicated to promoting human rights (p. 32). The new opportunities for access provided at the top offered openings for less legitimate groups to organize.

To some extent, Gorbachev's desire for liberalization was based on the idea of stimulating more open discussion *(glasnost')*. But he quickly realized that without a renovation of the political class, his plans would be stymied by official obstruction or inactivity and he might lose power altogether. As a result, he transformed the usually formalistic elections to the USSR Congress of People's Deputies into "the first even partially open and competitive national election in the history of the Soviet Union" (Fish 1995: 35–6). Although the election's rules reserved one-third of the seats for party-controlled representatives, it conferred on a few independently elected individuals the mantle of legitimacy. "Perhaps of greatest moment," writes Steven Fish, "the balloting engendered the closest thing that the populace had ever known to a real election campaign" (p. 35).

But the reformers were few and disorganized: lacking internal resources and possessing only weak ties and little mutual trust, they quickly divided into a number of competing factions and parties (Fish 1995: 35 ff.). They profited mainly from external support, like that accorded them when the secretary of the Moscow Communist Party Committee, Boris Yeltsin, gave informal approval to a conference of political discussion groups called "Social Initiative for Perestroika" (p. 32). External help also appeared in the form of the coal miners of the Kuzbass and the Donbass who went on strike in 1989, and from eastern Europe, where Gorbachev's reforms – and particularly his removal of the threat of Red Army intervention – triggered a wave of democratization movements (Fish, pp. 39–41). The role of these "allies," both conscious and involuntary, added immensely to the confidence of insurgents in the Soviet Union that true reform was possible.

This possibility grew more plausible as cracks appeared in the Communist Party elite. While the Supreme Soviet was approving a draft law in November 1989 opening up the media and legalizing free use of print by private individuals, a popular television program, *Vzgliad* (Viewpoint), was canceled, and special police units continued to repress public demonstrations. These inconsistencies began to reveal "a profound and systematic tension between . . . political pluralism and the statist and monopolistic essence of the regime" (Fish 1995: 40–1). The contradiction was deepened in early 1990 with the emergence of a reform movement within the Communist Party, "Democratic Platform," whose members wanted a more systematic program of reform within the party and called for the establishment of Western style parliamentary democracy (pp. 41–2). In reaction, party conservatives formed puppet organizations to seek support from within the public (p. 40).

As 1990 dawned, these developments were accompanied by a decline in the state's capacity – and even its will – to repress dissent. This was exacerbated by previous intraelite struggles, leading to divisions in the elite. Tolerance of the miners' strikes and the acceptance of the independent unions they produced were one startling expression of this decline, while another was the acceptance of large-scale demonstrations in the cities (Fish 1995: 45). Although repression continued here and there, Gorbachev's need for elections to renovate the political class legitimated popular discussion and debate. Even more than in the 1989 elections, the 1990 elections to the republican, oblast', city, and district councils "were a time of huge public demonstrations in many Russian cities" (p. 43).

These elections, and the discussions and demonstrations they produced, led to the formation of a number of new parties and movements. As Fish concludes:

> The center and the party could prevent, obstruct, and coerce; but they could no longer even pretend to initiate, create, and convince. . . . A motly conglomeration of autonomous social organizations, spearheading a popular movement for democracy, had rendered power visible. . . . In doing so, they had begun to push it toward its demise. (1995: 51)

But the appearance of widespread contention does not in itself constitute a social movement. Without a network of interpersonal ties or a collective identity, these organizations gained neither the ideological unity nor the organizational fiber to produce a sustained social movement. By 1992, torn by ideological and territorial decomposition, the regime crumbled, but, as it fell, the challengers divided and a former apparachnik, Boris Yeltsin, emerged on top. The challengers of 1989–91 had created opportunities for those within the system who were willing and able to exploit them.

This briefest of narratives on the emergence of the politics of contention in the former Soviet Union not only illustrates the importance of political opportunities in transforming the potential for mobilization into action; it also helps us to narrow down the concept and to identify a number of its key dimensions. Most important among them were: (1) the opening of access to participation for new actors; (2) the evidence of political realignment within the polity; (3) the appearance of influential allies; (4) emerging splits within the elite; and (5) a decline in the state's capacity or will to repress dissent. In the next section, we examine each of these dimensions in turn.

DIMENSIONS OF OPPORTUNITY

By the concept of political opportunity, I mean consistent – but not necessarily formal or permanent – dimensions of the political environment that provide incentives for collective action by affecting people's expectations for success or failure (Gamson and Meyer 1996). Compared with theorists of resource mobilization, with whom they are often confused, writers in the political opportunity tradition emphasize the mobilization of resources *external* to the group.[5] They also, for the most part, emphasize elements of opportunity that are *perceived* by insurgents – for structural changes that are not experienced can hardly be expected to affect people's behavior, except indirectly.

Political opportunities sometimes center on particular groups and evade others, as the foregoing examples of workers in the 1930s suggest, and opportunities for protest are sometimes greater in some regions or cities than in others (Agnew 1997: iv). But despite these variations, movements emerge because the conditions for mobilization have expanded in the polity in general, as was the case when the American peace, student, and women's movements of the late 1960s took advantage of a generally widening opportunity structure. Some movement sectors are particularly affected by changes in opportunities, as was the peace movement in the 1980s (Meyer 1990), but more often, opportunities signaled to some are also available to others. In the 1960s, most activists referred only to "*the* movement."

Political opportunities may not be apparent all at once to all potential challengers. In fact, an advantage of the concept is that it helps us to understand how mobilization spreads from people with deep grievances and strong resources to those with fewer ones and less resources. By challenging elites and authorities, "early risers" reveal their opponents' vulnerability and open them to attacks by weaker players. By the same token, the latter groups more easily collapse when opportunities decline because they lack the internal resources to sustain contention. This means that – although the term "structure" has frequently been used to characterize political opportunities[6] – most opportunities and constraints are situational, and cannot compensate for long for weaknesses in cultural, ideological, and organizational resources.

INCREASING ACCESS

Rational people do not often attack well-fortified opponents when opportunities are closed; gaining partial access to participation provides them with such incentives. But are people who possess full political rights any more likely to engage in contention? Peter Eisinger argues that the relationship between protest and political opportunity is curvilinear: neither full access nor its absence produce the greatest degree of protest. Taking his cue from Tocqueville, Eisinger (1973: 15) writes that protest is most likely "in systems characterized by a mix of open and closed factors."[7]

The expansion of access is most readily expressed through elections; Piven and Cloward show, for example, how the breakup of the "solid South" in the 1950s opened new opportunities for black electors (1977). Americans saw this again in 1992, when outsider Ross Perot built a movement to launch his presidential campaign. Similarly, the elections of 1994 in Italy gave rise to a new movement led by media magnate Silvio Berlusconi. Elections are an umbrella under which new challengers are often formed.

In democratic systems, elections are routine events and are usually dominated by institutional parties, which pass rules to maintain their monopoly of representation. It is in nondemocratic systems that newly opened access is most likely to trigger contention, as our Soviet example illustrated. In Czechoslovakia at the same time, it was the appearance of a Student Press and Information Center (STIS) that gave students in Prague a site in which they could make contact and the assurance that political action would be tolerated (van Praag 1992). In the former Yugoslavia, future nationalists were already poised to take advantage of the post-Soviet period by constitutional reforms that gave them greater institutional resources (Bunce, forthcoming). The narrower the preexisting avenues to participation, the more likely each new opening is to produce new opportunities for contention.

SHIFTING ALIGNMENTS

A second element that encouraged contention in the Soviet Union was the instability of political alignments. In pluralist systems, this is measured most centrally by electoral instability. Especially when they are based on new coalitions, the changing fortunes of government and opposition parties create uncertainty among supporters, encourage challengers to try to exercise marginal power, and may even induce elites to compete for support from outside the polity.

The importance of electoral realignments in opening opportunities could be seen in the American civil rights movement. Throughout the 1950s, racial "exclusionists" in the southern wing of the Democratic Party were weakened by defections to the Republicans, while the number of Democratic "inclusionists" was growing stronger (Valelly 1993). The decline of the southern white vote and the move of African American voters to the cities, where Jim Crow was less oppressive, increased the incentive for the Democrats to seek black electoral support. With its razor-thin electoral margin, the Kennedy administration was forced to move from cautious foot-dragging to seizing the initiative for civil rights.

It is not only in fully fledged democracies that political instability encourages contention. Peasants are most likely to rebel against authorities when windows of opportunity appear in the walls of their subordination. This is what Eric Hobsbawm found when he looked into the history of Peruvian land occupations (1974). The same was true of the peasants who occupied parts of the southern Italian *latifundia* after World War II. While their land hunger and resentment at landlord abuses were age-old, it was the collapse of Mussolini's Fascist regime, the presence of reform-oriented American occupiers, and changing partisan alignments that transformed their resentment into a struggle for the land (Bevilacqua 1980; Tarrow 1967). In less-than-democratic regimes, the lack of routinized competition makes any sign of political instability a signal and a source for contention.

DIVIDED ELITES

As we saw when a reform faction emerged in the Communist Party of the Soviet Union, conflicts within and among elites encourage outbreaks of contention. Divisions among elites not only provide incentives to resource-poor groups to take the risks of collective action; they encourage portions of the elite that are out of power to seize the role of "tribunes of the people."

History provides numerous examples of divided elites bringing resources to emerging movements. In Old Regime France, people like Lafayette and Mirabeau broke with their class to make common cause with the lower clergy and the third estate. Two hundred years after, splits within the elite played a key role in east central Europe, especially after Gorbachev warned the Communist states of the region that the Red Army would no longer intervene to defend them. This was seen by insurgent groups as a signal to organize and by many elite members as an inducement to defect. Splits were also important in the transitions to democracy in authoritarian Spain and Brazil in the 1970s and 1980s, where the divisions between soft-liners and hard-liners provided openings that opposition movements could exploit (Bermeo 1997; O'Donnell and Schmitter 1986: 19).

INFLUENTIAL ALLIES

A fourth aspect of political opportunity that was apparent in the emergence of contentious politics in the former Soviet Union was the presence of influential allies within the Communist Party elite. Challengers are encouraged to take collective action when they have allies who can act as friends in court, as guarantors against repression, or as acceptable negotiators on their behalf. Both through Yeltsin's apparent support for their efforts and through the independent activities of the miners and east European dissidents, challengers in the Soviet Union gained both confidence and models for collective action.

From William Gamson's book on contention in the United States (1990), there is historical evidence for similar processes in democratic systems. Gamson's research shows a correlation between the presence of influential allies and movement success. In the fifty-three "conflict groups" he studied, the presence or absence of political allies was closely related to whether these groups succeeded (1990: 64–6). And in studying American farm worker movements in the 1940s and 1960s, Craig Jenkins and Charles Perrow found a similar contrast: the advantage of the United Farm Workers in the 1960s lay in the presence of external constituencies that their predecessors in the 1940s had lacked (1977). One reason for the long "sliding May" in Italy was the presence of the Socialist Party in government, which styled itself for a time as the defender of those outside the gates (Tarrow 1989a).

Especially important allies for challengers in representative systems are political parties. Left-wing parties are generally more favorable to challengers than
moderate or conservative ones; and within the left, "New Left" parties – like the
European Greens – are more hospitable to "life-space" movements than the parties of the old left, which are more receptive to distribution-based movements
(Kriesi et al. 1995: ch. 3). Parties on the right are swayed by both new religious
movements – like the Christian Coalition – and by economic interest groups,
but the former may have more crucial marginal power because of their capacity
to appeal to voters across socioeconomic lines.

Influential allies have proved especially important in nondemocratic systems,
where new movements have access to few internal resources. For example, in
Central America, peasant movements profited from the presence of religious
workers, union organizers, revolutionary guerrillas, political party activists, and
development workers (Brockett 1991: 258). In Poland during the 1970s and
1980s, the Catholic Church helped to incubate resistance and protect activists
from retribution (Osa 1995). Allies within the system are an external resource
that otherwise resource-deficient actors can lean on, especially in authoritarian
and repressive environments.

REPRESSION AND FACILITATION

In Charles Tilly's definition, "repression is any action by another group which
raises the contender's cost of collective action. An action which lowers the group's
cost of collective action is a form of facilitation" (1978: 100). The development
of modern states produced powerful tools for the repression of popular politics,
but, as we saw in Chapter 4, some aspects of state development facilitated the
rise of movements.

Repression is a more likely fate for movements that demand fundamental
changes and threaten elites than for groups that make modest demands (Gamson
1990: ch. 4). It is also obvious that, whereas authoritarian states repress social
movements, representative ones facilitate them. But there are aspects of repressive
states that encourage some forms of contention, while some characteristics of
representative ones take the sting out of movements. We will have much more
to say about repression and facilitation later.

These aspects of changing political opportunity and constraint are arrayed dif-
ferentially in different systems and change over time – often independently but
sometimes in close connection with one another. For example, splits among elites
and political realignments work together to induce disaffected groups or even
governments to seek support from outsiders. When minority factions of the elite
ally with outside challengers, challenges from inside and outside the polity combine in major cycles of contention. But all of these changes must be seen in the
context of more stable aspects of opportunity and constraint.

STATES AND OPPORTUNITIES

These five aspects of political opportunity are specified as *changes* in opportunity; but there are also more stable aspects of opportunity–constraint that condition contentious politics. One set of factors revolves around the concept of "state strength"; a second deals with states' prevailing strategies toward challengers; while a third relates to the problem of repression and social control.

STATE STRENGTH AND PREVAILING STRATEGIES

Do strong states automatically ignore movements while weak ones must suffer their incursions? In its most common form, the argument from state strength runs like this: centralized states with effective policy instruments at their command attract collective actors to the summit of the political system, whereas decentralized states provide a multitude of targets at the base.[8] Strong states also have greater capacity to implement the policies they choose to support: when these are favorable to challengers' claims, the latter will gravitate to conventional forms of expression; when they are negative, violence or confrontation ensue.[9]

Because they invite criticism and participation, decentralized systems frequently "process" the most challenging elements out of popular politics, as the United States did following the race riots of the 1960s (Lipsky and Olson 1976). Federalism is a particular invitation to movements to shift their venues into institutions, because it provides so many alternative pockets for participation (Tarrow 1998c). In her research on the American temperance movement, Ann-Marie Syzmanski showed how the movement's leaders shifted strategically between levels of the federal system and from proposing constitutional amendments to local organizing (1997). Such strategic flexibility and "venue shopping" are less available in more centralized states.

Different degrees of state centralization were a major source of the contrasts between the French and American student movements of the 1960s. The first exploded only in early 1968, diffused rapidly, and soon moved rapidly into the political arena, triggering a political convulsion that threatened the Fifth Republic (see Chapter 10). The second produced a much longer, more decentralized series of protest campaigns at campuses around the United States and was diffused in the various rivulets of the New Left (Tarrow 1989a).

Differences in state strength were related to the differential pace and timing of the revolutions in east central Europe too. A state that was never completely stalinized, Poland produced the earliest and most vital movement in the Solidarity strikes of 1980, whereas Czechoslovakia, which was subjected to brutal stalinist control after 1968, was one of the last to rebel. Polish precociousness and Czechoslovak delay were related to the respective strength of state socialism in the two countries.

In authoritarian settings, while repression crushes resistance under most con-

	STATE STRENGTH	
PREVAILING STATE STRATEGY	Weak States	Strong States
Inclusive	United States	Sweden
Exclusive	Italy	France

Figure 5.2. State Strength and Prevailing State Strategies as Structuring Principles for Contentious Politics in Some Western Democracies (SOURCE: Adapted from Hanspeter Kriesi, R. Koopmans, J. W. Duyvendak, and M. G. Giugni, The Politics of New Social Movements in Western Europe *{Minneapolis: Universitiy of Minnesota Press, 1995}, p. 37.)*

ditions, the centralization of power offers dissidents an odd sort of advantage – a unified field and a centralized target to attack once the system is weakened. This was one of the contributing reasons for the rapidity of the collapse of state socialism in east central Europe after 1989. Where power is centralized and conditions are homogenized, once opportunities are opened, as they were when Gorbachev began his reforms, framing and organizing a social movement are facilitated. The weapon of the weak in such systems, writes Valerie Bunce, is that they have "a great deal in common" (1991:6).

If taken alone as a guide to action, the concept of state strength is somewhat wooden and lacks agency. Some states, whether strong or weak, have a prevailing strategy toward challengers that is inclusive, responding to and absorbing their demands (in Gamson's terminology, "pre-emption") and facilitating their entry into the polity (Gamson 1990: ch. 2), whereas others have an "exclusive" strategy. Hanspeter Kriesi and his collaborators see these "prevailing strategies" varying systematically in different countries (1995: 40–4).

Prevailing strategies intersect with state strength in interesting ways. In their research on protest events in four European countries, Kriesi et al. found that Switzerland (which they consider a "weak" state with an "inclusive" strategy) had a high level of mobilization and a low level of violence and confrontation. At the other extreme, France (which Kriesi and his collaborators use as an example of a "strong" state with an "exclusive" strategy) they found to have a lower level of mobilization and a higher level of confrontational protest (1995: 49).[10] Consider two other cases: Sweden, with a strong social-democratic state, has a more inclusive strategy toward challengers (Kitschelt 1986), whereas Italy, at least until the 1990s, had a weak state and an exclusive strategy toward the left. These properties of state strength and prevailing strategy intersect in the typology in Figure 5.2.

Kriesi's typology is useful, but we must beware of overschematization. It would be easier to use state strength as a global predictor of contention if it were in fact a constant. But "strength" and "weakness" are relational values that vary for different sectors and levels of the state. When Ann-Marie Szymanski's temperance activists found the national state too strong to crack, they turned to a strategy of "thinking globally, acting gradually." Is the American state "strong" or "weak"? That depends on where it is attacked; for example, Peter Eisinger found that urban protest was far more common in "unreformed" mayor-council cities than in reformed council-manager ones (1973).

The same caution must be expressed about the concept of "prevailing strategies." For example, the American state – "inclusive" where middle-class civic protests are concerned – has usually been quite "exclusive" in the face of attacks on property. As a result of this difference, the American state presents an open door to groups that advance modest goals – the so-called consensus movements studied by McCarthy and Wolfson (1992) – but sets up a barricade against those which challenge capital or national security.

Moreover, neither state strength nor prevailing strategies are exogenous of political factors, which change as the result of wars, elections, party realignments, and shifts in public opinion. A state that is "strong" in the hands of a unified majority or under a strong leader can become "weak" when that majority is divided or opposition to it grows. And a state that is strong when it enjoys the confidence of business weakens when inflation soars and capital moves abroad. When a new collective actor appears – as Islamic fundamentalism did in the late 1970s in Iran – an apparently "strong" state like the shah's can quickly wither.

Divisions in the political elite are easy to mistake for a structurally weak state. Thus, until the Civil War, the regionally divided American elite limited the growth of the American state. When that war reduced the South both militarily and politically, the state became much stronger – a "Yankee Leviathan," in Richard Bensel's terms (1990). Conversely, the "strong" French state under General de Gaulle weakened under his less charismatic and ideologically divided followers, as President Chirac learned in 1997.

MODES OF REPRESSION

Repression can either depress collective action or raise the costs of organizing and mobilizing opinion (Tilly 1978: 100–2). Though suppression is more brutal and frightening, there is evidence that increasing the costs of organization and mobilization is a more effective strategy in the long run. For example, when Steven Barkan compared southern cities that used the courts to block civil rights activities with those which used the police to suppress them, he found that the former were able to resist desegregation longer than the latter (1984). Similarly, during the McCarthy era, American conservatives found it easier to increase the cost of membership in the Communist Party than to ban strikes or demonstrations.

But suppressing the preconditions of collective action is not always easy to accomplish. Since raising the costs of organization is nonselective, the first impediment is the cost – both financial and administrative. The second is that repressing organizations silences constructive critics as well as opponents of the regime and blocks information flow upward. Finally, in conditions of generally depressed organization, when collective action does break out, it turns from a trickle into a torrent as people learn for the first time that others like themselves have taken to the streets (Kuran 1991).

Jailing protesters and potential protesters remained the major response to contention until after World Wars I and II, when, first, the citizens of the occupied Ruhr, then Gandhi, and then American civil rights leaders invented civil disobedience. Filling the jails to capacity and gaining public sympathy for protesters were effective forms of pressure (Ackerman and Kruegler 1994; Sharp 1973). From that time on, nonviolent civil disobedience has become a major political weapon in the armory of contention (see Chapter 6).

In response to the growing success of nonviolent protest in the 1960s, both in the United States and in Europe the police and the courts began to accept as legitimate forms of action that had previously been seen as threatening to civil order. Thus, the sit-in, punished almost universally by incarceration when it was first employed, was increasingly accepted in the 1960s as a form of speech. Diffused among progressive and liberal groups in the 1960s, sit-ins spread to their ideological enemies in the 1980s, as the antiabortion movement gained ground (Staggenborg 1991).

State toleration for nonviolent contention is a double-edged sword. On the one hand, it provides a relatively risk-free means of assembling large numbers of people and giving them the sense that they are acting meaningfully on behalf of their beliefs. But on the other hand, it deprives organizers of the potent weapon of outrage. Violent and capricious police who throw sincere young protesters into jail are easier to mobilize against than reasonable-sounding public authorities who organize seminars for demonstrators and protect their right to free speech against opponents (della Porta and Reiter 1997).

The ease of organizing opinion in representative systems and finding legitimate channels for its expression induces many movements to turn to elections. The dynamic runs something like this: a movement organizes massive public demonstrations on behalf of its demands; the government permits and even facilitates its continued expression; numerical growth has its most direct effect in electing candidates to office; thereafter, the movement turns into a party or enters a party in order to influence its policies.

This logic led the American women's movement into a permanent alliance with the Democratic Party in the 1970s and 1980s (Costain and Costain 1987). The same logic split the Italian extreme left in the mid-1970s, when parts of it turned from confrontation to the formation of New Left parties (della Porta 1995; Tarrow 1989a). At its most successful, the electoral strategy produced Green parties in parts of northern Europe, parties that rapidly became part of the parliamentary game of politics. In Switzerland, the use of direct democratic institutions appears to moderate the actions of social movements and favors moderate movements at the expense of others (Kriesi and Wisler 1996).

REPRESSIVE PARADOXES

That authoritarian states discourage popular politics is implicit in their very definition. But their success in repression can produce a radicalization of collective action and a more effective organization of opponents, as moderate dissenters defect into private life and more militant ones take center stage. It was, after all, not in democratic Britain or republican France that nineteenth-century anarchists turned to terrorism, but in autocratic Russia and semiconstitutional Italy and Spain. And we know how the repressive atmosphere of czarist Russia contributed to the closure and radicalization of social democracy in that country (Bonnell 1983).

Not all repressive states are equally effective in closing off opportunities for contention. For example, in Fascist Italy, anti-Fascist groups in Catholic Action organized resistance under the legitimate umbrella of the Fascist-Vatican Concordat (Webster 1960: chs. 10, 11). In Communist Poland, books and articles by Solidarity writers continued to be published even during the martial law period (Laba 1990: 155).

The systematic repression of collective action has the perverse result of lending a political coloration to even ordinary acts. "V.E.R.D.I.," scrawled on the walls of Milan in 1848, not only stood for the name of the nationalist composer, Giuseppe Verdi, but was an acronym for the slogan "Vittorio Emmanuele Re d'Italia" (Victor Emmanuel, king of Italy). And to any Russian who could read, graffiti scribbled on the walls of Moscow in the 1980s communicated the extent of alienation in Russian society (Bushnell 1990).[11]

In less determinedly authoritarian states, even how people tip their hats or the forms of address they employ indicate dissent, as James Scott found in his research in Malaysia (1985: ch. 7). These "hidden transcripts" seldom produce organized collective action, but they undermine consensus in a way that is difficult to repress, because no single instance crosses the line from resentment to opposition. Repressive states depress collective action of a conventional and a confrontational sort, but leave themselves open to unobtrusive mobilization which can signal solidarity that becomes a resource when the opportunities arise.

While authoritarian states systematically repress contention, the absence of regular channels for expressing opinion turns even moderate dissenters into opponents of the regime and forces them to pose the problem of regime overthrow as the condition for reform. As Marx wrote in 1843 of the difference between the relatively liberal French monarchy and the repressive Prussian state, "In France partial emancipation is the basis of universal emancipation. In Germany, universal emancipation is the *conditio sine qua non* of any partial emancipation" (1967: 262–3). This is particularly true when repression aims at the collective survival of threatened groups.

THREATS AND OPPORTUNITIES

Thus far, we have talked mainly of the opportunities for and constraints upon collective action. These perceived variations and changes induce people who might otherwise stay at home to engage in costly, frustrating, and possibly dangerous collective action. But there is another order of variables, about which we know much less, that logically appears to stimulate contention: the threats to interests, values, and, at times, survival that different groups and individuals experience.

We can best begin by regarding contention as a collective action problem and those considering it faced with a series of costs and obstacles. From a simple resource mobilization point of view, those most likely to engage in contention would be people with the least to lose, since it is they who possess the greatest resources. But from the point of view of asking who tries to seize external opportunities, it is those with the most to lose who are most likely to engage in contention, since they face the greatest threat from inaction.

Consider the expansion of Jewish settlements around Jerusalem that was announced by Israeli Prime Minister Netanyahu in early 1997, flying in the face of the Oslo peace agreement that his government was sworn to uphold; this move threatened the integrity of the future Palestinian state and could not fail to trigger an outraged response from Arab residents of Jerusalem and the newly formed Palestinian Authority. The threat of suffocating in the grip of Israeli "created facts" was a major incentive to Palestinian protest. Indeed, it might be said that Netanyahu's outrageous move provided an opportunity for popular protest that Yassar Arafat's government could not have mustered on its own.

One way of theorizing the importance of threat in triggering contention is suggested by the "prospect theory" of the late Stanford psychologist Amos Tversky (see Quatrone and Tversky 1988). Tversky and his collaborators argue that individuals react differently to prospective gains and losses. They claim that individuals employ different decisional heuristics that are contextually contingent. "An individual's attitude toward risk depends on whether the outcomes are perceived as gains or losses, relative to the reference point" (p. 722).

Applying Tversky's insights to collective action theory, Jeffrey Berejikian has argued that gains and losses have different potential for triggering contention, and that potential cost – or threat – is far more energizing than the hope of gain (1992). Though no field research has been designed to test this hypothesis, Berejikian interprets a number of historical cases in support of his thesis. In particular, he argues that "revolutionary collective action" is particularly likely to be triggered by the "threat of losses." He writes that "peasants living through social-structural transformations that lead, for example, to increased vulnerability to subsistence crisis . . . would view a choice in favor of status quo not as neutral but as a loss" (p. 653).

But three cautions can be raised against Berejikian's claim. First, empirically, there are a number of fairly obvious cases in which contention was mounted under no immediate threat, by people who most observers would agree were not seeking gains in their status or position. Consider the American civil rights movement: most of the northern whites who went south to help the movement faced no risk to life or property. On the contrary, by engaging in contention, they increased their risks substantially (McAdam 1986).

Second, it is not clear whether "gains" and "losses" (e.g., in tverskian terms, the individual's "reference point") can ever be objectively defined and observed. Is a peasant who occupies the land of a landholder seeking a gain, since it is someone else's land he occupies, or rectifying a loss, since he may claim that the land in question was stolen from his grandfather? If we cannot observably distinguish between the prospect of a gain and the threat of a loss, we will be at the analytic mercy of collective actors whose claim of losses suffered cannot be taken at face value.

Finally, the strongest objection to the argument that fear of loss produces more contention than the hope of gain is that Tversky's theory assumes individualistic incentives to collective action. When we turn to recent transnational movements in Chapter 11, we will note that many are mobilized by conscience constituents on behalf of what Dieter Rucht calls "distant issues" – to which the question of personal loss or gain is hardly relevant (Rucht 1998a).

The most important implication of tverskian theorizing is not to explain the behavior of individuals but what Berejikian calls "framing by revolutionary organizations." For if a subject population is more likely to respond to the fear of losses than to the hope of gain, "then the initial task for a revolutionary organization is to adopt a worldview that effectively communicates to individual peasants the understanding that existing social-structural arrangements are worse than in some 'normal' past" (Berejikian 1992: 653). We turn to these issues of framing in Chapter 6.

MAKING AND DIFFUSING OPPORTUNITIES

Unlike conventional forms of participation, contentious collective action demonstrates the possibilities of collective action to others and offers even resource-poor groups opportunities that their lack of resources would deny them. This occurs when "early risers" make claims on elites that can be used by those with less daring and fewer resources. Moreover, collective action exposes opponents' points of weakness that may not be evident until they are challenged. It can also reveal unsuspected or formerly passive allies both within and outside the system. Finally, it can pry open institutional barriers through which the demands of others can pour.

Once collective action is launched in part of a system, on behalf of one type of goal, and by a particular group, the encounter between that group and its antagonists provides models of collective action, master frames, and mobilizing structures that produce new opportunities. These secondary effects take three general forms: in the expansion of a group's own opportunities and those of cognate groups; in the dialectic between movements and countermovements; and in the creation of opportunities for elites and authorities.

EXPANDING OTHERS' OPPORTUNITIES

One of the most remarkable characteristics of contentious politics is that it expands the opportunities of others. Protesting groups put issues on the agenda with which other people identify and demonstrate the utility of collective action that others can copy or innovate upon. For example, as we will see in the next chapter, the American civil rights movement expanded the doctrine of rights that became the "master frame" of the 1960s and 1970s (Hamilton 1986). Collective action embodies claims in dramatic ways that show others the way.

This expansion of opportunities not only affects a movement's "alliance system"; it also affects its actual and potential opponents. A movement that offends influential groups can trigger a countermovement (Meyer and Staggenborg 1996). Movements that employ violence invite physical repression. Movements that make extreme forms of policy demand can be outmaneuvered by groups that pose the same claim in more acceptable form. And when a movement's success threatens another group in a context of heightened mobilization, it can lead to outbidding and counterprotests. For example, in Italy in the 1960s, extreme left and extreme right fed upon one another, producing terrorist campaigns from both extremes in the 1970s (della Porta and Tarrow 1986).

The spiral of conflict between the American pro-choice and pro-life movements in the 1980s and early 1990s is an example of how movements create opportunities for opponents. The access to abortion rights that was decreed by the Supreme Court in the early 1970s galvanized Catholics and fundamentalist Protestants to organize against abortion clinics. This pro-life movement became so dynamic that it was a major force in the defeat of the equal rights amendment in the 1980s (Mansbridge 1986). Eventually, an offshoot of pro-life called "Operation Rescue" used such radical direct tactics in the early 1990s that it stimulated a countermobilization campaign by the usually legalistic pro-choice forces (Meyer and Staggenborg 1996).

MAKING OPPORTUNITIES FOR ELITES

Finally, protesters create political opportunities for elites: both in a negative sense, when their actions provide grounds for repression, and in a positive one, when politicians seize the opportunity created by challengers to proclaim themselves tribunes of the people. As we will see in Chapter 10, perhaps the most enduring outcome of the French May movement was an educational reform on which the protesters had only minimal impact. Protesters on their own seldom have the power to affect the policy priorities of elites. This is both because their protests often take an expressive form and because elites are unlikely to be persuaded to make policy changes that are not in their own interest. Reform is most likely when challenges from outside the polity provide a political incentive for elites within it to advance their own policies and careers (see Chapter 10).

Political opportunism is not a monopoly of either left or right, parties of movement or parties of conservation. The conservative Eisenhower administration responded in essentially the same way to the civil rights movement as the liberal Kennedy administration for the simple reason that both were concerned with electoral realignment and wished to minimize the foreign policy damage of American racism (Piven and Cloward 1977: ch. 4).

When are parties and interest groups most likely to take advantage of opportunities created by social movements? They appear to do so mainly when a system is challenged by a range of movements, and not when individual movement organizations mount challenges that can be easily repressed or isolated. That is to say, reformist outcomes are most likely when political opportunities produce general confrontations among challengers, elites, and authorities, as in the cycles of contention that are examined in Chapter 9.

DECLINING OPPORTUNITIES

The opening of opportunities provides external resources to people who lack internal ones; openings where there were only walls before; alliances that did not previously seem possible; and realignments that appear capable of bringing new groups to power. But because these opportunities are external – and because they shift so easily from initial challengers to their allies and opponents and, ultimately, to elites and authorities – political opportunities are fickle friends. The result is that openings for reform quickly close or allow new challengers with different aims to march through the gates that the early risers have battered down.

Thus, the 1989 revolutions in eastern Europe that many thought would bring democracy to a part of the world that had been denied freedom produced a few working democracies, several neo-communist states, and a number of countries that quickly disintegrated into ethnic conflict. Even in East Germany, rapidly absorbed into a stable Western democracy, the democratic Civic Forum that led the way to unification in 1989 was swept aside by the established political parties, while the successor to the old Communist Party remains an electoral force. Movements are evanescent because they influence political changes that precipitate their own demobilization.

The shifting nature of political opportunities does not mean that they do not matter in the formation of social movements. Just as it was the result of a political opportunity that the Bolsheviks came to power in 1917, it was the opportunities provided by Gorbachev that stimulated collective action in the former Soviet Union and in east central Europe in 1989. But if opportunities migrate from challengers to their allies, from movements to countermovements, and from outside the polity to elites and parties within it, then something more durable is necessary to turn contention into sustained social movements. Three other kinds of resources are necessary to turn contentious possibilities into sustained social movements: the forms of contention that people employ to gain support and impose their will on opponents; the collective action frames that dignify and justify their actions; and the mobilizing structures that reinforce challengers on the line of fire and link center to base. These are the powers of movement that are analyzed in the next three chapters.

6

ACTING CONTENTIOUSLY

The Serbian nationalist regime of Slobodan Milosevic would seem to have been the last to be undermined by a social movement. A wily Leninist quick to sniff the winds of change blowing across east central Europe well before 1989, Milosevic undermined what was left of Yugoslav unity by fomenting a war with Croatia and attacking the vulnerable state of Bosnia-Herzegovina through his agents, the Bosnian Serbs. When the horrors of Bosnian genocide led to reaction from the West, Milosevic made a deal with the Americans and western Europeans that left his Bosnian henchmen dangling in the wind.[1]

Politically unassailable as long as he controlled the army and the media, Milosevic's position weakened as the costs of the Bosnian war became clear. But with ruthless cunning, continued control of the press, and the remnants of the old Communist apparat to support him, Milosevic seemed secure in his power until November 1996, when the formerly divided opposition parties mounted a coalition list, *Zajedno* (Together), for the local elections of 1996. When they won fourteen of the country's local elections, including that of the country's capital, the government declared these victories illegal.

Such a tactic could only work if three things were true: if it was backed by a credible threat of force, if the media were under state control, and if no one from outside the country was watching. But, as it happened, those conditions no longer held. Although the police were daily arrayed on the streets, the army (perhaps still smarting from Milosevic's retreat from Bosnia) stayed on the sidelines. If the official media refused to publicize the opposition's victory or tactics, private radio and television and the foreign media more than made up for it. And finally, using the potential wedge of trade sanctions, the Organization for European Security and Cooperation found that *Zadedno* had won in all fourteen cities (*Le Monde*, February 13, 1997, p. 2).

That is the background of the cycle of contentious politics that began with

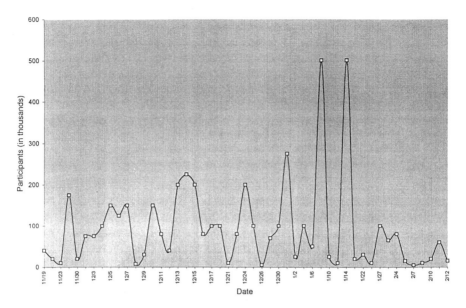

Figure 6.1. Participation in Belgrade Protest Events, November 19, 1996–February 12, 1997 (SOURCE: Reuter's Press Releases. Note: The data in the graph represents only those dates for which Reuter's provides estimates of actual participation.)

the stolen electoral victories and lasted until three months later, when the opposition's victories were recognized. From November 19, 1996, until mid-February 1997 – when the Serbian parliament finally conceded its victories – *Zajedno* mounted a nightly campaign of contention that threw the regime off balance, kept the eyes of an international audience glued to its television screens, and severely weakened Milosevic and his regime. At the same time, Belgrade's university students organized a separate resistance each day; though their fiery rhetoric distanced them from the *Zajedno* militants, they in fact helped to confront the regime with challenges from several directions (Garton Ash 1997).

Was this the Balkans exploding in violence once again? Some of the protests did turn violent, first as protesters pelted the state media with eggs for refusing to broadcast news of the protests, and then as police, trying to drive the opposition off the streets, attacked the demonstrators and wounded one of their leaders (*Le Monde*, February 13, 1997, p. 2). But from the beginning, the centerpiece of the campaign was the peaceful nightly marches through the center of Belgrade. For almost two months, thousands of demonstrators marched, sang, blew whistles, listened to speeches, alternatively heckling and fraternizing with the police, and went to court to keep the pressure on Milosevic. In the semidictatorial conditions of post-1989 Yugoslavia, the protest march – heir to two hundred years of contentious politics and virtually a part of institutional politics in the West – took on a special power. Figure 6.1, drawn from Reuter's press reports, gives a rough idea of the magnitude of the demonstrations in Belgrade.[2]

It was not just the fact of marching that expressed popular power in Belgrade: the determination of the protesters was matched by their creativity. "The regime was 'fired at' with eggs, blown at with whistles, banged at with pots and pans, and ridiculed by clowns" (Vejvoda 1997: 2). When the police demanded that only ordinary pedestrians use the streets of downtown Belgrade, thousands of people appeared walking their pets and pretending to be on the job; when the state-controlled media refused to publicize the protests, marchers blowing whistles filed past their headquarters nightly and accessed the international media; when New Year's Eve arrived, 300,000 demonstrators turned their protest into a street party; when the winner of a beauty contest was chosen, she named one of the policemen facing the demonstrators the "cutest cop" and handed him a bouquet of flowers. Without the nightly spectacle of thousands of citizens marching in the cold, laughing and singing, the world would probably have left Serbia to its fate.

The Serbian story illustrates the three major aspects of publicly mounted contention that will be analyzed in this chapter. The first, violent encounters, is the oldest we know of and the most direct; the second, the organized public demonstration, represents the main type of contentious politics in the world today – conventional collective action; the third, creative disruption, exists on the shifting frontier between convention and contention. Though violence, disruption, and conventional protest differ in a number of ways, they share a common thread: all are to some degree public performances.

THE PERFORMANCE OF CONTENTIOUS POLITICS

In his work on Britain and France and his theoretical essays (1983, 1984b), Charles Tilly has focused on the repertoires of contention that people typically use in a given time and place to express their claims. In Chapter 2, the concept of the repertoire helped to place contentious politics in a broad historical and comparative framework. But, thus far, much of the research on protest is limited to its quantitative dimensions: how often a particular form of contention is used; under what conditions it is replaced by another; its connection with industrialization and state building and with cycles of hunger, unemployment, and war; who typically uses which forms of action and against whom.[3] Recent advances in computerized text analysis have made it easy for scholars to reduce the study of repertoires to numbers and to study them over long periods of time (Franzosi 1989), but make it difficult to see them as public performances with emotional and cultural content.

But are all the variants of contentious politics equally performative? In what I called the "old" repertoire in Chapter 2, there were elements of performance – for example, in the carnival (Le Roy Ladourie 1980). The destruction of icons and statues in the wars of religion was also a performance, if only for the benefit of a celestial audience (Davis 1973). But local, parochial, and direct forms of contention were aimed mainly at extracting claims directly from antagonists or taking vengeance upon them. Only in the modern world – when public opinion and national states began to mediate between claim makers and their targets – has contention become a true performance for the benefit of third parties.

This was already evident in the French Revolution, when forms of dress and public display became politicized (see Chapter 7). The nineteenth century – with its development of the political march, the public demonstration, and the turnout – reinforced the trend to ritualized public performance. But it is only in our century, with the development of the mass media and the growing role of states and third parties in determining the outcomes of protest, that the performance of political contention has become both routine and professional. Even some forms of violence – the most elemental of the forms of contentious politics – reveal elements of performance.

THE CHALLENGE OF VIOLENCE

Violence is the most visible trace of collective action, both in contemporary news coverage and in the historical record. This is not surprising, because violence makes news and concerns those whose job it is to keep order. But violence also has a morbid fascination for most people, who are simultaneously repelled by and attracted to it. Finally, violence is the easiest kind of collective action for small groups to initiate without encountering major costs of coordination and control. Whereas organizers of a protest demonstration need to work hard to bring together a following, fomenters of violence need no more than bricks, bats, or chains, the sound of breaking windows, or the crunch of batons on victims' heads. Their solidarity is the solidarity of the gang.

Traditional forms of collective action centered on violence or on the threat of violence because it was the easiest form of collective action for isolated, illiterate, and enraged people to initiate. But violence is also used deliberately by larger movements to weld supporters together, dehumanize opponents, and demonstrate a movement's prowess. Hitler's Brownshirts attacked Communists and Jews not only to fight their way to power but to create a collective identity based on virility and power.

Given how easy it is to initiate violence, it is striking that it has become more rare in contemporary democracies than the other forms of collective action we will examine here (della Porta 1995: 216). The change begins with the rise of the national state in the West, as it suppressed private violence and took control of organized violence. We see evidence of the change in Tilly's research on British collective action, as Britons shifted from the brawls and rick burnings of the mid-eighteenth century to the petitions and demonstrations that dominate the historical record in the nineteenth (1995a, 1995b). But we see it most clearly in our own century in the growing acceptance of nonviolent protest on the part of governmental authorities.

INTERACTIVE VIOLENCE

Although violence has often been seen as an expression of psychological or social dysfunction, it is better understood as a function of the interaction between protesters' tactics and policing. The modern European record, writes Charles Tilly, shows a rough division of labor: "repressive forces do the largest part of the killing and wounding, while the groups they are seeking to control do most of the damage to objects" (1978: 177). These relations are interactive; as della Porta concludes from her study of political violence in Italy and Germany, "the escalation of protest repertoires involved *tactical adaptations* between the two main actors: demonstrators and the police" (1995: 211).

Such a "normalization" of protest does not often extend to nondemocratic states. It was in such states as czarist Russia that terrorism first developed – largely because protesters lacked access to legitimate means of participation and were forced into clandestinity, where their only means of expression was violent. But even in democratic states, the isolation of extremist groups and their clashes with police often leave them with no other protest resource than the recourse to violence (della Porta 1995).

Violence sometimes becomes habitual for certain groups and in certain ritualized intergroup interactions. Southern French winegrowers have used violence against property so consistently in their struggles to maintain prices and keep out foreign wine that dumping wine on the roads and invading government offices is, for them, virtually an institutionalized form of protest (Mann 1990). Violent conflicts between Protestant Unionists and Catholic nationalists in Northern Ireland are routinely triggered by violent Catholic reactions to provocative "Orange" marches in Catholic neighborhoods – which is exactly why the Protestants choose to march through these neighborhoods.

Violence has a polarizing effect on conflict and alliance systems. It transforms the relations between challengers and authorities from a confused, many-sided game of allies, enemies, and bystanders into a bipolar one in which people are forced to choose sides, allies defect, and the state's repressive apparatus swings into gear.[4] The threat of violence is a major power in movements but it turns into a liability when potential allies become frightened, elites regroup in the name of social peace, and the forces of order learn to respond to it. The main reason why the organizers of the nightly marches in Belgrade begged their supporters not to engage in violence was to limit this polarization and to give the authorities no pretext for repression.

Movements repeatedly split over whether or not to use violence. The struggle between the Girondins and the Jacobins in the French Revolution was triggered by a dispute about executing the king, with the Girondins – who opposed regicide – soon following him to the scaffold. On the European left, anarchists and social democrats argued about the violence of the former and the bureaucratization of the latter. In 1960s America, the most important of the left-wing student organizations, the Students for a Democratic Society (SDS), collapsed when conflict increased and the underground Weathermen emerged from the wreckage (della Porta 1995: 212).

Although violence impresses people, it has a severe limitation in the formation of movements, for it restrains and frightens off sympathizers. As long as violence remains only a possibility behind protesters' actions, uncertainty reigns and collective actors gain psychological leverage vis-à-vis opponents. But where violence occurs or is even likely, this gives authorities a mandate for repression (Eisinger 1973) and turns nonviolent sympathizers away. When that happens, organizers are trapped in a spiral of military confrontation with authorities that, in the modern age, it is virtually impossible for them to win. This may be why practically all of the modular forms of collective action that have developed as staples of the contemporary repertoire in democratic states are nonviolent. Or more specifically, they are divided between conventional forms of contention and disruption.

DISRUPTION AND THE INSTABILITY OF PROTEST

Disruption is the archtypical expression of challenging groups. It has taken a variety of forms, from the attack on a wrongdoer's house and the assault on a miller's grain store in the eighteenth century to the barricades of the nineteenth and the sit-ins and sit-down strikes of our own century. In its most direct forms, disruption is no more than a threat of violence: "If you do not produce grain or money," the challenger says, "or do not cease to use the machines that are destroying our livelihood, you may suffer physical harm."

But disruption has a more indirect logic in contemporary forms of contention. First, it is the concrete performance of a movement's determination. By sitting, standing, or moving together aggressively in public space, demonstrators signal their identity and reinforce their solidarity. At the same time, disruption obstructs the routine activities of opponents, bystanders, or authorities and forces them to attend to protesters' demands. Finally, disruption broadens the circle of conflict. By blocking traffic or interrupting public business, protesters inconvenience bystanders, pose a risk to law and order, and draw authorities into a private conflict.

Disruption need not threaten public order. In the United States, first the civil rights movement and then the women's movement taught Americans that political causes can be advanced through personal means. What would be non-disruptive for one set of social arrangements can be highly disruptive in another. For example, a primary battlefield for American feminism has been in the family – even on the part of nonmilitant women who would not consider themselves feminists. Another recent arena is the Catholic Church, where "women religious" developed a discursive but highly disruptive critique of hierarchy and patriarchy (Katzenstein 1998: ch. 6).

While the characteristic nineteenth-century form of confrontation was the barricade, the twentieth century has added its own forms to the repertoire of disruption. To the march ending in a demonstration in a public place were added the tools of nonviolent direct action and the sit-in – perhaps the major contributions of our century to the repertoire of contention. In places as far apart as preindependence India, the American South, and Greenham Common, England, nonviolent direct action has become a staple of protesters all over the world (Ackerman and Kreugler 1994; Sharp 1973).

Although there is evidence of nonviolence far back in history,[5] the practice first received formal theorization by Gandhi after he and his followers used it against South African discrimination and British colonial rule in India (Ackerman and Kreugler 1994: ch. 5). Although his movement's tactics were peaceful, Gandhi was quite clear about its disruptive aims. In initiating the 1930–1 nonviolence campaign in India, he wrote to the British viceroy: "It is not a matter of carrying conviction by argument. The matter resolves itself into one of matching forces" (quoted in Sharp 1973: 85).

Although it began as a tool of anticolonial nationalism, nonviolent direct action was truly modular, spreading to a variety of movements in the 1960s and 1970s as a tool of strategic choice, even where it was not formally theorized (Ackerman and Kruegler 1994: xxi). It was used in the American civil rights movements, during the Prague Spring and the student movements of 1968, by the European and American peace and environmental movements, by opponents of the Marcos regime in the Philippines, and by opponents of military rule in Thailand and Burma. Its capacity to spread from one kind of movement to very different ones is dramatically demonstrated by its use by antiabortion protesters in the United States. Here, a movement that rejects much of the cultural and ideological baggage of the New Left adopted the tactic of blocking the entrances of abortion clinics and resisting nonviolently as its militants were being carried off by the police.[6]

In authoritarian systems, where nonviolent protest would be smartly repressed, opposition movements have become skilled at mounting unobtrusive, symbolic, and peaceful forms of disruption that avoid repression while symbolizing contention. When Nazi occupation made street demonstrations risky in Denmark, Danes organized community songfests, walking tours, and the wearing of national symbols.[7] And long before state socialism collapsed in the former Soviet Union and east central Europe, opponents of those regimes had developed a broad repertoire of symbolic actions, passive resistance, and graffiti (Bushnell

1990), which avoided violence or any hint of it. The more closed is citizens' access to legitimate participation, the more sensitive they become to symbolic forms of protest.

THE POWER OF DISRUPTION

There is a paradox in disruptive forms of contention: because they spread uncertainty and give weak actors leverage against powerful opponents, they are the strongest weapon of social movements. But when we analyze modern cycles of collective action, we see that disruptive forms are not the most common (Tarrow 1989a: ch. 4). For sustaining disruption depends on a high level of commitment, on keeping authorities off balance, and on resisting the attractions of both violence and conventionalization. In all three ways, disruptive forms of contention are powerful but unstable.

First, as we will see in Chapter 8, commitment in social movements is difficult to maintain over long periods, except through formal organizations, which movements do not like, can seldom master, and – when they do – often turn them away from disruption. This was what Piven and Cloward found for the National Welfare Rights Organization they studied in the 1960s. So determined were its leaders to make it into a mass membership organization that the disruptive source of the movement's power was lost (1977: ch. 5).

Second, through disruption, movements attempt to keep authorities off balance, but this can seldom be sustained for very long, especially when police are determined and elites united. Each invention of a new tactic is ultimately met by new police tactics. Short of violence, organizers soon run out of ways to challenge authorities, embolden supporters, and keep the public interested and amused. In particular, the police practices designed and perfected since the 1960s routinize protest and remove much of its sting.

Third, faced by determined police and unified governments, the less committed members of social movements – usually in the majority – tend to slip back into private life, leaving the field in the hands of the most militant, who are more likely to choose violence than to maintain an uncertain relation with authorities. Disruption splits movements into militant minorities tending toward violence and moderate majorities heading toward convention. This too makes it unstable as a form of contention.

CONVENTIONAL COLLECTIVE ACTION

It is easiest for people to employ a form of collective action they know how to use, and this is what best explains the predominance of conventional forms over all others.[8] Most modern forms of contention have become part of a repertoire that is generally known and understood. Coordinated through a process that resembles the "contracts by convention" outlined by Russell Hardin

(1982), they involve at least the tacit coordination of participants' implicit expectations (Schelling 1960: 71). And because they require relatively little commitment and involve low risk, they can attract large numbers of participants. These are the major appeals of conventional forms of contention like the strike and the demonstration.

STRIKES AND DEMONSTRATIONS

The strike offers a good example of how forms of contention that began historically as disruptive confrontations become modular and ultimately conventional. The first use of the term "strike" in English seems to date from the actions of the eighteenth-century sailors who "struck" the sails of their ships as a sign of their unwillingness to work (Linebaugh and Rediker 1990: 240). But the emergence of the term in many European languages about the same time suggests that the strike had multiple origins (Tilly 1978: 159).

Though by now associated with industry, the strike predates industrialization and often included a variety of social actors, none of whom could be regarded as "proletarian."[9] Unlike the peasant revolt, which was inseparable from the seignorial system, once the strike was invented it was not tied to any particular occupation. As it became generally known that strikes could succeed, striking spread from skilled to unskilled workers, from the large factory to smaller firms, from the withholding of labor to the withholding of produce, from industry to agriculture, and from there to the public services. By now, the strike has become a virtual part of the institutions of collective bargaining, with its own jurisprudence, rituals, and expectations among both challengers and opponents.

Strikes developed as a means for workers to put pressure on management, but in the course of the nineteenth century, they became a source of class solidarity. This was reflected in the increasing offering of mutual support across occupational and geographic lines (Aminzade 1981: 81–2) and in the growing ritualization of the strike, which was designed to enhance solidarity. Strikers would parade within the precincts of the factory, carrying banners and tooting horns, chanting slogans, and singing songs of solidarity to induce their workmates to join them. Solidarity was also sometimes imposed, by "sending to Coventry" a worker who refused to down his tools.

Strikes could be employed in combination with other forms of contention: occupations, marches, industrial sabotage, petitions, and legal actions. Assemblies prepared the workers and elected strike committees; organizers in an especially militant sector would try to bring out other workers; pickets blocked the gates of the plant to keep raw materials out. Strikers who wanted to gain community solidarity would march from the factory through working-class neighborhoods in "turnouts," which – at their most successful – induced merchants to close their shutters and housewives to join their marches. From a spontaneous withdrawal of labor, the strike became the major means through which workers built and expressed solidarity, demonstrated their challenges, sought external support, and negotiated their differences with opponents from a position of enhanced, if temporary, power.

Like the strike, the demonstration began as a disruptive direct action that was eventually institutionalized. Owing much to the form of the religious procession, it seems to have developed when challengers moved from one target to another, either to attack opponents or to deliver demands.[10]

It became distinct from processions when secular demands were made, but its symbols resembled religious icons. Public demonstrations are connected historically with democratization; it was in the democratic phase of the 1848 revolution that the demonstration appeared in its full modern form,[11] for the leaders of the new French Republic could not refuse the people the right to present their petitions (Favre 1990: 16). From then on, the typical form through which all kinds of French movements made themselves known was the peaceful demonstration in a public place. By the late nineteenth century, the demonstration had become the major means by which unions and mass parties publicized their demands and demonstrated their strength in numbers.

Unlike strikes, which required some relationship to the withholding of labor or of a product to attract supporters, demonstrations could spread rapidly from place to place and combine many social actors. They could be employed on behalf of a claim, against an opponent, to express the existence of a group or its solidarity with another group, or to celebrate a victory or mourn the passage of a leader. Demonstrations thus became the classical modular form of collective action.

As demonstrations were legalized, like the strike, they gave rise to a jurisprudence and a culture (Champagne 1996; Hubrecht 1990). Rather than allowing the police to manhandle demonstrators, organizers began to employ their own parade marshals (Cardon and Huertin 1991: 199), developed a repeated sequence of routes, slogans, and signs, and had a regular marching order. Different ideological families favored one route or another, so that the political coloration of the group could often be determined from its itinerary. Even the role of nonparticipants – the press, the forces of order, bystanders and opponents – eventually became part of the demonstrative performance (Favre 1990: 18–32).

Repressive states almost always regard demonstrations as potential riots, which leads to the savage repression of peaceful protesters and sometimes – as in the events of January 1905 in Russia – to revolution. Constitutional states have come to accept demonstrations as a normal, and even an advantageous practice, as indicated by the fact that demonstrators receive police protection and even guidance. In Washington, D.C., in Rome, and in Paris, organizers are offered friendly advice by the police on how best to run a demonstration (della Porta, Fillieule, and Rieter 1998; McCarthy and McPhail 1998). From the unruly movement of protesters from one place to another, the protest demonstration has become the major nonelectoral expression of civil politics.

ITINERARIES OF REPERTOIRE CHANGE

Over time, there have been many changes in the repertoire of contention, some resulting from the kinds of environmental changes described in the preceding chapters, like print and association, state building and industrialization. Others have resulted from the internal unfolding of particular forms of contention and their institutionalization. Still others were invented by new movements and emerged from their particular composition and claims. We can chart the itineraries of repertoire change within four major categories: the institutionalization of disruptive forms of contention, innovation at the margins of inherited forms, tactical interaction with police and other actors, and paradigmatic change.

THE INSTITUTIONALIZATION OF CONTENTION

We saw earlier how the strike and the demonstration became part of the existing repertoire. The pattern of institutionalization is almost everywhere the same: as the excitement of the disruptive phase of a movement dies and the police become more skilled at controlling it, movements institutionalize their tactics and attempt to gain concrete benefits for their supporters through negotiation and compromise – a route that often succeeds at the cost of transforming the movement into a party or interest group.

At times, forms of disruption that invite repression are discarded as participants learn to avoid them. Such was the case for the "armed demonstrations" used by the French Montagnards during the 1851 insurrection against Louis Napoleon's coup d'etat.[12] At other times, forms of confrontation are themselves institutionalized as authorities learn to tolerate them or facilitate their use. To win concessions that supporters demand or authorities proffer, leaders move from confrontation to cooperation. This is particularly true when a political ally comes to power, as occurred in the democratization of South Africa in the mid-1990s (Klandermans, Roefs, and Olivier 1998).

The familiar pattern of goal displacement that observers since Michels have found in social movements runs parallel to this shift in tactics. But there are compensations for groups that choose the institutional path. Ordinary people are more likely to participate in forms of collective action that they know about than risk the uncertainty and potential violence of direct action. Police are less likely to charge an unarmed demonstration than one made up of people carrying clubs and brandishing chains. Once a movement's chosen form of action crystallizes into convention, it becomes a known and expected part of the repertoire. As Kafka wrote in one of his most prescient fables: "Leopards break into the temple and drink to the dregs what is in the sacrificial pitchers; this is repeated over and over again; finally it can be calculated in advance, and it becomes a part of the ceremony" (Kafka 1937: 92–3).

INNOVATION AT THE MARGINS

Even within inherited forms of collective action, there is incremental innovation and spontaneity. For instance, using the modular skeleton of the demonstration, demonstrators can march in costume, brandish pitchforks or monkey wrenches to display their militancy (Lumley 1990: 224), or carry props that symbolize their goals. Feminists wear witches' costumes to ridicule feminism's stereotyping by male opponents (Costain 1992: 49). Peace marchers don skeleton outfits to symbolize their fear of nuclear holocaust. Parisians opposing a strict immigration law march with cardboard suitcases to connect their protest with Nazi deportations. And protesters against sexual crimes against children march in white clothing – as they did in Belgium in 1996 – to symbolize the purity of the victims.

In the short run, innovations at the margins may simply enliven a conventional form of collective action by adding elements of play and carnival or ferocity and menace to its basic form. But over the long run, innovations can crystallize into wholly new forms. For example, French truckers in the 1990s blocked the roads with their vehicles, much as students in the 1960s had blocked university buildings – but to more devastating effect (Courty 1993).

TACTICAL INTERACTION

Innovation in collective action forms often results from the interaction between protesters and their opponents. This can be seen in the history of industrial relations: when employers used the tactic of locking their workers out of a factory to defeat a strike, workers invented the sit-down strike and added the factory occupation to their repertoire (Spriano 1975). By the time of the French Popular Front in 1936, the factory occupation had itself become routine, with its characteristic rituals, roles, and activities (Tartakowsky 1996: 56–7). Lockouts were eventually made illegal in most countries, to protect the legality of the strike and defend factories from potentially damaging occupations, but the occupation remained in use.

The same interactive process occurred between the American civil rights movement and the southern police trying to repress it. Doug McAdam determined from a detailed analysis of the movement's actions that each time its leaders approached a crisis in participation or opposition, it raised the threshold of collective action to a new level, using its tools selectively and creatively to outguess opponents and increase participation (1983). New forms often emerge from a dialectic of action and reaction by the state.

PARADIGMATIC CHANGE

Given the long, slow, historical evolution of the repertoire of contention, it may seem surprising to use the term "paradigmatic" change for the forms that people use to express their claims. And indeed, given the need to root collective action in cultural expectations, paradigmatic change is rare. That it does occur, however, can be gathered from the examples that have been used in this chapter and the preceding ones. The shift from rigid to modular forms of contention in the eighteenth century; the invention of the strike and the demonstration in the nineteenth; the development of nonviolent forms of resistance in the twentieth century: these could not be explained if there were no major breakthroughs in the way people mount claims and how authorities respond to them.

When a new form is "discovered," its appropriateness to a new situation is immediately obvious, and it is widely taken up, spreads rapidly, and gives the impression of a dramatic breakthrough. For example, part of the reason for the rapid diffusion of the democratization movements in eastern Europe in 1989 was the discovery that many citizens felt the same way, and that ordinary means of public expression would be tolerated and could succeed (Kuran 1991; Lohmann 1994).

An important mechanism for repertoire breakthroughs are what Aristide Zolberg calls "moments of madness" – the peaks of protest cycles – when "all is possible," "the wall between the instrumental and the expressive collapses," "politics bursts its bounds to invade all of life," and "political animals somehow transcend their fate" (1972: 183).[13] May 1968 in France was such a moment. New actors and frames of meaning came onto the scene; new forms of collective action were invented on the spot and experimented with; even after the cycle had collapsed in disillusionment and recrimination, some of its innovations remained, albeit in much reduced form.

Such an innovation was the change in the mood of the French street demonstration after 1968. Before the May events, demonstrations were large, orderly affairs led by mass parties and unions and mounted as set-piece performances in the name of general programs and demands. Demonstrators marched in serried ranks with great seriousness and near military discipline. After 1968, street demonstrations became far less orderly affairs. Full of ludic symbolism, outlandish costumes, and popular song, they are frequently mounted on behalf of single issues rather than the broad programs of the past (Ernst 1997; Fillieule 1997: 194–5). Often occasions for outings of family and friends, such demonstrations are as likely to be surrounded by street vendors selling hot dogs as by riot police, and are more likely to be followed by the green-clad sanitation workers than by *casseurs* overturning autos. Paradigmatic change, in Zolberg's words, is "like a flood tide which loosens up much of the soil but leaves alluvial deposits in its wake" (1972: 206).

MULTIFORM MOVEMENTS

Social movements are not limited to particular types of action but have access to a variety of forms, either alone or in combination. This flexibility allows them to combine the demands and the participation of broad coalitions of actors in coalitional campaigns of collective action and to shift their focus both outside and inside the political process.[14] This was already true in the nineteenth century. As historian Jack Blocker writes of the American temperance movement, its members "conducted surveys, prayed and sang, marched on saloons, marched in parades, marched in demonstrations, and attended meetings and conventions, . . . petitioned, circularized candidates, canvassed, voted, and watched the polls" (1989: xiv).

Contemporary movements are even more flexible in their tactics. Comparing the ecological movement in France and Germany, Dieter Rucht found that, at one time or another, antinuclear protesters in both countries used forms of collective action that were expressive or instrumental, confrontational, violent, or conventional, and brought people together in campaigns, skirmishes, and battles (1990). The same flexibility can be seen in the American women's movement. When the Reagan administration came to power, "movement groups changed from working inside the institutions of government . . . to more electorally focused events and rising political protest" (Costain 1992: 126–7). Activities ranged between "teas held at churches to discuss change in the laws and endless trips to the state legislatures" and "counter-hearings" and "speak-outs" (Staggenborg 1991: 29, 44). The modern social movement is a multiform phenomenon, ranging from protests that physically and symbolically attack the dominant system to those that bring movements within the range of conventional politics.

CONCLUSIONS

The repertoire of contention offers three basic types of collective action: violence, disruption, and convention. They combine in different degrees the properties of challenge, uncertainty, and solidarity. The first form, violence, is the easiest to initiate, but under normal circumstances it is limited to small groups with few resources who are willing to exact damage and risk repression. The opposite form, convention, has the advantage of building on routines that people understand and that elites will accept or even facilitate. This is the source of its numerical predominance in the repertoire, but also of its institutionalization and lack of excitement. The third form, disruption, breaks with routine, startles bystanders, and leaves elites disoriented, at least for a time. Disruption is the source of much of the innovation in the repertoire and of the power in movement, but it is unstable and easily produces violence or becomes routinized into convention.

Such movements as ecology, civil rights, and feminism combine challenge, solidarity, and uncertainty in their protests. They have maintained support and grown so well over the past three decades, in part because they had available a known, well-understood repertoire of modular forms to build upon. They adapted well to change because their leaders innovated on these basic models with skill and creativity to produce protest performances that gained followers, attracted attention from third parties, and challenged opponents.

But the presence of even a large number of protest events does not, in itself, constitute a social movement. As Mario Diani writes, unless these events are *perceived* to be part of a broader movement by supporters and opponents alike, however dramatic, they will remain isolated and noncumulative (1995: 3). Challengers must frame their demands in ways that will attract followers and build on social networks, and connective structures must link them to one another with a shared definition of reality, of "us" and "them," and of fundamental goals through changing seasons of opportunities and constraints. These are the main "internal" powers through which social movements are constructed and maintained; we turn to them next.

7

FRAMING CONTENTION

In Year V of the French Revolution, the commissioner of the revolutionary executive power in Grenoble wrote:

> It is a contravention of the constitutional charter . . . to insult, provoke, or threaten citizens because of their choice of clothing. Let taste and propriety preside over your dress; never turn away from agreeable simplicity . . . Renounce these signs of rallying, these *costumes of revolt*, which are the uniforms of an enemy army.[1]

The commissioner was in a position to know. In the decade in which he wrote, the French produced the first systematic attempts to reshape political culture around new forms of dress, holidays, salutations, public works, and monuments.[2] As the revolution spread, so did its symbols. Austere dress marked off republicans from aristocratic display (Hunt 1984: 75–6); supporters of the Revolution would challenge citizens who dared to be seen on the street in elegant dress; even the king had a Phrygian bonnet stuck on his head before he lost it after the failure of his flight to Varennes (Schama 1989: 603–4).

Attempts at symbolic mobilization accompany every modern social movement, from the donning of simple military tunics by the Russian and Chinese Communists, to the pagan glitter of the Italian Fascist hierarchs, to the simple khaki cloth of Indian nationalists, and the scruffy beards of Latin American *guerrilleros*. Since social movements attempt to replace "a dominant belief system that legitimizes the status quo with an alternative mobilizing belief system that supports collective action for change" (Gamson, Fireman, and Rytina 1982: 15), movement leaders proffer the symbols of revolt to gain support and mark themselves off from opponents.

But there is a paradox in the symbolic politics of social movements: between developing dynamic symbols that will create new identities and bring about

106

change, and proffering symbols that are familiar to people who are rooted in their own cultures. This was hard enough for French revolutionaries dealing with a largely illiterate population; it has been rendered more complex by the barrage of information that competes with movement messages through books, newspapers, and especially the mass media. This is one reason why their public actions increasingly take the form of "performances": they are competing for public space with entertainment, news, other movements, and the government's attempts to monopolize the formation of opinion. The major symbolic dilemma of social movements is to mediate between inherited symbols that are familiar, but lead to passivity, and new ones that are electrifying, but may be too unfamiliar to lead to action.

This dilemma produces three sets of problems for analysts and practitioners of social movements.

First, most scholars agree that meanings are "constructed."[3] But what is the relationship between symbol formation and underlying conflicts of interest in turning contention into movements? Do movements start from the changing terrain of interest and conflict, using and modifying cultural materials as a costume aimed at animating their supporters? Or do they frame collective action with symbols created out of whole cloth – as a certain kind of poststructuralist scholarship would seem to suggest?

Second, how do the intended subjects of social movements interpret the symbols challengers array? Intellectuals can interpret symbolic materials for their intended recipients, but can we be sure that they are "read" in the same way by ordinary people? In particular, how can we infer the emotional valence on the receiving end of symbolic communication from social subjects whose voices are muted?

Third, we often hear the term "identity politics" when social movements are discussed, by which is meant that contention is fought in the name of collective identities. But are these identities inherited like old clothes and applied to contention – "essentialist," in the current jargon – or are they sewn together for purposes of struggle? Few individuals possess single, unified identities; most people juggle and combine, categorical and political, embedded and disjoined identities (Tilly 1997a: ch. 7). From such checkered materials, how do movements weave the unity and dynamism they need to construct fully integrated mass movements?

At the heart of these questions is a basic problem for the cultural study of social movements.[4] If the struggle between movements and their opponents were merely cognitive and symbolic, then a social movement could be understood as no more than a symbolic message center, either recycling inherited meanings of spinning out new ones. In that case, we could read the interaction between movements and authorities as a kind of literary text – a contest between competing tropes. But if meaning is constructed out of social and political interaction with supporters and opponents, then we must ask how the "text" of movement messages relates to the *con*text of interests and conflicts in play (Glenn 1997; Kertzer

1988: 175) and to the emotions of the people appealed to. How symbolic discourse takes shape in the process of struggle is the final question that animates this chapter.

FROM POLITICAL CULTURE TO STRATEGIC FRAMING

In the past decade, cultural historians, sociologists of culture, and political anthropologists have returned to the concept of political culture to study revolutionary change. An important forerunner was George Mosse in his reconstruction of the nineteenth-century creation of a German national myth. In his book *The Nationalization of the Masses* (1975), Mosse took his cue from how the Jacobins manipulated the symbols of the French Revolution. Turning from France to Germany, he saw the entire tradition of mass politics as a species of theater, fixed in ritual and inherently antiparliamentary to the extent that it posited an unmediated relationship between the people and its leaders (p. 2).

But if meanings are "fixed" by rhetorical renderings, was it enough to establish a discourse in order to provide the meaning for future mobilizations? Even if we assume that the basic content of a movement is its symbolism, how is that message received and interpreted over time and across space among different social subjects? Will it be applied in its original form like holy scripture? Must it be reworked and readdressed to local constituents according to their cultural preconceptions? Or will it be applied selectively and in combination with indigenous cultural symbols by movement entrepreneurs? The modification and appropriation of marxism as it spread across the globe can help us to answer this question.

VARIATIONS ON A MARXIST THEME

The original doctrine propounded by Marx and Engels placed great hope in the mass action of the working class in its inevitable clash with concentrating capital. But it left open the question of agency. Because it was combined with a historical epistemology, marxism could be interpreted as a form of inevitablism – waiting for the masses to mature to a point when they could take advantage of ripening historical conditions – which tempted later social democrats to build up their organizations and wait for the contradictions of capitalism to ripen.

So long was the wait that, for some, building the organizational weapon to seize the moment of capitalism's collapse began to take precedence over advancing its date (Michels 1962). And while waiting, adaptation to existing conditions – for example, in embracing both trade unionism and nationalism (Roth 1963), adapting to the conditions of peasant societies (Tarrow 1967), or wooing the middle class (Hellman 1975) – ate away at the movement's revolutionary élan.

That was the case until marxism moved eastward, where Lenin, faced with an authoritarian state and an immature proletariat, appropriated marxism's revolutionary message but substituted for the mass action of the proletariat the conscious direction of the party – interpreting the latter as the "head" of the movement of which the workers were the body. Both Russian conditions and Lenin's creative constructivism changed the framing of marxism from a theory of mass working-class revolution to one of elite-led organization and mobilization.

As marxism spread around the world, its obsession with the working class lost much of its immediacy, for in the largely peasant colonies and semicolonies of the world, how could a revolution be built with a proletariat that was largely lacking? Lenin's vanguard notions also came under challenge, first as the movement spread into rural areas where it blended with peasant eschatologies (Hobsbawm 1959); and, second, when the strategy came into contact with civil societies more resilient than czarist Russia's (Gramsci 1971). When the Chinese Communist Party was smashed by Chiang Kai-Shek in the Shanghai rebellion of 1927 (Perry 1993: ch. 5), vanguardism and workerism came into question.

It was at this point that an entirely new variant of marxism was fashioned by Mao Tse-tung – "the mass line." No simple return to Marx's workerism, nor a rejection of leninist organization, maoism reframed marxism as the struggle of colonial peoples based in the countryside of the world against the parasitic cities, under the leadership of a vanguard group rooted in the peasantry. Mao also mobilized a following around Chinese cultural symbols, making the movement infinitely more effective when it faced a foreign invader than when it faced domestic capitalists and landholders (Johnson 1962).

What these examples from the history of marxism show is that changes in the symbolism of a movement are neither derived directly from culture nor woven out of the whole cloth of ideology, but are the result of its strategic interaction in its various and changing settings. The symbols of collective action cannot be simply read like a "text," independent of the conditions in which they struggle. Nor are they simple projections of indigenous culture into political strategies. Out of a cultural reservoir of possible symbols, movement entrepreneurs choose those that they hope will mediate among the cultural understandings of the groups they wish to appeal to, their own beliefs and aspirations, and their situations of struggle (Laitin 1988). To relate text to context, the grammar of culture to the semantics of struggle, we need a concept suited to the interactive nature of social movements. A contemporary group of scholars offers such a concept in the idea of collective action "frames."

COLLECTIVE ACTION FRAMES

In his synthesis of the concept of collective action frames, Bert Klandermans writes: "The transformation of social issues into collective action frames does not occur by itself. It is a process in which social actors, media and members of a society jointly interpret, define and redefine states of affairs" (1997: 44). In an important series of papers, sociologist David Snow and his collaborators have adopted Erving Goffman's (1974) concept of framing to collective action, arguing that there is a special category of cognitive understandings – collective action frames – that relate to how social movements construct meaning for action.[5] A frame, in Snow and Benford's words, is an

> interpretive schemata that simplifies and condenses the "world out there" by selectively punctuating and encoding objects, situations, events, experiences, and sequences of actions within one's present or past environment. (1992: 137)

Collective action frames are accentuating devices that either "underscore and embellish the seriousness and injustice of a social condition or redefine as unjust and immoral what was previously seen as unfortunate but perhaps tolerable" (Snow and Benford 1992: 137). Social movements are deeply involved in the work of "naming" grievances, connecting them to other grievances and constructing larger frames of meaning that will resonate with a population's cultural predispositions and communicate a uniform message to power holders and others (p. 136).

Movement entrepreneurs cannot simply adapt frames of meaning from traditional cultural symbols: if they did, they would be nothing more than reflections of their societies' values and would be inhibited from challenging them. Like Lenin and Mao, they orient their movements' frames toward action in particular contexts and fashion them at the intersection between a target population's culture and their own values and goals. This is what Snow and his associates call "frame alignment" (1986). In their 1986 article, they describe four alignment processes through which movements formulate their messages in relation to the existing culture. The first three make only incremental innovations in symbolism. Through "frame bridging," "frame amplification," and "frame extension," movements link existing cultural frames to a particular issue or problem, clarify and invigorate a frame that bears on a particular issue, and expand the boundaries of a movement's primary framework to encompass broader interests or points of view (pp. 467–76). The most ambitious strategy is the fourth – "frame transformation." It is the most important framing device in movements that seek substantial social change (p. 474).

The process of frame alignment is not always easy, clear, or uncontested. First, movement leaders compete with other movements, with media agents, and with the state for cultural supremacy – competitors with immensely powerful cultural resources at their disposal. Second, movements that adapt too well to their societies' cultures lose the power of opposition and alienate their most militant supporters – for what society has dominant values that do not support existing power arrangements? Third, ordinary people often have their own "reading" of events that differs from those constructed by their leaders, often assimilating the interpretation that elites give to their failings. A considerable effort at cognitive mobilization is often necessary to break constituents of this habit of thought (McAdam 1982). In doing so, two kinds of appeals are often employed.

INJUSTICE AND EMOTIONALITY

A recurring mode of discourse in contentious politics is built around what William Gamson calls an "injustice frame" (1992a: 68, 73). In the same vein, writes Barrington Moore Jr., "any movement against oppression has to develop a new diagnosis and remedy for existing forms of suffering, a diagnosis and remedy by which this suffering stands morally condemned" (1978: 88). Similarly, Doug McAdam argues that "before collective action can get underway, people must collectively define their situations as unjust" (1982: 51). "Injustice," concludes Gamson, "focusses on the righteous anger that puts fire in the belly and iron in the soul" (1992b: 32).

But it is no simple matter to convince timid people that the indignities of everyday life are not written in the stars – that they can be attributed to some agent and that the actions they take collectively can change that condition. "Different emotions can be stimulated by perceived inequalities – cynicism, bemused irony, resignation" (Gamson 1992b: 32). Contention may point to a grievance, identify a constituency, and name an enemy. But, writes Gamson, "it is insufficient if individuals privately adopt a different interpretation of what is happening. For collective adoption of an injustice frame, it must be shared by the potential challengers in a public way" (1992a: 73). Inscribing grievances in overall frames that identify an injustice, attribute the responsibility for it to others, and propose solutions to it is a central activity of social movements.

Much of the "work" of framing is cognitive and evaluative – that is, it identifies grievances and translates them into broader claims against significant others. But framing work should not be reduced to the sterile cogitations of ideologues; no significant transformation of claims into action can occur without tapping or creating emotional energy. Emotions, writes Verta Taylor, are the "site for articulating the links between cultural ideas, structural inequality, and individual action" (1995: 227). She writes, "it is emotions that provide the 'heat', so to speak, that distinguishes social movements from dominant institutions" (p. 232).

Some emotions, like love, loyalty, reverence, are clearly more mobilizing than others, such as despair, resignation, and shame. Some, like anger, are "vitalizing," and are more likely to be present in triggering acts of resistance, whereas others, like resignation or depression, are "devitalizing," and are more likely to be present during phases of demobilization.[6] The high points of contention produce emotional pivots around which the future direction of the movement turns. Over time, movement entrepreneurs will strain to reevoke these emotional pivots through rhetoric, ritual, and gatherings at the sites of injustice or of past victories.[7]

Because it is so reliable a source of emotion, religion is a recurring source of social movement framing. Religion provides ready-made symbols, rituals, and solidarities that can be accessed and appropriated by movement leaders (Smith 1996). The same is true of nationalism: lacking the fine mechanical metaphors of class dialectics, nationalism possesses a much greater emotional potential. As Benedict Anderson ironically asks, contrasting the many monuments to nationalism with the lack of memorials to social class, can one even imagine "a Tomb of the Unknown Marxist" (1991: 10)?

More than any other recent movement, it is feminism that has led to a recognition of the force of emotionality in social movements. Feminist "popular and scholarly writings brim with accounts of the intense feelings that underlie participation in the women's movement" (Taylor 1995: 226–7). "Scholars of the women's movement," writes Verta Taylor, "have pointed to both the love and caring, on the one hand, and the anger, pain, and hostility, on the other, that characterize feminists' interactions" (p. 229).[8]

Sociologist Arlie Hochschild has pointed out that particular groups form "emotion cultures" (1990). Many movements are built around the deliberate cultivation of hatred or anger. The long and tortured struggle between Catholics and Protestants in Northern Ireland cannot be understood except as the deliberate stoking of mutual hatreds. The deliberate use of the rape of Muslim women by Bosnian Serbs was aimed at least as much at desensitizing their own soldiers as at humiliating their victims (Eisenstein 1996: 167). Even racial pride – cultivated by a sector of the Black Power movement in the United States in the 1960s – involved formalized expressions of verbal violence (Gitlin 1995: ch. 1). The link between mobilization and anger is perhaps most explicit in the case of Act-Up, the movement to defend AIDS victims. "Anger," writes one of its leaders, "is something that is created; Act Up is a machine for the construction of anger" (quoted in Ernst 1997: 3).

The culture of collective action is built on frames and emotions oriented toward mobilizing people out of their compliance and into action in conflictual settings. Symbols are taken selectively by movement leaders from a cultural reservoir and combined with action-oriented beliefs in order to navigate strategically among a parallelogram of actors, ranging from states and social opponents to militants and target populations. Most important, they are given an emotional valence aimed at converting passivity into action.

CONSENSUS MOBILIZATION AND MEDIA FRAMING

The symbols of collective action take hold through two main processes: over the long run, they enter people's consciousness through a capillary process of consensus formation and mobilization; and in the shorter run, they impress people through the transformations wrought by collective action itself. The first set of processes can be seen in how movements interact with autonomous sources of culture and the media, whereas the second require attention to the performative elements in the process of contention itself.

In a 1988 article, Bert Klandermans makes the important distinction between consensus formation and consensus mobilization. Consensus formation results from the unplanned convergence of meaning in social networks and subcultures and takes place outside anyone's direct control. Within these networks and subcultures, writes Klandermans, "processes of social comparison produce collective definitions of a situation" (1988: 175). These collective definitions often lie hidden behind official culture – for example, the profound alienation of citizens in eastern Europe was hidden behind people's formal acceptance of state socialism until 1989 (Kuran 1991). As for Western societies, Tom Rochon sees a two-stage process of movement expression: the first, a process of consensus formation through "critical communities" with no necessary movement vocation; the second, as explicit consensus mobilization, directed at goals that follow from the "culture moves" created by criticism (1998).

Consensus formation produces collective definitions of a situation but does little more than that. It neither produces collective action nor does it provide clues to action for those who wish to guide people into a social movement. For that to occur, consensus *mobilization* is necessary (Klandermans 1988: 183–91). Consensus mobilization consists of deliberate attempts to spread the views of a social actor among parts of a population (p. 175). Movement organizations are among the actors that attempt to do this (p. 184). In so doing, they compete with other organizations, with churches and governments, with the media, and with widespread cultural predispositions. That contest is often unequal, as the following example suggests.

COSTUMES OF CONSENSUS

When the Iraqi army invaded Kuwait and the American and other Western governments prepared to counterattack, peace demonstrations were organized in Washington and on the West Coast (*New York Times*, December 27, 1991, p. 17). During these rallies, a variety of physical symbols drew on the oppositional subculture that had maintained itself since the antiwar movement of the 1960s. But in a climate of public opinion that was supportive of the president's war policy, the dominant symbolism with which the demonstrators tried to frame their protest was patriotic. As the *Now National Times* summed it up for its readers:

> There were American flags, there were yellow ribbons, and there were concerned mothers and fathers, wives and husbands, sisters, brothers and friends

who understood that the best way to support our troops in the Middle East is to bring them home alive. (March–April 1991, p. 1)

What is happening in this protest? Surely not a mechanical aping of the inherited symbols of the American dream, but rather a self-conscious strategy by movement leaders to extend consensual symbols into oppositional meanings. The attempt was ingenious, but in contesting the wave of popular support for a just war waged by a popular president against an opponent framed as a hitlerian villain, the barrage of consensual symbolism made not the slightest difference. The costume of consensus cannot mobilize consent against the system that has produced it.

Why does it seem so difficult to construct truly oppositional symbols? One reason may be that movement leaders genuinely wish to remain within the boundaries of a political consensus – this was certainly true of most of the American peace protesters. Another is that the reach of the state is so great that even messages of rupture are framed in terms of consensus. But a third reason relates more directly to the structure of communication in today's societies: movements that wish to communicate with a broader public must either have the internal resources to "perform" protest (Glenn 1997; Meyer and Gamson 1995), or use the media in order to do so. But the media are far from neutral in the symbols that they select and transmit.

MEDIA FRAMING AND MOVEMENT STRATEGY[9]

In the fall of 1996, a set of gruesome murder cases of teenage girls was exposed in Belgium, along with a history of police incompetence, indifference, and possibly even complicity involving the activities of pedophiles. With little advance planning or coordination, and led by the parents of the victims, hundreds of thousands of Belgians of both Flemish and French-speaking background marched and assembled in the streets of Brussels dressed in white to symbolize the innocence of the victims (Rihoux 1997). Several months later, the supporters of the parents were publishing a newsletter – *La marche blanche* – to seek out corruption in high places and diffuse the message of the movement.

When Eric Hobsbawm studied "primitive" rebellion in the 1950s, it was common to ascribe the use of such symbolic ritual to the "pre-political" nature of these movements (1959: p. 2; ch. 9). But the role of visual symbolism has been vividly reinforced by the role of the media, and particularly of television. One reason for the use of visual symbolism is to help in the construction of collective identities; another to project an image to bystanders and opponents of a movement's mourning or joy, ferocity, or spirit of play (Lumley 1990: 223). The primary mechanism for both processes is the mass media.

The role of radio in information diffusion should not be ignored. For example, the May 1968 events in France were dutifully reported on government radio, informing people in different parts of the country about marches, strikes, and factory occupations and helping the movement to spread. During the cold war, the BBC and Radio Free Europe played an important role in diffusing information to eastern Europe, especially after dissidents in those countries learned how to get press releases out to these media sources. But it was television, with its unique capacity to encapsulate complex situations in compressed visual images, that brought about a revolution in movement tactics.

The extent of this revolution first became evident during the 1960s in the United States. The civil rights movement, write Kielbowicz and Scherer, "was television's first recurring news story largely because of its visual elements" (1986: 83). The coincidence of the movement's appearance with on-site television news-casting helped it in three ways: first, television brought long-ignored grievances to the attention of the nation, and particularly to viewers in the North; second, it visually contrasted the peaceful goals of the movement with the viciousness of the police; third, television was a medium of communication for those inside the movement. It helped diffuse knowledge of what the movement was doing by the visual demonstration of how to sit-in at a lunch counter, how to march peacefully for civil rights, and how to respond when attacked by police and fire hoses.

The student movement was the second major testing ground for the impact of television. The co-occurrence of student demonstrations all over the West in 1968 – using many of the same slogans and forms of action (McAdam and Rucht 1993) – was in part the result of the impact of television. As two scholars of the media's effect on movements conclude, "for members of the audience whose own experiences resemble those of the televised cases, such media attention can serve to cultivate a collective awareness, laying the groundwork for a social movement" (Kielbowicz and Scherer 1986: 81).

A third phase was the popularization of political religion in the 1970s and 1980s through the mass media. In places as diverse as Iran and the United States, religious figures became adept at using the media to diffuse their political mes-sages. In Iran, the Ayatollah Khomeini and his followers used radio and tape cassettes to diffuse their anti-Western critique of the shah's government, while Christian fundamentalists in the United States broadcast their messages from venues as diverse as the pulpits of neighborhood churches and the gridirons of football stadiums.[10]

The most dramatic example of the role of the media was global: the staging of a massive demonstration by Chinese students in Tienanmen Square in protest against Communist Party corruption and authoritarianism (Esherick and Was-serstrom 1990). Chinese students not only drew on traditional symbols of Chinese political theater; as in other episodes of the 1989 revolutions, they used theatrical forms strategically to gain the sympathy of the international media audience that they knew was their only hope of putting external pressure on authorities (Cal-houn 1994a: ch. 3). The monument to freedom that they rolled on to the square at one point had roots in Chinese political culture; but it also had a disarming resemblance to the Statue of Liberty that French republicans had presented to their American cousins in New York harbor.

The media provide a diffuse source for consensus formation that movements on their own cannot easily achieve. New information, and mainly new ways of interpreting it, often first appear in public space, only later giving rise to collective action frames on the part of movement entrepreneurs. For example, when William Gamson studied the coverage of two nuclear accidents in the American press in the 1950s and the 1980s, he found that there had been a radical change in how reporters treated the issue (1988).

Once formed, movements can take advantage of coverage by sympathetic journalists (Gitlin 1980: 26). More often, however, the media choose to frame a story in a certain way because it sells newspapers or attracts viewers. Thus, in a 1997 strike against a plant closing by Renault in Belgium, when large numbers of French and Spanish Renault workers crossed the border to protest the decision in Brussels, it was the press that labeled the protest a "Eurostrike" (Imig and Tarrow 1997). Its motive was not sympathy for the strikers as much as the desire to frame the story in a newsworthy way for an international audience.

This story highlights a major problem for social movements: the media are far from neutral bystanders in the framing of movement events. While the media may not work directly for the ruling class (Molotch 1979: 75), they certainly do not work for social movements. In a capitalist society, at least, the media are in business to report on the news and they stay in business only if they report on what will interest readers or viewers, or in what editors think will interest them.

How movements are covered by the media is affected by the structure of the media industry. As Kielbowicz and Scherer write, movements are affected by the media's preference for dramatic, visible events; by journalists' reliance on authoritative sources; by news cycles or rhythms; by the influence of reporters' professional values or orientations; and by how the media environment – mainly the degree of competition – influences the news (1986: 75–6). As a result, the capacity of movement organizations to appropriate the media for their own purposes is limited.

The influence of the media on the perception of movements' actions is double-edged. On the one hand, a growing "frame" of the media is that public life is corrupt, a point of view that is comfortable for readers or viewers because it justifies inaction or demobilization.[11] On the other hand, the interest of movement-mounted dramatic activities quickly fades for the media unless they change or escalate their routines. When protests escalate, the media will continue to offer coverage, but are quick to give priority to their violent or bizarre aspects.

The media tend to focus on what "makes" news. This reinforces the shift from disruption to violence often found in protest cycles (Gans 1979: 169). The single student in a peaceful antiwar protest who throws a rock at a police line or the transvestite marching in garish drag in a gay rights march makes better copy than no matter how many marchers parading peacefully down a city street. In this way, the media "accentuate the militant strains found in any collection of activists" (Kielbowicz and Scherer 1986: 86), providing incentives for disruptive or violent elements in otherwise peaceful movements.[12]

CONSTRUCTING CONTENTION

Both existing cultural frames and the role of the media constrain movement formation. Yet new movements are constructed all the time, and the most successful of them transcend their societies' cultural frames and – in some cases – produce revolutions. It is not consensus mobilization or media framing that accomplish this but the process of contention itself. The case of the American civil rights movement will show how inherited cultural frames are combined with strategic choices within the process of contention.

REFRAMING RIGHTS IN AMERICA

It is striking how naturally Americans frame their demands in terms of rights – whether they be the rights of minorities, women, gays, animals, or the unborn.[13] But for African Americans, rights have most often been honored in the breach; why then did the civil rights movement of the 1960s draw upon this frame so centrally? And why did "rights" then become the "master frame" of many other movement sectors during the cycle of contention of the 1960s (Snow and Benford 1992)?

The first outcome resulted from the historical fact that the earliest terrain of the movement was in the courts, beginning from the concept of equal educational rights. Rights were not an idiom that came automatically to black Americans convinced of the ingrained racial injustices of the system; but seeking rights had been a successful strategy *before* the most conflictual period of the movement. As Charles Hamilton writes, this context "created a cadre of constitutional lawyers who became in a real sense the focal points of the civil rights struggle" (1986: 244).

A second reason why rights became the central frame for civil rights was strategic: equal opportunity was a useful bridge, based on traditional American political rhetoric, between the movement's main internal constituency, the southern black middle class, and the white liberal "conscience constituents" whose support bolstered it from the outside. For the black middle class, equality of opportunity was a worthy enough goal, while white liberals were most offended by the contradiction between the value Americans placed on rights and the denial of equal opportunity to African Americans. Rights had the dual function of building on previous court successes and bridging the white liberals and the black middle class from which the core of the movement came.

But was the civil rights movement's concept of "rights" no more than the traditional costume of American consensus? If so, why did the movement have to await the 1960s to act and how did it achieve as much as it did? The answer is that only when combined with an innovative form of action in a changing opportunity structure did rights become the central collective action frame of the movement.

From the late 1950s on, the modest equal opportunity rights frame was accompanied by a highly dramatic and confrontational protest *practice* – nonviolent direct action. If the doctrine of rights bridged the gap between the traditional subaltern status of southern blacks and their white liberal supporters rhetorically, nonviolent direct action transformed black middle-class quietism into activism. Rather than oppose a frame of risky revolt to police violence, the movement's leaders elaborated a practice of militant quiescence within the most traditional institution they possessed – the black church. It was not the inherited grammar of rights but the action of nonviolent resistance that turned cultural quiescence into action.

From the beginning, the transformation of the rights frame was interactive. Two key actors played a critical role: a generation of college students who had grown up in the cities where the worst practices of Jim Crow were absent, and the agents of the white power structure whose behavior played into the hands of the movement – on television! While the students in their neat suits and demure dresses sat-in, marched, demonstrated, sang, and prayed, the police responded to nonviolence with violence, meeting the doves of peace with the police dogs of war. The more violent and un-Christian the behavior of white power holders, the greater the moral superiority of the students' tactic and the more reasonable the movement's program. It was in the process of struggle that the inherited rhetoric of rights was transformed into a new and broader collective action frame.

The lesson of the civil rights movement is that the symbols of revolt are not drawn like musty costumes from a cultural closet and arrayed before the public. Nor are new meanings unrolled out of whole cloth. The costumes of revolt are woven from a blend of inherited and invented fibers into collective action frames in confrontation with opponents and elites. And once established, they are no longer the sole possession of the movements that produced them but – like the modular forms of collective action described in Chapter 6 – become available for others to wear. As Snow and Benford point out, once enunciated in the context of a period of general turbulence, a successful collective action frame becomes a "master frame" (1992). In the case of civil rights, as the result of the pathbreaking framing work of civil rights, "we began to see the heightened politicization of other groups, notably feminists, environmentalists, the elderly, children, the handicapped, and homosexuals organizing and demanding their 'rights' " (Hamilton 1986: 246).

FRAMES AND IDENTITIES

"Two distinct, but not unrelated, features of culture are relevant to comparative politics," writes Marc Howard Ross:

> first, culture is a system of meaning which people use to manage their daily
> worlds . . . ; second, culture is the basis of social and political identity which

affects how people line up and how they act on a wide range of matters.
(1998: 42)

Thus far, we have dealt mainly with the first meaning of culture; but lurking
beneath the surface is the question of how existing identities constrain and vitalize
movements and how new ones may be formed in the process of contention.[14] We
can summarize the main issues surrounding collective identity in four brief
points.

First, "natural," or inherited, identities are often the basis of aggregation in
social movements, as we saw earlier in discussing the importance of religion in
framing contention. But movements often struggle to change the meaning of
these identities – as Israeli Zionists fought to discard the eastern European image
of the Jew as urban, mercantile, and cowardly for a new one that would be rural,
productive, and courageous, or as African Americans worked to create a new and
more positive image of blackness, in a community in which lightness of skin
color had been seen as a sign of status.

Second, social movements require solidarity to act collectively and consistently; creating or accessing identities around their claims is one way of doing
so. Thus, feminists identify themselves with woman's oppressed fate since the
dawn of time; environmentalists present themselves as the representatives of most
of humanity; and well-paid, skilled "aristocrats of labor" present themselves as
the suffering proletariat. Sometimes the myths create what Tilly calls "lineaments
of durable connection among core participants." But, he concludes, "most social
movements remain far more contingent and volatile than their mystifications
allow" (Tilly 1997a: 133).

Third, while such "categorical" identity claims are often the outward apparel
that movements wear to mark their members off from others, the solidarity of
their militants is often based on more intimate and specialized communities: like
the "communities of discourse" that Mary Katzenstein found among American
Catholic women (1995); or the workplace solidarity that Rick Fantasia found
among the workers he studied (1988); or the personalized community building
that Paul Lichterman found in American local communities (1996).

Fourth, building a movement around strong ties of collective identity,
whether inherited or constructed, does much of the work that would normally
fall to organization; but it cannot do the work of mobilization, which depends
on framing identities so that they will lead to action, alliances, interaction. In
fact, identity politics often produces insular, sectarian, and divisive movements
incapable of expanding membership, broadening appeals, and negotiating with
prospective allies. This is the trenchant critique that Todd Gitlin makes of contemporary American "identity politics" in his *Twilight of Common Dreams* (1995)
– a weakness he does not find in the class politics of the past.

The link between exclusiveness and weakness also works in the opposite
direction: it is frequently observed of weak movements and toward the ends of

protest cycles that militants raise the walls of their collective identity higher and higher, defining themselves through increasingly narrow definitions of identity and rejecting alliances as a form of "selling out." In Gitlin's withering epigram, weak movements often "march on the English Department while the Right takes the White House" (1995: ch. 5).

Finally, we should not regard the collective identity of a social movement as either permanent or impermeable to external influence. Just as their repertoires of contention, their programs, and their emotional valence evolve, identities are not simply woven out of whole cloth, but respond to changes in political opportunity and constraint, strategic needs, and available cultural materials, as we will see in this final example.

CATHOLICS AND WORKERS IN POLAND

In his fresh treatment of Solidarity in the years 1980–1, Roman Laba describes the depth of the religious symbolism that he found in the propaganda of the movement that was to become Solidarność (1990: ch. 7). Laba reproduces a cartoon of Lech Walesa with his fist raised in the workers' salute alongside the pope with his hand lifted in a papal greeting (p. 141). He reproduces a poster from the Gdansk shipyard strike showing a crown of thorns that was used to memorialize the martyrs of past industrial conflicts (p. 150). Never did the practice of revolt appear to draw so heavily on inherited symbols of consensus.

Poland had witnessed a number of political usages of Catholic ritual during the 1970s, beginning with the contested marches of the Black Madonna of Czestochowa and ending with the spectacle of a Polish pope celebrating a public mass in a Communist country (Kubik 1994: ch. 5; Osa 1995). But from the outset, Solidarity was not so much a mass movement of a Catholic people as a movement of industrial workers seeking a free trade union and using Catholic symbols to mobilize consensus (Laba 1990: ch. 8). The strategy that guided the Gdansk workers in 1980 used religious imagery to recall and draw energy from an earlier wave of strikes. In December 1970, workers had attacked Communist Party headquarters in Gdansk and several were killed by the army (Garton Ash 1984: 12–13; Laba 1990: ch. 2).[15] "The myth of the martyrs grew in the fertile subsoil of the national conscience," writes Timothy Garton Ash (1984: 12).

These symbols emerged periodically as a resource with which to build solidarity and frame new demands. As early as December 1970, the fusion of the images of martyred Poland and suffering proletarians appeared in the strikes of Gydina and Gdansk. In 1971, workers in the Gdansk May Day parade carried a banner demanding a plaque to commemorate the dead of the previous year's strikes (Laba 1990: 126). In 1977, the groups that later founded the Free Trade Unions of the Baltic and the Young Poland movement took up the same cry (p. 136). The Lenin shipyard electrician who seized the leadership of the Gdansk movement in the summer of 1980 considered it a duty – almost an obsession –

to honor the memory of the martyrs. Lech Walesa first gained notoriety at the 1979 demonstration at the Lenin shipyard. Evading arrest to come to the demonstration, he had "erupted on the scene" demanding the construction of a monument to honor the dead of 1970. "Everyone should come back the next year, same place, same time," he said, "and *each carrying a stone*." If the authorities refused to build a monument, they would build it themselves out of the stones in their pockets (Garton Ash 1984: 31).

The events that led to the occupation of the Lenin shipyard in July 1980 were sparked by the issue of the martyrs of 1970. When a popular Free Trade Union militant, Anna Walentynowicz, went to a local cemetery to find candle stubs to burn in memory of the victims of 1970, she was fired by the plant management, adding a spark of human outrage to the simmering flames of worker dissatisfaction. At dawn on August 14, Free Trade Union militants of the group slipped by plant guards with posters demanding the reinstatement of Walentynowicz and a thousand zloty flat pay raise for all. Plastering them around the shipyard, they set off on an internal march, picking up supporters as they went. Thus began the chain of events that would lead to the establishment of Solidarność and its temporary triumph over the government (Garton Ash 1984: 39).

FRAMING THROUGH CONTENTION

The Catholic symbols that surrounded the Polish workers' movement when it burst out on the Baltic coast in 1980 certainly show that symbolism must be culturally resonant to fire people's minds. But these symbols were available in Catholic Poland for decades. As in the case of the American civil rights movement, it was not a symbol inherited from the past that took the movement into its most radical phase, but a new one – the symbol of workers' solidarity – that emerged in the course of struggle and served a strategic purpose for militants locked in combat with powerful opponents.

The most important success of the Gdansk strikers and of their external supporters was not their ability to invoke the essentialist symbols of Catholic piety but to construct solidarity between workers in different factories and sectors through symbolic mediation among Catholic and workerist elements. It was this that defeated the government's strategy of offering wage concessions to some workers and not to others. In fact, the very symbol of "Solidarity" was a product of struggle. As the designer of the Solidarność symbol later wrote:

> I saw how Solidarity appeared among the people, how a social movement was being born. I chose the word [Solidarność] because it best described what was happening to people. The concept came out of the similarity to people in the dense crowds leaning on one another – that was characteristic of the crowds in front of the gate [of the Lenin shipyard]. (Quoted in Laba 1990: 133)

CONCLUSIONS

What can we learn from the cases of the civil rights movement and the Gdansk workers' movement about the power of symbolism in collective action?

First, cultural symbols are not automatically available as mobilizing symbols but require concrete agents to turn them into frames of contention. Just as nonviolent direct action in the South gained its power from the ability of the National Association for the Advancement of Colored People (NAACP) to expand rights through a decade of judicial decisions and the practice of nonviolent resistance, Solidarity gained its success when its leaders joined the religious symbol of their slain comrades to their strike demands to build solidarity across factory walls.

Second, inherited political culture did little in either Poland or America to decide which symbols would dignify and energize collective action and which would not. Rights in America and Catholicism in Poland had been available for generations without visibly helping African Americans or Polish workers throw off their oppression. It is the combination of new frames embedded within a cultural matrix that produces explosive collective action frames. Combining them depends on the actors in the struggle, the opponents they face, and the opportunities for collective action.

Finally, it is in struggle that people discover which values they share, as well as what divides them, and learn to frame their appeals around the former and paper over the latter. Often they fail, but when they succeed, a movement like Solidarity results. As Laba writes in his *Roots of Solidarity*,

> Solidarity has usually been assumed to be simply a nationalist movement, its symbolism merely a continuation of nineteenth-century prewar tradition. Such an analysis misses the innovative quality of Solidarity – *the extent to which the dominant symbols were invented during the strikes*, and the degree to which dominant symbols and rituals were lifted from nationalist and socialist tradition and transformed. (1990: 128, emphasis added)

8

MOBILIZING STRUCTURES AND CONTENTIOUS POLITICS

Social movements do not depend on framing alone; they must bring people together in the field, shape coalitions, confront opponents, and assure their own future after the exhilaration of the peak of mobilization has passed. This takes us to the third type of resource that movements muster: mobilizing structures. Ever since social movements became a force for change in the modern world, observers and activists have puzzled over the effects of organization on their capacity for contention. Some theorists have argued that without leadership exercised through organizations, rebellion remains "primitive" and soon disintegrates (Hobsbawm 1959). Others are persuaded that, far from inspiring people to action, organizational leaders can deprive them of their major power – the power to disrupt (Piven and Cloward 1977).[1] The theoretical support for this position comes from Robert Michels's "Iron Law of Oligarchy," which holds that, over time, organizations displace their original goals, become wedded to routine, and ultimately accept the rules of the game of the existing system (Michels 1962).

But as must be obvious, some leaders, working through certain kinds of organizations in particular situations, *do* transform contention into movements and sustain conflict with opponents, while others do not. Equally obvious, some movements emerge without formal leadership, often producing leaders out of the experience of struggle – or from cognate groups from which they borrow resources. How are we to explain this diversity of organizational roles?

Part of the reason for the confusion is that we often fail to distinguish among three different aspects of movement organization. The dominant meaning of the term is *formal hierarchical organization* – what Zald and McCarthy define as "a complex, or formal, organization that identifies its goals with the preferences of a social movement or a countermovement and attempts to implement those goals" (1987: 20). A second meaning is *the organization of collective action at the point of contact with opponents*. These range from temporary assemblies of challengers, to informal social networks, to formal branches, clubs, and even military-like cells. They can be either controlled by formal organizations, by coalitions of organizations, or by no one in particular. Social networks at the base of society have emerged as the most common sources of recruitment into social movements (Gould 1995; McAdam 1988).

The third meaning of organization refers to the *connective structures* that link leaders and followers, center and periphery, and different parts of a movement sector, permitting coordination and aggregation between movement organizations and allowing movements to persist even when formal organization is lacking (Diani 1995). Only when such connective structures are internalized in a movement organization and collective action is controlled by its leaders is a social movement coterminous with a single organization. More often, formal organizations only imperfectly reflect the informal connective tissue of a movement. Yet without some degree of organization, although movements can reach great peaks of contention, they frequently fade away or dissipate their energies.

The problem for movement organizers is to create organizational models that are sufficiently robust to structure sustained relations with opponents, but are flexible enough to permit the informal connections that link people and networks to one another to aggregate and coordinate contention. The argument of this chapter is that the most effective forms of organization are based on partly autonomous and contextually rooted local units linked by connective structures, and coordinated by formal organizations. The following cases from the nineteenth-century history of European contention illustrate the importance of all three in the modern history of social movements.

A FAILURE AND TWO NONSOLUTIONS

In the early morning hours of December 2, 1851, troops loyal to President Louis Napoleon occupied the French National Assembly, launching the coup d'etat that history has remembered as the Eighteenth Brumaire.[2] In Paris, where hundreds of republicans were rounded up, resistance was quickly overcome. But in France's South and West, where a loose network of Montagnard republicans had grown up, in the days following the coup, an armed insurrection broke out. "These provincial rebels," writes Ted Margadant, "proclaimed revolutionary commissions in over one hundred communes; they seized control of an entire department as well as a dozen *arrondissement* capitals; and they clashed violently with troops or gendarmes in thirty different localities" (1979: vii). But by December 10, the army had the rebels on the run. Their organizations crumbled rapidly and the form of collective action they favored – the armed demonstration – fell apart before armed force.

In many of its particulars, the 1851 insurrection seems like one of Hobsbawm's "primitive rebellions" (1959). The pattern is familiar: news of some outrage, real or imagined, arrives in a village. Suffering economic distress and aggrieved at abuses of their rights, the villagers gather at the sound of the tocsin, arms at the ready. Emboldened by their numbers and their leaders' rhetoric, they confront authorities at some central place, are mown down by superior force, and the survivors return to their farms to lick their wounds and wait for the opportunity to fight another day.

But this insurrection was neither "rural" nor primitive. It combined republicans from the cities and towns with rural peasants and workers (Margadant 1979: 29) and its themes were national and political and not local and parochial.[3] It also showed a substantial interdependence of action and belief among a variety of social groups, urban and rural units, peasants and craftsmen, leaders and followers, who were united in confronting power holders. It was in many ways a modern social movement.

Was the movement organized? That depends on what we mean by organization. At the summit, there was a scattering of tight republican organizations led by middle-class leaders who had participated in the 1848 revolution and remained active as the Republic moved to the right. At the base were the centers of collective action that attacked the *mairies*, fought with troops, and roused other villages to action. These were not random collections of rural hooligans, but came from stable village social and family networks – many of them incubated in local *chambrées* and drinking clubs (Agulhon 1982). But it was the connective structures linking these republican leaders to the local units that were weakest.

First developed on the basis of commercial links between the towns and villages and, after the declaration of the Republic in 1848, taking political shape in republican election organizations (Margadant 1979: 115–16), these linkages were effective enough to launch the struggle. But once the local armed bands appeared in public, "poor communications and administrative countermeasures limited the extent of concerted regional action" (pp. 232–3). Local leaders were more likely to respond to word of a successful uprising elsewhere than to orders from unseen bourgeois republicans. The lack of stable and trust-creating connective structures linking center and periphery was the movement's major disability. It was to the solution of this problem that the next phase of European contention turned.

THE SOCIAL DEMOCRATIC SOLUTION

In the decades following the failure of the 1848 revolutions, a new social actor appeared – the industrial proletariat – naturally forming a new organization at the base geared to collective action in the factory and linked to a new set of organizations at the summit. Mainly middle-class organizers and intellectuals took charge of the socialist and labor parties with links to trade unions, cooperatives, mutual insurance schemes, and even recreation centers. In the most well developed form, the Social Democratic Party of Germany (SPD), these sprawling structures gave the imposing impression of a "state within a state" (Roth 1963).

But between the centralized movement organizations of European social democracy and the networks of workers at the base, there was no natural or social set of connective structures. In some countries, like France, the distance between syndicalist-oriented workers and parliamentary socialists was so great that competing organizations were formed. The German social democrats, with characteristic determination, undertook to formalize relations between summit and base and make them permanent. The result was to create a single organizational hierarchy, frighten the imperial regime to the point of temporarily banning the party for a time, but ultimately to vitiate the movement of its spontaneity and its energy and leave it incapable of facing the threats that arose in the early twentieth century. The SPD's vote for war credits in 1914 and its lack of preparation to fight national socialism in the 1930s were the ultimate outcome.

A formal connective structure was of course far from lacking: Social Democrats encapsulated their members into permanent federal structures, which rose from local branches through provincial and regional federations to central committees and national executives. Discipline was expected of those who joined, and collective actions were periodically organized to advance the movement's goals. From a scattered network of insurgent groups and secret societies, the workers' movement grew into a vast, formal, and centralized organization. Such was the prestige of the SPD that its organizational model was imitated to different degrees in central, northern, and eastern Europe.[4]

This was this model of organization – the central European working-class movement, with its panoply of unions, cooperatives, and popular services – that Michels had in mind when he formulated his "Iron Law." In such an organization, he argued, organizers became more wedded to the survival of the organization than to the ultimate victory of the proletariat, with all the risks it imposed. If the movement's militancy melted away once representation for the lower classes was achieved, no one should have been surprised. One group of competitors was anything but surprised.

THE ANARCHIST COUNTERMODEL

Even as German Social Democrats were building a "state within a state," in other parts of Europe and in America some were developing different organizational models to challenge it. The most serious challenge came from the anarchists, whose political theory and practice were opposed to social democracy in every respect. Where the social democrats were led by politicians and intellectuals and aimed at taking over the bourgeois state in the name of disciplined workers in formal organizations, anarchists distrusted politics and sought to destroy the state from below. Social democracy they dismissed as "authoritarian" and castigated its leaders as traitors to the cause.

The anarchists resisted the tendency to become a party. Their instinctive organizational model was provided by Proudhon, who had theorized that a network of workers' associations, democratically organized and loosely linked in a voluntary federation, could eventually replace both the state and capitalism.[5] But lacking an organizational template like that of their opponents, they surged into different forms in different parts of Europe in close approximation to local economic and political conditions.[6]

It was where economic conditions were most backward and political organization least developed, in eastern and southern Europe, that anarchism became a mass movement. The Russian *narodniki* had first hurled themselves at the czarist power structure, imagining that their courage and bravery would unleash the rebellious potential that they thought lay hidden in the peasants. The latter responded with indifference, if not hostility, and long prison terms and doleful memoirs were the lot of many of these populists. What remained of the populist dream was transformed, first, into a network of terrorist groups, and then into the Social Revolutionary Party – the largest to emerge in the Constituent Assembly of 1918 but no match for Lenin's Bolsheviks.

In Italy, the story ended differently. Hounded by the police and the authorities, the Italian anarchists encapsulated themselves into tight cells in which they hatched utopian schemes and plotted the overthrow of the state. As Daniel Guérin writes:

> Free rein was given to utopian doctrines, combining premature anticipations and nostalgic evocations of a golden age. . . . The anarchists turned in on themselves, organized themselves for direct action in small clandestine groups which were easily infiltrated by police informers. (Guérin 1970: 74)

Just as the dream of the general strike inspired their French counterparts, the illusion that the state was bound up in the person of its rulers led the Italian anarchists to engage in acts of violence, but a wave of bombings only cast suspicion on the entire left and isolated them still further. Where the hierarchy of social democracy turned movements into parties, the anarchists' obsession with action and their allergy to organization transformed them into a sect.

RECURRING POLARITIES

The polarization between institutionalization and disruption that we saw in social democracy and anarchism is particular to European history, but it is a recurring story in the history of modern social movements. It was relived in the movements of the 1960s in both Europe and the United States. By the early 1960s, most of the American civil rights movement was highly institutionalized (Piven and Cloward 1977: ch. 4). From the streets of Selma, the battle for civil rights gravitated to the lobbies of Congress and to neighborhood community organizations subsidized by government and foundations and was soon constrained by the rules of the game of ordinary politics (ch. 5). Not even the riots following the murder of Martin Luther King turned mainstream civil rights organizations away from their institutional path.

The same shift into institutions could be seen in the New Left in both Europe and America. Both began in an exhilarating cycle of protest in which mass, disruptive forms of action predominated. But from the sit-ins and draft card burnings of the mid-1960s, many U.S. anti–Vietnam War activists moved into the public interest groups and peace lobbies that flourished in America in the 1970s and 1980s. From battling the police and organizing the urban poor, French and Italian student organizers formed political organizations and entered the trade unions and the Communist Party (Lange, Irvin, and Tarrow 1989).

But just as anarchism had measured its progress in competition with social democracy, more determined American activists of the 1960s, critical of the institutional strategy of their elders, split off into radical organizations to carry the fight to the heart of organized capitalism. And, in western Europe, parts of the New Left critical of the "long march through the institutions" drew sharp lines between their own militancy and the moderation of their opponents. Some, like their anarchist predecessors, ended up in clandestine cells from which they launched armed struggle (della Porta 1990; 1995: ch. 8); others competed for worker support with the party-linked trade unions. The nineteenth-century polarity between anarchism and social democracy was replayed in the shadow of the New Left.

BETWEEN HIERARCHY AND DISRUPTION

Social democracy and anarchism were not the only forms of social movement organization that developed in the nineteenth century – nor did the radical and moderate branches of the 1960s movements monopolize the field. Where the social democrats internalized movement within organization, and the anarchists foreshortened organization into action, American civic movements that fought slavery and alcohol and advanced the causes of women's suffrage and agrarian populism built flexible organizations based on informal connective structures that kept these movements alive through fat seasons and lean. Helped in this direction by the structure of American federalism, these loose umbrella organizations coordinated constituents at the base and did not attempt to internalize them. This allowed them to reside in the structures of everyday life – for example, in the churches – and mobilize or demobilize supporters according to political conditions. It built on the "free spaces" in which ordinary citizens could take local initiatives that more centralized organizations would have tried to monopolize (Evans and Boyte 1992).

The connective structures of these movements ranged from informal contacts among public-spirited women and men, to churches and fraternal orders, to farmers' cooperatives, to political movements like the Populists. Coordination varied from informal communication between militants, lecture tours, and prayer meetings, to newspapers and magazines, to state federations and political parties. Most were informal or paid their own way, requiring little or no centrally controlled resources to maintain them.

Formal organizations rose and fell with cyclical frequency, along with the waves of movement whose enthusiasm they reflected. In times of stress or de-moralization, they relapsed into the latent ties among friends, relations, and fellow church members (Rupp and Taylor 1987). Because they could draw on existing social networks, they could mobilize supporters rapidly and put pressure on the state through established institutions. When reforms were accomplished or mobilization declined, activists disappeared into "abeyance structures" like churches or lodges. When a new cycle of contention appeared, informal contacts served to revive old ties (Blocker 1989; Buechler 1986). To an extent, activism within movements created networks and connective structures for the future.

Though more permanently organized than their American cousins, nine-teenth-century European cooperatives followed a similar model. Begun on the left, under the doctrine of social Christianity, cooperatives were adopted by Cath-olic laymen with the approval of the church. Especially in semidemocratic systems like Italy and imperial Germany, cooperatives and mutual-aid societies were dif-ficult to repress because their functions were overtly nonpolitical; however, they supported socialist activities and helped the left to maintain ties during lean times that could be revitalized when political opportunities opened up.

BREAKING THE IRON LAW

In both western Europe and the United States, such loosely coordinated organi-zations presaged a model of democratically decentralized movements that Amer-icans and western Europeans theorized in the 1960s and 1970s (Evans and Boyte 1992; Rosenthal and Schwartz 1990). In 1970, Luther Gerlach and Virginia Hine had deduced from such organizations a model of "decentralized, segmented, and reticulated" groups. By decentralization, Gerlach and Hine meant the lack of a single leadership and the absence of card-carrying membership. By segmentation, they meant that the movement "is composed of a great variety of localized groups or cells which are essentially independent, but which can combine to form larger configurations or divide to form smaller units" (1970: 41). And by reticulation, they referred to a weblike connective structure "in which the cells, or nodes, are tied together, not through any central point, but rather through intersecting sets of personal relationships and other intergroup linkages" (pp. 34–55).

These decentralized movements not only provided "abeyance structures" be-tween periods of mobilization; they created spaces for autonomous participation that helped keep people involved in the movement and provided experiences they could use at later stages. As Evans and Boyte argue, at the heart of successful democratic movements there are "environments in which people are able to learn a new self-respect, a deeper and more assertive group identity, public skills, and values of cooperation and civic virtue" (1992: 17–18).

In many ways the prototypes of these decentralized organizations were the teams of activists sent to the South by the younger branch of the civil rights movement, especially by the Congress on Racial Equality (CORE) and the Stu-dent Nonviolent Coordinating Committee (SNCC). But the same informal and decentralized forms of organization reappeared in the "new" social movements of the 1970s in western Europe, which replayed many of the organizational themes of their American predecessors (Calhoun 1995; d'Anieri, Ernst, and Kier 1990). Fashioning a variety of organizational innovations, they insisted on the virtues of decentralization against the monopoly of power by centralized party bureaucrats. If they exaggerated the "newness" of their movements, this was no more than what every new wave of movements does.

American community organizers extended the model of decentralized, segmented, and reticulated organization into practical activism in the disintegrating matrix of the American city. First theorized by activists like Saul Alinsky (1971) and Harry Boyte (1980), community action organizations took a variety of forms, including individual membership organizations, coalitions, and church-based organizations (McCarthy and Castelli 1994).[7] Decentralization was also the watchword of many of the women's organizations that evolved out of the 1960s movements (Ferree and Martin 1995).

In western Europe as well, even formally organized groups, like the Italian environmental organizations studied by Diani, developed informal links (1995). In France, radical *coordinations* have been formed to compete with the big party-linked union confederations. And in Germany, local community organizations provide services and put pressure on local authorities, not unlike the practices of the new generation of community organizers in the United States.

THE TYRANNY OF DECENTRALIZATION

However, such loose patterns of organization as the ones described here have the defects of their virtues. While encouraging the autonomy of the base and exhilarating activists with their aura of participation, they permit – indeed, encourage – a lack of coordination and continuity. For example, while the women of the Greenham Common peace camp kept the British army at bay for months during the peace movement of the 1980s, their devotion to internal democracy led to bitter fights over the issue of whether to allow male comrades to spend the night there (Rochon 1988: 82). Similarly, in the women's groups that Judith Hellman studied in Italy, personalism became a kind of "tyranny" that made formal decision making difficult and left noninitiates excluded (1987: 195–6).

Nor could these groups always maintain themselves as their predecessors had done through "abeyance structures" like churches, cooperatives, or trade unions. Some became semigovernmental social assistance groups, accepting grants from local authorities and routinizing their activities; many disappeared into private life, turning their values into life-style choices; some fractionated as a natural result of the looseness of their organizations (Meyer 1990); others eventually combined into various Green parties, building formal organizations and running candidates for office while continuing to deny their institutional nature.

Whereas European social democracy solved the problem of coordination by encapsulating the working class into permanent organizations, and the anarchists tried to inspire mass revolt by mounting dramatic attacks on authority, community-based movements thrive because they need no special organized efforts to maintain them over time and across space. But their weakness is that autonomy at the base sometimes excludes strong connective ties between center and periphery, making it difficult for leaders to implement coherent strategies.

ORGANIZATIONAL INNOVATIONS

The 1960s was a watershed for organizational innovation, but not only because that decade produced a tidal wave of new movements. The period saw the development of internal innovations in movement organizations that suggest a more differentiated dynamic of change than previous students detected. These movements also arose amid technological and social changes in the world at large that gave them new and expanded resources and connections with which organizers could work.

EXTERNAL RESOURCES

The most important of the external developments was the expansion and availability of the mass media, especially of television. From civil rights marchers braving police dogs and hoses, to the New Left's public draft card burnings, to the spectacle of gay or lesbian activists "coming out": television's appetite for dramatic visual images was a tool that was nurtured and exploited by movement organizers. If movements could transmit their messages to millions of people across the airwaves, encouraging some to follow their example and larger numbers to take sympathetic notice of their claims, it was possible to create a movement without incurring the costs of building and maintaining mass organizations.

A second set of changes revolved around the increased amount of money, free time, and expertise available to young people in the postwar boom years (McCarthy and Zald 1973; 1977). Not only did disposable family income rise substantially all over the West; by the 1960s, young people were targeted as a choice market for consumer goods and as the center of a new youth culture (McAdam 1988: 13–19). Both in Europe and America, they were entering universities in much larger numbers, where they had more free time and were exposed to broader currents of ideas than young people in the past. If nothing else, this produced many more "conscience constituents" to lend their numbers and skills to minority movements (Marx and Useem 1971) and many others who could afford to dedicate themselves to "distant issues" (Rucht 1996).

A third set of external changes was the financial and administrative resources available to some movements from foundations, local governments, and even, in some cases, from business and civic groups (Jenkins and Eckert 1986; McCarthy and Zald 1973).[8] Particularly for the Third World "nongovernmental organizations" that blossomed in the 1980s, American and western European foundations were major funding sources, as were the United Nations and a number of international human rights groupings (Keck and Sikkink 1998a, 1998b; Smith, Chatfield, and Pagnucco 1997).

INTERNAL INNOVATIONS

Organizers have not been passive beneficiaries of these external changes. They have been quick to take advantage of the same advances in communication and fund raising as more conventional political and interest groups – first through the mimeograph machine, then through computerized direct mailing lists, and more recently with the fax, the camcorder, and the use of the internet. As a result of these and other changes, organizers can now mount and coordinate collective action across a broad sweep of territory in competition with parties, interest groups, and governments.

Movement organizations have also learned to draw on the appeal of celebrities – the rock stars, folk singers, and movie stars who lend their names and their talents to movement campaigns (Meyer and Gamson 1995) – and on professionals such as scientists and technical experts, who lend their authority and their expertise to the ecological, antinuclear, and peace movements (Nelkin 1975). The American women's and gay movements in the 1980s increasingly depended on the professional services of feminist or gay lawyers who lent a legalistic tone to many of their activities (d'Emilio 1992: 192; Mansbridge 1986).

Professionalization was nothing new for the large mass parties and movements of the past; it was what had worried Michels about the SPD. But what we see today is a new type of professionalization not dependent on large, bureaucratic organizations – the diffusion of organizational and communications skills among movement activists. The widespread possession of such skills makes it possible to mobilize a large reservoir of support at short notice, allowing movement organizations to be both small *and* professional.[9] But it also diffuses movement activities into the broader society.

SOCIAL CAPITAL DEFICITS?

If affluence and mass communications give movement organizers new resources and new opportunities, they have nevertheless deprived movements of the steady participation at the base that prewar movements could count on. People who watch television in the evening and go off for long weekends will be less interested in attending meetings and marching in Sunday demonstrations than their parents were (Allardt 1962). While some movements, like the French and Italian Communists, attempted to maintain their formal structures well into the 1980s, participation became more and more formalistic and was soon more expensive to maintain than to abandon (Hellman 1988).

Are social movement organizations suffering a social capital deficit? In a series of works not centered directly on movements, Robert Putnam has discerned a declining level of social participation in American society (Putnam 1995).[10] Putnam finds a strong correlation between the intrusion of television into private life and the tendency of Americans to retreat from group activities and interactions with others. The same tendency for traditional sectors of voluntary organization to lose membership and active participation has been noted in France, despite its long tradition of militance (Ion 1997).

The effect of this decline of "social capital," however, may be less severe for social movements than for voluntary associations. For while the latter depend on steady membership participation, sustained activities within institutions, and distribution of selective incentives, the main activities of movement organizations today are periodic, rapidly organized mass demonstrations, small-scale disruptive actions carried out by teams of trained militants, and publicity-gaining media activities. None of these require the day-to-day work of membership participation, but rather depend on the capacity to assemble mass support for brief and often exhilarating performances.

Consider one of the most successful new American movement organizations, the "Promise Keepers," which has created a constituency opposed to gender equality – especially within the family (Conason, Ross, and Cokorinos 1996). Capable of assembling hundreds of thousands of men for quasi-revivalist assemblies in football stadiums, the organization is run by a small national group in alliance with a number of like-minded, Christian fundamentalist organizations, and operates at the base through what it itself calls "small groups" of activities.

Beyond national boundaries, similarly light, inexpensive to maintain but highly professional organizations can be seen in the "transnational issue networks" studied by Margaret Keck and Katherine Sikkink (see Chapter 11). Focusing on one type of issue – whether human rights, the environment, women's rights, or indigenous people's rights – these transnational networks have flimsy organizations, but can become effectively active on single issues because of their ties with donor agencies, foundations, and movement groups within particular countries.

An emerging international pattern of social movement organization seems to be appearing: a combination of small professional leaderships; large but mainly passive mass support; and impersonal networklike connective structures. In this pattern, members of the organization communicate by mail, fax, or e-mail with leaders; they participate in large but rare mass demonstrations; and they take part by "proxy" in small, lightninglike demonstrative strikes by cadres of militants. The prototype for this model is, of course, Greenpeace, which claims millions of members but in fact limits their role largely to financial contributions and depends on a small cadre of professional militants for their dramatic exploits at sea.[11]

In response to the problems of gaining broad support bases without having to build large organizations, many movements have "franchised" local organizations, which remain independent but use the name of the national organization and receive their publicity in return for financial contributions and cooperation

in joint campaigns (McCarthy and Wolfson 1992). Franchises allow a small national umbrella organization to coordinate the activities of a much broader base
without expending scarce resources on maintaining the formal connective structures of a large mass organization. A spectacularly successful case of such "franchising" was that of the Committee for Nuclear Disarmament (CND) in Britain
in the 1980s (Maguire 1990).

In addition to franchising, many contemporary movements draw upon the
resources of allied organizations and associations not created primarily for collective action. This allows them to both use the infrastructures of more stable organizations and to mobilize, for brief periods, people who would not be interested
in permanent activism. The role of the churches in the Dutch peace campaigns
of the 1980s and of the black church in the American South both show how
movement organizations can access the resources of large *non*-movement-based
institutions (Klandermans 1997: ch. 6; Morris 1984).

Movements often develop *within* institutions, using their structures and ideologies to develop contacts among networks of dissidents and employing their
ideologies – literally conceived – against their official bearers (Zald and Berger
1978). With its sprawling structures and official dogma, the Catholic Church
has long provided a home for emergent heterodox movements. In the 1960s and
1970s, Christian "base communities" developed in Catholic Europe (Tarrow
1988) and in Latin America (Levine 1990); more recently, a movement for gender
equality has developed among the historically most passive sector of the American
church – its female monastic orders (Katzenstein 1998).

CAMPAIGNS AND COALITIONS

If the newer, lighter, externalized movement organizations described here have
a major weakness, it is their lack of a permanent cadre of grass-roots activists. It
is in part for this reason that they cultivate ties with like-minded groups, attempting to compensate for the weakness of their constituency base by assembling concentrated numbers at strategic places and occasions around particular
issues. In the United States, the antiwar coalitions of the late 1960s, the pro-
abortion movements of the 1980s, and the peace movement developed this technique of campaign collaboration to a high level. Even before the 1960s, because
of its numerical weakness, the peace movement had perfected the technique of
organizing through coordinated campaigns (Kleidman 1992). By the 1970s,
writes Tom Rochon, in both Europe and the United States "many of these were
federations of existing organizations, pulled together to take advantage of the
new possibilities for mobilization" (1988: 79).[12] By the 1980s, coalitional campaigns were the major strategy of the American nuclear freeze movement (Meyer
and Rochon 1997).

Environmental organizations frequently join forces to put pressure on authorities or to organize mass "Earth Days" or green outings. Though many of
these organizations have deep ideological differences – for example, between tra-

ditional conservation groups and radical environmentalists – the informal connections among their activists allow these ideological chasms to be crossed. Even in Italy, where the gap between the Catholic and marxist subcultures was once deep, Mario Diani found that informal ties between members of different environmental organizations helped to develop a common collective identity among their members (1995).

So common is the practice of joint campaigning by coalitions of organizations that Jürgen Gerhards and Dieter Rucht coined a new word to describe it – "mesomobilization" (1992). The two campaigns they studied in Berlin possessed organizational flexibility that allowed ideological, social, and political pluralism to flourish. They mounted a variety of activities, giving each group the chance to stress its particular interests and not feel lost in the crowd. But when the campaign was over, no permanent organization remained.

Similar campaigns mounted by coalitions of organizations have recently appeared in French and American politics. In France, a campaign against the fascist National Front in 1997 showed a pattern of rapid coordination and dissolution similar to what Gerhards and Rucht found in Germany.[13] In Washington, D.C., in 1993, a massive march of gay and lesbian Americans under the loose leadership of a coalition of organizations was mounted on behalf of gay rights and against discrimination. The informal ties between members of different organizations in protest campaigns can eventually produce broader social networks and an overarching collective identity among members of different movement organizations (Diani 1995).

ORGANIZATIONAL DIFFUSION AND DIFFERENTIATION

The wide variety of organizational patterns we see in social movements today leads us to look more carefully at the dynamics of organizational change. Michels's "Iron Law of Oligarchy" helped him to understand the dynamics of change in social democratic organizations at the turn of the century, as they grew out of small groups of grass-roots cadres into large mass organizations, and hardened into institutionalized unions and parties. But it explained neither the very different logic of anarchism, nor the grass-roots groups that developed in nineteenth-century America, nor the diversified organizational models we see today. This is because Michels had only one organizational model in mind: the type that attempted to internalize a movement's connective structures within large, centralized, and bureaucratic organizations and to control collective action at the base.

As we have seen, the spectrum of movement organizations was never this simple, and the changes in the postwar world have complicated the picture even further. In response to this complexity, and based on the wide spectrum of "new" social movements he studied in western Europe, Hanspeter Kriesi has proposed a broader array of organizational types (1996). In Kriesi's conception, classical

	MODE OF PARTICIPATION	
ORIENTATION	Indirect	Direct
Constituency	Autonomous Firms, Cooperatives	Women's Self-Help Groups
Public Authorities	Green Parties	Social Movement Organizations

Figure 8.1. Typology of Movement-Related Organizations (SOURCE: Adapted from Hanspeter Kriesi, "The Organizational Structure of New Social Movements in a Political Context," in D. McAdam, J. McCarthy, and M. Zald, eds., Comparative Perspectives on Social Movements *{Cambridge: Cambridge University Press, 1996}, p. 153.)*

social movement organizations (SMOs) combine two factors: the direct participation of constituents in action and an orientation that makes claims on authorities. But this is only one type of movement-oriented organization: Kriesi identifies three other types that vary on both the dimension of whether constituents participate directly or indirectly and on whether they aim their activities primarily at authorities or within society. This produces a four-cell typology of movement-related organizations, which is reproduced in Figure 8.1 with some examples of each.

Kriesi's typology allows us to examine different types of movement-related organizations without relegating any to a residual category. For example, the women's self-help groups studied by Verta Taylor are not oriented primarily at authorities but – like SMOs – involve the direct participation of constituents and build consensus around common goals (Taylor and Van Willigen 1996). Conversely, the European Green parties and American public interest groups that evolved out of the movements of the 1960s no longer participate in direct action but are oriented toward public authorities and share many of the goals of the movements that gave rise to them. Finally, the so-called autonomous sector that developed in West Germany after the 1960s involves neither direct constituency participation nor orientation to authorities, but it provides services that have helped to preserve "free spaces" away from the logic of the market.

In addition to helping us consider a broader range of movement-related organizations than are normally included in studies of social movements, Kriesi's typology has two other uses. First, it suggests a way of tracing organizational diffusion within the social movement sector, for many of the kinds of organizations it points to developed historically out of the main trunk of the 1960s SMOs. Second, it can help to understand how the relatively small, weak, and impermanent movement organizations of today can mobilize support for large demonstrations at short notice: if militants in classical SMOs maintain informal connective links with activists in these other types of organizations, they can draw upon them to mount demonstrations when political opportunities or threats arise. Gerhards and Rucht's "mesomobilization" takes its strength not only from coalitions of SMOs, but from alliances and friendly relations among SMOs and other forms of movement-oriented groups.

This perspective also suggests the variety of ways in which movement militants can partially "exit" from activism into less demanding venues without opting out or deserting their goals. By joining self-help groups, working for service organizations, and supporting parties and interest groups linked by connective tissue to their original movement homes, activists may keep up their contacts with old comrades in movement organizations, remain available for mobilization at times of stress or opportunity, and keep the flame of activism alive for another day.

CONCLUSIONS

There is no single model of movement organization. Heterogeneity and interdependence are greater spurs to collective action than homogeneity and discipline. The encapsulation of the European working class into mass parties and unions was a solution for the long term that left the workers unprepared for contention when crisis struck. The anarchist countermodel was an organizational weapon for the short term that left its proponents isolated from their purported base and provided little infrastructure in the long run. Contemporary innovations of transitory teams, professional movement groups, decentralized organizations, and coalitional campaigns are variations on and combinations of these experiences. What underlies the most successful of them is the role of informal connective tissue operating within and between formal movement organizations.

Such movements cannot be instantly formed; nor can they be maintained in a permanent state of readiness. The dilemma of hierarchical movement organizations is that, when they permanently internalize their base, they lose their capacity for disruption, but when they move in the opposite direction, they lack the infrastructure to maintain a sustained interaction with allies, authorities, and supporters. This suggests a delicate balance between formal organization and autonomy – one that can only be bridged by strong, informal, and nonhierarchical connective structures.

A similarly delicate balance must be maintained with respect to the other powers in movements discussed in the three preceding chapters. In Chapter 5 we saw that movements form in the context of widening opportunities and collapsing constraints; but in making opportunities for others and for opponents, movements may create the conditions for their own irrelevance or repression.

Similarly, in Chapter 6, we saw that it is disruption – not violence or contention – that characterizes insurgent movments. But movements that rely only on disruptive mass action risk conflict with the police and degeneration into violence, whereas those which adopt conventional forms of action may suffer from co-optation of their goals and decline as activists defect.

In parallel fashion, Chapter 7 showed that collective action frames are also built on an uneasy balance: between inherited but passive mentalities and action-oriented but unfamiliar new elements. Movements that rely only on tried-and-true cultural symbols lose their capacity for insurgency, while those which propose radically new "frame transformations" can lose support through the unfamiliarity of their goals. Movements rest on a razor's edge between institutionalization and isolation.

Chapter 7 also explored the importance of collective identity in movement formation and maintenance. Whether inherited as categorical identities or created in conflict with opponents, collective identity is a crucial process in the formation of movements, but it contains within it the seeds of isolation, sectarianism, and "the twilight of common dreams" (Gitlin 1995).

Does this mean that social movements are doomed to instability and eventual disappearance? When considered in isolation, the difficulty they experience in sustaining confrontations with opponents, maintaining a broad support base, and containing fissiparous tendencies suggests just such an outcome. But movements seldom *do* appear in isolation; they most often come in clusters, and it is within the widening spiral of cycles of contention that their major successes appear. Let us turn to these cycles as we begin our analysis of movement outcomes.

PART III

THE DYNAMICS
OF MOVEMENT

9

CYCLES OF CONTENTION

Whatever the source of contentious claims, it is political opportunities and constraints that translate them into action. They produce social movements by accessing known and flexible repertoires of contention; by developing collective action frames and collective identities; and by building mobilizing structures around social networks and organizations. While the opportunities and constraints in their environments give challengers incentives to mobilize, it is their cultural, organizational, and practical resources that are the foundations for social movements.

But three things are missing from this two-stage image of contention and movement formation. First, it deals with social movements as if they emerged, made claims, and evolved all on their own. Second, it ignores the fact that the shifting of opportunities and constraints does not cease with the triggering of collective action. Third, it leaves out authorities, who do not sit idly by as challengers contest their rule: they respond weakly or strongly, selectively or generally, intelligently or stupidly to the emergence of contention, setting a pattern of interaction that affects other challengers too.

These additional factors establish broader waves of contention than the individual movements that have filled most academic treatments of contentious politics. In combination, they determine whether a burst of contention will sputter out like a roman candle or ripen into a cycle of contention – or even a revolution. It is to understanding when and how contention broadens into general cycles that this chapter is devoted.

A special aspect of the problem of cyclicity relates to the differences between cycles of contention and revolutionary ones (Goldstone 1997). While we cannot deal in detail with revolutions in this space, the distinction will help us raise the question of whether a single cyclical dynamic can be used to describe all waves of contention; or whether revolutionary cycles are so different from others that they demand separate treatment; or if they invite us to develop analogical or path-dependent methods to compare them with other kinds of cycles.[1]

Our treatment of cycles devotes little space to the regularity, sequencing, and frequency of historical cycles, although these are all fascinating questions. Instead, we devote our attention, first, to the definition and elements within cycles; then, to four sets of processes that describe the broadening of contention into general waves of conflict; and, finally, to three related processes – exhaustion and factionalization, repression–facilitation, and radicalization–institutionalization – that mark cyclical decline. The cases of the first major international cycle – the 1848 revolution in Europe – and of the 1960s New Left illustrate these factors. The chapter closes with brief reflections on the analogy between social movement cycles, revolutionary cycles, and democratization.

DEFINITION AND ELEMENTS OF CYCLES

By a "cycle of contention," I intend a phase of heightened conflict across the social system: with a rapid diffusion of collective action from more mobilized to less mobilized sectors; a rapid pace of innovation in the forms of contention; the creation of new or transformed collective action frames; a combination of organized and unorganized participation; and sequences of intensified information flow and interaction between challengers and authorities. Such widespread contention produces externalities that give challengers at least a temporary advantage and allows them to overcome the weaknesses in their resource base. It demands that states devise broad strategies of response that are either repressive or facilitative, or a combination of the two. And it produces general outcomes that are more than the sum of the results of an aggregate of unconnected events.

BETWEEN AND WITHIN CYCLES

When we turn to social scientists' research on cycles, we find an odd paradox. Though recognizing their importance for social movements, scholars have been more apt to pay attention to individuals, movements, and movement organizations than to the broad waves of contention that mark much of modern history. Even students of revolution have often ignored the relationship between revolutions and other forms of collective action (but see Goldstone 1997: 2). This is in part because of the tendency to see revolutions as events rather than processes (Goldstone 1991). Once we understand them as processes, their analogies with and differences from cycles are set in relief.

But if cycles are such major watersheds of social and political change as I have claimed, why do we have so few studies of such periods? One reason is that movement organizations are easier to trace than broad waves of contention and are more readily open to investigators – many of whom come from within their ranks. Cycles of contention often begin within institutions, spread into confrontations among ordinary people, and bring the scholar face-to-face with some of the less edifying aspects of collective action – the crowd, the mob, the armed insurrection. When they end in repression and disillusionment, they make for depressing reading. "Post coitum omnia animal triste," writes Aristide Zolberg, quoting the old adage to reflect how disillusionment follows the end of waves of contention (1972: 205–6).

Another reason for the relative neglect of cycles is that they occupy no clearly demarcated space with respect to institutional politics. Students of "collective behavior" distinguished their subject from behavior in institutions. But insurgencies often begin *within* institutions and even organized movements become rapidly involved in the political process, where they interact with interest groups, unions, parties, and the forces of order (Burstein 1998). To encompass cycles, our accounts must bridge institutional and noninstitutional conflict, and this requires interaction between the tools of political scientists who most often focus on institutions and the sociologists and social historians who study movements.

The idea that entire systems go through cyclical dynamics has been found among three main groups of scholars: cultural theorists, who see changes in culture as the source of political and social change (Brand 1990; Rochon 1998); political historians and historical economists, who look for regular cycles of political or economic change (Hirschman 1982; Schlesinger 1986); and social theorists, who see changes in collective action resulting from changes in states and capitalism (Elias 1994). The first group of scholars emphasizes the globality of cycles, the second their regularity, and the third their derivation from configurations of structural change. All three can prove useful, but they mainly examine the progression *between* waves of contention; few stop to examine the structure and dynamic of the cycle itself – which is what provides the externalities that nourish and transform movements.

Within such periods, organizations and authorities, movements and interest groups, and members of the polity and challengers interact, conflict, and cooperate. The dynamic of the cycle is the outcome of their interaction. "Actions," writes Pam Oliver, "can affect the likelihood of other actions by creating occasions for action, by altering material conditions, by changing a group's social organization, by altering beliefs, or by adding knowledge" (1989: 2). These actions create uncertainty and transmit information, opening the way for new actors and undermining the calculations on which existing commitments are based. This leads regime supporters to trim their sails and opponents to make new calculations of interest and alliance. The outcome depends less on the balance of power between and the resources of any pair of opponents than on the generalized structure of contention and the responses to it of elites, opponents, and potential allies. This is why, as we will see, though the beginnings of such cycles are often similar, their endings are far more disparate. In what follows, I sketch the main elements in the mobilization phases of cycles of contention to help us understand how they unfold.

THE MOBILIZATION PHASE

The generalization of conflict into a cycle of contention begins when political opportunities are opened for well-placed "early risers," when their claims resonate with those of significant others, and when these give rise to objective or explicit coalitions among disparate actors and create or reinforce instability in the elite. This co-occurrence and coalescence is furthered by state responses rejecting the claims of the early risers, thereby encouraging their assimilation to other possible claimants, while lowering constraints and offering opportunities for broader contention.[2]

The early demands that trigger a cycle of contention are often narrow and group-specific. They do three important things. First, they demonstrate the vulnerability of authorities to contention, signaling to others that the time is ripe for their own claims to be translated into action. Second, they "challenge the interests of other contenders, either because the distribution of benefits to one group will diminish the rewards available for another, or because the demands directly attack the interests of an established group" (Tilly 1993: 13). Third, they suggest convergences among challengers through the enunciation of master frames.

Although cycles do not have a uniform frequency or extend equally to entire populations, a number of common features characterize such periods in recent history.[3] These include heightened conflict, broad sectoral and geographic diffusion, the expansion of the repertoire of contention, the appearance of new organizations and the empowerment of old ones, the creation of new "master frames" linking the actions of disparate groups to one another, and intensified interaction between challengers and the state, lending to particular state responses a key pivoting role in determining which direction the cycle will take.

CONFLICT AND DIFFUSION

Cycles of contention are characterized by heightened conflict, not only in industrial relations but in the streets, and not only there but in villages and schools. In such periods, the magnitude of contention of all kinds rises appreciably above what is typical both before and after. Particular groups recur with regularity in the vanguard of waves of social protest (e.g., miners, students), but they are often joined at the peak of the cycle by groups that are not generally known for their insurgent tendencies (e.g., peasants, workers in small industry, white-collar workers).

Cycles have broad paths of diffusion, some of which are traceable from large cities to the rural periphery or from periphery to center. They often spread from heavy industrial areas to adjacent areas of light industry and farming, along river valleys, or through other major routes of communication. They spread among members of the same ethnic or national group whose "embedded" identities are activated by new opportunities and threats, as was the case among Serbs, Croats, and Muslims in the former Yugoslavia in the early 1990s. Widespread contention brings about uncertainty and fear; the breakdown of functional transactions that this produces increases the salience of preexisting ties like ethnicity, religion, or other forms of mutual recognition, trust, and cooperation.

What is most distinctive about such periods is not that entire societies "rise" in the same direction at the same time (they seldom do), or that particular population groups act in the same way over and over, but that the demonstration effect of collective action on the part of a group of early risers triggers a variety of processes of diffusion, extension, imitation, and reaction among groups that are normally more quiescent and have fewer resources to engage in collective action.

Diffusion is misspecified if it is seen only as the "contagion" of collective action to similar groups making the same claims against equivalent opponents. A key characteristic of cycles is the diffusion of a propensity for collective action from its initiators to both unrelated groups and to antagonists. The former respond to the demonstration effect of a challenge that succeeds – or at least escapes suppression – whereas the latter produce the countermovements that are a frequent reaction to the onset of contention (Meyer and Staggenborg 1996). This is why movements like ethnic nationalism or the declaration of "difference" spreads – not because people like to imitate what other people do but because the mobilization of one ethnic identity triggers reactions in the part of others who fear their survival or interests will be threatened.

REPERTOIRES AND FRAMES

Cycles are the crucibles out of which new weapons of social protest are often fashioned. The barricade construction moving beyond neighborhoods in the French revolution of 1848, the factory councils in the Russian revolution of 1905, the sitdown strikes of the French Popular Front and the American New Deal, the "direct actions" of the 1968–72 period: in the uncertainty and exuberance of the early period of a cycle of mobilization, innovation accelerates and new forms of contention are developed and diffused.

To some extent, this is no more than an acceleration of the trends of innovation we saw in the repertoire of contention in Chapter 6. But because cycles bring a variety of new actors onto the scene, there are possibilities for aggregation and interaction that are not as likely in less agitated times. Thus, the creativity and energy of the Serbian protests against election fraud we saw in Chapter 6 were the result of the copresence of a variety of actors in the streets, some with little in common. The Italian cycle of the late 1960s brought together the energies of the students with the discipline of the working class to produce a qualitatively new form of contention – *autoriduzione* – that spread from the factories to universities, and from there to rent strikes and refusal to pay utility bills (Tarrow 1989a).

Of course, not all the innovations that appear in these periods of generalized contention survive past the end of the cycle. Some are directly linked to the peak of contention, when it seems as if anything is possible and the world will be transformed (Zolberg 1972). Others depend on the high level of participation

and information flow characteristic of cycles, and cannot be sustained when mobilization declines and information sources turn to other topics. And some result
from the temporary paralysis of the forces of order as they face unexpected masses
of challengers on the streets; when they regroup, tactics that seemed unassailable
at the height of the cycle are easily crushed.

It is with similar logic that cycles produce new or transformed symbols,
frames of meaning, and ideologies to justify and dignify collective action. These
"master frames" typically arise among insurgent groups, which was how movements in the 1960s transformed the traditional American concept of "rights"
(see Chapter 7). Cycles of contention are the crucibles within which new cultural
constructs born among critical communities are created, tested, and refined (cf.
Rochon 1998). These enter the culture in more diffuse and less militant form,
where they can serve as sources for the symbols of future movements.

OLD AND NEW MOVEMENT ORGANIZATIONS

Cycles of contention almost never fall under the control of a single organization.
The high point of the wave is marked by the appearance of "spontaneous" forms
of action, but even at this phase, both previous organizational traditions and
newly organized movements shape their direction and outcomes. Nor do "old"
organizations necessarily give way to new ones in the course of the cycle: many
existing organizations, like the NAACP at the height of the civil rights movement, adopt the radical tactics of their competitors and adjust their discourse
into a broader, more aggressive public stance.

Whereas older organizations soon return to more traditional forms of action,
as the NAACP did after the early 1960s, organizations born in periods of intense
contention are likely to continue to use it, for contention is the bridge they have
constructed between them and their followers. This is one reason why contention
will not cease just because a particular group's claims have been satisfied or its
hopes dashed. Contention is how they first gained support, and they use it to
maintain it and compete with other groups.

INCREASED INFORMATION AND INTERACTION

Finally, during periods of increased contention, information flows more rapidly,
political attention heightens, and interactions among groups of challengers and
between them and authorities increase in frequency and intensity. Conflicts between elites widen into deeper cleavages between social groups; new centers of
power – however temporary and ephemeral – develop, convincing insurgents that
they are effecting the collapse of the old system and producing new and sometimes bizarre alliances between challengers and some of its former supporters.

These alliances sometimes form the bases of new governing coalitions, but
more often they split apart as some branches of the movement seek more radical
change, others try to institutionalize their gains, and moderates grow frightened

of disorder and desert former allies. The array of actors that forms against and around the state produces loosely connected coalitions. When buttressed by effective organizations and broad master frames, these coalitions can polarize society. And this takes us to the dynamics of demobilization.

THE DEMOBILIZATION PHASE

Early students of revolutionary cycles, like Crane Brinton (1965), posited set successions of stages, much like those that characterize biological development or the stages of a disease. We now know that too many factors vary around the central processes of widespread contention for such unilinear models to help in comparing different revolutions, let alone in allowing us to understand the broader universe of cycles of contention. If nothing else, external actors can intervene, shifting the internal balance of power and bringing the cycle to an abrupt close.

Perhaps reacting against such unilinear cyclical thinking, some students of revolution have neglected the internal processes by which cycles of contention develop, either by focusing on the recurring conditions that lead to revolution (Skocpol 1979, 1994; Wickham-Crowley 1992) or retreating into historical narrative, often richly filled with evidence about agency or accident. The best of these studies either theorize narratives for relatively short periods and condensed events (Sewell 1996) or construct general narratives out of sets of personal stories (Selbin 1993). But it is rare to find a theorized narrative that explains why a cycle moves inexorably forward up to a certain point and then just as surely declines.

We do not possess a powerful enough theory to allow us to delineate all the recurring dynamic elements in all cycles of contention. If we did, it might so flatten the different species of contention as to be of little use. What we can do is propose a series of causal processes that seem to be present in the "tipping points" of cycles. Three sets of processes appear to be present in a wide range of cases: exhaustion and factionalization, institutionalization and violence, and repression and facilitation.

EXHAUSTION AND POLARIZATION

The simplest reason why mobilization declines is probably exhaustion. Although street protests, demonstrations, and violence are exhilarating at first, as movements organize better, and divide into leaders and followers, they involve risk, personal costs, and, eventually, weariness and disillusionment. What results is a decline of participation, one that can be encouraged when political authorities and the forces of order are intelligent enough to bide their time.

But participation does not decline at an equal pace for all sectors of a movement. Those at the periphery of a challenge, lacking strong reasons to support it, are the most likely to defect, while those close to its core, who have strong reasons to support it, are most likely to persist. As a general rule, the former are more moderate in their actions; as they defect, their absence removes a brake on extremism; conversely, because the latter are more militant, they are more likely to support violent confrontations. Unequal rates of defection between center and periphery of a movement shift the balance from moderate to radical claims and from peaceful to violent protest.

This unequal decline of participation poses a dilemma for movement leadership. Aware that their strength lies in numbers, they may respond to the decline of participation by embracing more moderate demands and attempting to compromise with opponents. Conversely, to keep the support of militant elements, they may attempt to keep the fire alive by making radical claims and intensifying contention. In either case, the differential decline of support leads to polarization between those willing to compromise with authorities and those who seek continued confrontation.

Factionalization takes different forms in different historical cycles. For example, the coalition that began the Dutch Patriot movement in the 1780s with massive – but moderate – petition drives led to the formation of a provincial network of citizens' committees and militias (te Brake 1997: 6). Frightened by the fear of disorder, "the original coalition of disillusioned elites and popular political activists had begun to disintegrate." The result was polarization in the original Patriot coalition, the formation of an essentially counterrevolutionary one against it, and a revolutionary split in the country. As te Brake concludes, "Those who remained in the Patriot coalition began to realize that the breakdown of apparent consensus within the local political arena would require them to take forceful revolutionary action to achieve their goals."[4]

A very different outcome could be seen in the Tienanmen Square uprising in China in 1989. There, a peaceful petition drive by students against corruption attracted the support of a mass of dissatisfied students and other citizens of Beijing and other cities. Factionalization occurred as a group of radicals entered the square with their white headbands and militant slogans, opposing the moderates who were ready to compromise with the Communist leadership. These splits paralyzed the movement, providing time for the party to regroup and send fresh troops to repress the movement.[5]

VIOLENCE AND INSTITUTIONALIZATION

The splits that developed among both Dutch Patriots and Chinese students were mainly over goals. But splits between radicals and moderates often take the form of a conflict over violence. When moderate leaders institutionalize their tactics to retain mass support, radical competitors employ confrontational tactics to gain the support of the militants and prevent backsliding. The former have a repugnance for violence, whereas the latter often use it and sometimes elevate it to a higher form of politics to justify its use against their enemies.

The battle between the Girondins and the Jacobins in the French Revolution is a good historical example of such conflicts. It was triggered by a dispute about the execution of the king, with the Jacobins calling for regicide and the Girondins, who opposed it, soon following Louis XVI to the guillotine. Within the British Chartists, there was a long debate about the virtues of physical versus moral action. And as we have seen, on the European left, anarchists and social democrats argued about the violence of the former and the moderation of the latter.

In recent decades, movements have produced similar polarizations over violence. Even within the largely peaceful American civil rights movement, the debate between the older, moderate wing of the movement and the young firebrands who challenged it for leadership was both about violence and the wisdom of pushing for radical economic gains, as opposed to consolidating the political rights won in the early 1960s. Each phase of the movement led to increased disputes between its older and the younger branches. As the original forms of disruptive politics were consumed and the movement's center of gravity shifted from South to North, a mass movement gave way to the practice of organized violence and thence to movement collapse. But here we must bring a third element into play – the reactions of the state.

FACILITATION AND REPRESSION

Although factionalization grows up within the elements of a mass movement, it can be either encouraged or discouraged by different governmental strategies. Governments that give in rapidly to insurgents' demands may find themselves replaced, as these demands escalate with every sign of the regime's weakness. This was the case in eastern Europe in 1989, as the revealed weakness of the regimes led challengers to broaden their demands from reforms within state socialism to its liquidation.

Conversely, governments that categorically reject all challengers' claims and back their rejection with force will either destroy the opposition – where repression is effective – or bring about a revolutionary polarization where it is not. The former was the outcome in the Chinese student rebellion of 1989, whereas the latter was the case in the 1905 revolution in Russia, where an absolutist regime lacked the repressive capacity to enforce its refusal of insurgents' demands.

But these extreme forms of repression are less typical of contemporary cycles than they were in the eighteenth and nineteenth centuries. Far more common today are the selective facilitation of some groups' claims and the selective repression of others. For example, Jack Goldstone points out how rulers in the Philippines, Colombia, and Kenya successfully worked to split off elites from peasants and workers (1997: 20).[6] By negotiating with some elements among a spectrum of contenders, governments encourage moderation and split off the moderates from their radical allies.

Especially when it coincides with the decline of mass support and with factionalization inside the movement, this policy of facilitation and selective repression pushes radicals into more sectarian forms of organization and more violent forms of action and encourages moderates to defect. At the extreme, the combination of partial demobilization, factionalization, and selective repression and facilitation produces terrorism (della Porta 1995: ch. 6). Goldstone, paraphrasing Sabine Katstedt-Henke, describes the process in Germany in the 1970s:

> Initially, the state overreacts to protest, but represses poorly and ineffectively; this provokes further protest. However, as the state gains more knowledge of the protest, it is able to split the protesters by offering moderate concessions. These attract the moderates in the movement to legitimate action, but frustrate the radicals who seek greater change. The radicals then strike back with more extreme violence, creating a spiral of terror and counter-terror that ends with the radical extreme suppressed or driven underground. (1997: 11–12)

Even short of terrorism, repression encourages extremism. When, following the French Revolution, British authorities began to repress Painite and Radical groups on the theory that they were pro-French and republican, "what remained of English radicalism committed itself to the pursuit of those subversive, clandestine and republican objectives which its more moderate leaders had hitherto consistently repudiated" (Goodwin 1979: 416). A similar dynamic could be seen in America in the late 1960s, when the demonstration against the Vietnam War at the 1968 Chicago Democratic convention led to violent encounters with the police. The mass movement collapsed, leaving behind "a congeries of smaller single-issue movements" in some of which "frustrated revolutionists built bombs, turning reveries of freedom into cruel, ineffectual outbursts of terrorism" (Miller 1987: 317).

But not all governments have the political control and self-possession to engage in selective repression and facilitation. This is most obviously true of authoritarian regimes, where elites may feel that giving in to even a trickle of moderate claims will lead to a torrent of more threatening ones. Even in more pluralistic regimes, as fear of disorder mounts among property-holding groups, reaction can become general and waves of contention are followed by global repression. One such cycle illustrates all of these processes and something else as well – the risk of external intervention when regimes weaken and challengers temporarily take control.

THE FIRST MODERN CYCLE[7]

In the winter and spring of 1848, rebellions broke out all over Europe. In parts of the continent, the bad crop yields of the previous years were the main cause of the uprisings, but in other areas, harvests had been improving since the disastrous one of 1846.[8] In some countries, disputes over the suffrage were the trigger for the agitations, but in others the suffrage had already been expanded and in still others it only became an issue after agitation broke out. Finally, religious and ethnic cleavages were the source of important struggles in some countries, while in others there was no visible communal conflict.[9]

Although they sprang from a variety of sources, from the start the uprisings of early 1848 struck observers as a single event of continental importance. Engels, from England, devoted considerable resources to raising insurrections in Germany. Mazzini made his way to Rome, where he helped hasten the end of the Roman Republic, while Garibaldi returned from Latin America to raise insurrections in the Italian states. Although the first stirrings of revolution came in Switzerland and Italy, everywhere the shadow of the first French Revolution loomed large.

That revolution had been primarily focused on political rights; but, as this new one gathered force, the social question began to intersect with questions of political representation. In his 1847 program for the moderate opposition, Tocqueville had foreseen this expansion of claims: "The time is coming," he prophesied, "when the country will again be divided between two great parties. Soon the political struggle will be between the haves and the have-nots; property will be the great battlefield" (1987: 12–13).

Tocqueville exaggerated; the 1848 revolution was not yet the social revolution of the future, as Marx shrewdly understood.[10] But following the effervescent tumult of its early weeks, it frightened the parliamentary liberals, middle-class democrats, and constitutional monarchists who feared a class war, bringing them back from flirtation with reform to support for reaction. After a period of retreating before the mobilized masses, governments recovered their self-control, called in allies, and swept the insurgents from the field.

In every major European country, by the middle of 1848 regimes were threatened or overturned, people marched, met, organized assemblies and committees, and erected barricades. Governments scurried to places of safety or rushed through reforms to forestall further rebellion. Figure 9.1 demonstrates the dramatic rise and fall in conflict and response by combining the number of contentious public events from Jacques Godechot's (1971) chronology for all the major European states for which he provides information for the years 1847 through 1849.[11]

Godechot's time-series begins in March 1847, when the first open conflicts occurred, and continues for thirty months through the end of August 1849. He includes a detailed outline of events of national importance for Austria-Hungary, Belgium, Britain, France, the German and Italian states, the Netherlands, Poland, Spain, and Switzerland. Some of these events were highly contentious and violent; others were routine electoral and legislative acts; others were the actions of public authorities; still others the interventions of foreign powers. His chronology allows us to record only the *number* of events, and not their duration or the number of participants in them, but it provides us with a graphic picture of what a cycle of contention looked like in mid-nineteenth-century Europe.

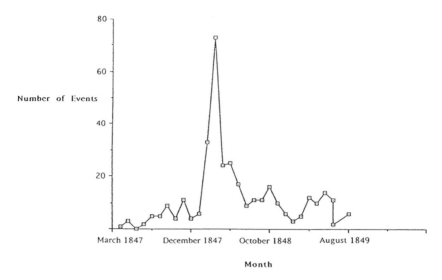

Figure 9.1. 1848 Events by Month, March 1847–August 1849 (SOURCE: Sarah Soule and Sidney Tarrow, "Acting Collectively, 1847–1849: How the Repertoire of Collective Action Changed and Where It Happened," paper presented to the annual conference of Social Science History Association, New Orleans, Louisiana, 1991.)

CREATING OPPORTUNITIES

Although the most dramatic memories of the 1848 revolution would come from Paris, in fact, the cycle began almost a year earlier in Italy, where a reform-minded new pope triggered a wave of agitation in Rome and in the South; then in Belgium, where a liberal government had just been sworn in; and in Switzerland, where the liberal Protestant cantons imposed their will on the mainly Catholic rural cantons of the confederation. No less French a historian than Elie Halèvy would assert that "the revolution of 1848 did not arise from the Parisian barricades but from the Swiss Civil War" (quoted in Sigmann 1973: 193).

As in many of the cycles that followed, the peak of contention in the spring of 1848 was marked by an expansion of the forms of collective action. In 1848, these were mainly public meetings, demonstrations, barricades, and violence against others. The co-occurrence of these collective action forms tells us much about the breadth of the coalition; as liberal and conservative gentlemen were holding sober meetings and learned conferences, republicans were organizing demonstrations, workers and artisans were building barricades, and peasants were attacking landlords and taking over forest reserves.

The barricades were the disruptive centerpieces of the various uprisings (Traugott 1990; 1995). The first were mounted in the February days in Paris when the monarchy was overthrown. They were built again in April, in Rouen, when socialist workers refused to accept the defeat of the republican candidates they had supported in the elections; during the June days, when the Assembly dissolved the national workshops; and again, a year later, when the French army landed at Civitavecchia to reinstate the pope. Barricades spread rapidly across Europe wherever the revolution took on a radical character.

The peaks of protest cycles are also marked by an increase in violence. The attacks on Jews in France in the spring of 1848 were a presentiment of the ethnic conflicts that marked the passage of the revolution to Hungary and the Balkans. In Germany the first months of the revolution were marked by scores of attacks on Jews. When Hungarian landowners shook off the rule of Vienna, they were quickly faced by an uprising of subject Serbs, whom they quickly repressed. As in Yugoslavia after the 1989 revolutions, the breakdown of order provided opportunities for advantage for ambitious local elites under cover of ethnic memories.

But the revolutions also produced endless public meetings, learned conferences, and parliamentary gatherings. What did the Sicilian rebels do when they took over Palermo in January 1848? They formed committees for restoring order, ensuring provisions, securing finance, and controlling information (Tilly, Tilly, and Tilly 1975: 130). How did German liberals respond when the king of Prussia dissolved the Landtag in June 1847? They met in Offenberg in September and in Oppenheim in October to debate (Godechot 1971: 199–200). Even in Austrian-ruled Serbia, Croatia, and Transylvania, the revolutionary events of February and March 1848 produced meetings and committees. The most long-lasting and the least productive meeting was the "professors' parliament" in Frankfurt, which was at first tolerated but eventually broken up by Prussia when the threat of insurrection had ebbed.

Mass demonstrations were a third important part of the repertoire of 1848 – in fact, it was in that year that the demonstration came into its own (Favre 1990). If we can assume a resemblance between Godechot's term *"manifestation"* and our term "demonstration,"[12] we will find in Godechot's chronology thirty-one major demonstrations in the twelve months from July 1847 to June 1848. But it was from February through April 1848 – the peak of mobilization – that we find the greatest density of demonstrations. As in many recent cycles, the peaceful occupation of public space, the public meeting, and the barricade, as well as traditional attacks on others, were all hallmarks of the intensive peak of the cycle.

WIDENING CONFLICT IN PARIS

The 1848 revolutions may have begun in Europe's periphery, but the core of radical politics had always been Paris. The Parisian events show how conflict begins within institutional circles and spreads outward like a widening gyre. By the early 1840s, most central and western European regimes, including France's, had semiconstitutional governments that provided a good deal of scope for elite debate focused increasingly around the issue of the suffrage (Anderson and Anderson 1967: 307–17).

The first stage in the unraveling of the Orleanist regime was its response to the parliamentary opposition's demand for suffrage reform. Rejection of their modest proposals threw the moderates into the arms of the republicans, launching the campaign of "banquets" that were thinly disguised demonstrations for reform and taking the debate from the Chamber of Deputies to the streets and from Paris to the provinces. Because these banquets were sponsored by the legitimate opposition and were entirely peaceable – even in 1848, the French loved to eat – the government hesitated to repress them. But because they bridged the interests of parliamentary and extraparliamentary groups, liberals and republicans, the banquet campaign passed by rapid stages from the parliamentary opposition into the hands of a coalition of extraparliamentary agitators and journalists (Tocqueville 1987: 26–7).

Faced by this republican move, the moderates tried to pull back, but it was too late and the initiative passed into the hands of the National Guard and the urban poor (Tocqueville 1987: 20). Before the moderates knew what was happening, barricades were going up on the streets of Paris, diligent drivers were taking advantage of the tumult to destroy the railway lines, Jews were attacked in the eastern provinces, and forest preserves were invaded. The walls of the monarchy had been sapped from within before they were attacked from without.

CYCLICAL DECLINE

As the 1848 revolutions progressed beyond the effervescence of the spring of 1848, the peaceful demonstration and the public meeting begin to disappear from Godechot's chronology, to be replaced by terms like "attack," "clash," "dissolve," "intervene," and "defeat." The last public demonstration he lists was a demand for work in Berlin on October 31, followed soon after by the retraction of the reforms that the kaiser conceded in the previous spring. People stopped demonstrating and turned to armed violence when force began to be employed against them.

The shift to violence in the streets – in part spontaneous and in part in response to repression – helped to destroy the revolutionary coalitions that were formed in the early spring. With his withering prose, Marx describes the process through which, in the interests of the preservation of property, the parliamentary liberals and then the republicans peeled away from support for the new French Republic, opening the way for Louis Napoleon to become, first, its president, and then emperor of France (1963a: 42–3).

Increasingly, the armed clashes in Godechot's chronology took on an international dimension. Austrian armies attacked the liberals in northern Italy, the French intervened in Rome, and Russian troops moved against the Hungarians in aid of the Hapsburgs. By the end of 1848, there emerges a picture of almost unrelieved armed strife, foreign intervention, and a collapse of popular collective action. Military force, backed by conservative reaction and the pulling back of the moderates, carried the springtime of peoples into a winter of discontent.

Like many other protest cycles, the 1848 revolution left the most bitter memories where the hopes it had generated were highest. At first welcomed by radicals and democrats across Europe, the 1848ers were soon denounced for their "hollow rhetoric, their mystical idealism . . . and their generous illusions" (Sigmann 1973: 10). In Germany, the year was soon labeled "das tolle Jahr" (the crazy year), while the British ambassador to Paris wrote that 1848 left "almost every individual less happy, every country less prosperous, every people not only less free but less hopeful of freedom hereafter" (quoted in Postgate 1955: 266). In Italy, even today, the expression to "fare un quarantotto" means to create confusion. "What we remember most" after the intoxication of such moments of madness, writes Aristide Zolberg, "is that moments of political enthusiasm are followed by bourgeois repression or by charismatic authoritarianism, sometimes by horror but always by the restoration of boredom" (1972: 205).

THE 1960s NEW LEFT

Many of the characteristics found in the 1848 revolutions can be found in more recent confrontations, in periods like the strike waves and revolutionary movements of the post–World War I period, that of the Popular Front in France and the New Deal in the United States, the eastern European democratization cycle that began in Poland in 1980 and ended in the collapse of the USSR in 1991, and the radical movements of the 1960s in western Europe and the United States. We will briefly examine the last period to illustrate some commonalities with the earlier cycle, as well as the difference in outcomes.

From 1968 to 1972, a wave of student and labor unrest arose in many countries in Europe that would eventually envelop almost every area of these societies. We still lack the systematic data to trace this cycle quantitatively over this half decade, but numerous qualitative studies and a few quantitative ones leave little doubt that the societies of Europe were undergoing a major cycle of contention.[13]

Two movements in particular reached historic proportions in 1968: in France, the short but explosive "movement of May" nearly toppled the self-assured Gaullist regime, while, in Czechoslovakia, a short spring of reform was followed by a brutal military crackdown under Soviet leadership. At about the same time, an Italian *maggio* shut down schools and universities, touching off a "sliding May" that lasted into the early 1970s (Salvati 1981; Tarrow 1989a); and, in Germany, a wave of protest jarred that country's complacent political class (della Porta 1995).

In the United States, the years of hope began earlier, in the civil rights movement of the early 1960s and in the anti–Vietnam War agitations that culminated in the "days of rage" at the Chicago Democratic Party convention.[14] As in Europe, university students were in the vanguard of the movements, but the workers who were key catalysts in France and Italy were missing, as were most of the African American young people who had been active earlier in the decade. These were largely absent from the recruitment pool of affluent college students who staffed the movement against the Vietnam War.

In both America and western Europe, diffusion was rapid and geographically widespread. Depending in part on the "transitory teams" of activists who had met earlier in the civil rights movement (McAdam 1988), it employed the newly discovered tools of cheap air travel and television, the former making it possible to assemble teams of leaders rapidly where conflict was brewing, the latter to communicate conflict across the country without strong mass organizations. In western Europe, the smaller size of the societies and the centralized nature of their educational systems made it possible to diffuse the movement rapidly across the national territory. In highly centralized France, it took only a few days for the confrontation between police and students at the Sorbonne to close universities all across the country (Schnapp and Vidal-Naquet 1988).

What is most striking in the movements of the 1960s was the common "master frames" on both sides of the Atlantic, in what Doug McAdam and Dieter Rucht call "the cross-national diffusion of movement ideas" (1993). Not only ideas, but sit-in and obstruction tactics crossed the Atlantic quickly in the 1960s. Though the 1960s movements were far from revolutionary, they aptly illustrate what Tilly writes about the cross-national diffusion of revolutionary situations; in a world in which communication is rapid, "the demonstration that one important state is vulnerable . . . signals the possibility of making similar demands elsewhere and makes available transferable expertise and doctrine" (1993: 14).

In both Europe and America, the movements of the 1960s combined organizations inherited from the "old" left with new ones using more decentralized forms of mobilization (Isserman 1987). In the United States, the Students for a Democratic Society were the most visible "New Left" group, but others of more traditional marxist and social-democratic coloration were also active. In France and Italy, students who had learned their politics in the "old" Communist and Catholic lefts were the creators of the "New Left" movements of the latter part of the decade. "Maoism" gave these movements a new allure, but many had reverted to leninist types of organization by the early 1970s (Bobbio 1979; Tarrow 1989a).

The repertoire of contention of the 1960s movements expanded rapidly too, shifting from the set-piece demonstrations that the students inherited from their marxist forebears to the nonviolent resistance tactics and sit-ins learned from the civil rights movement. For rejecting the leadership of the old left also meant rejecting its peaceful tactics – in part to demonstrate their difference from their elders, and in part to gain attention from the press, from other students, and from authorities.

In each country, a spiral of broad claims spun outward from confrontations that began as concrete conflicts of interest. As the protests spread, coalitions of challengers tried to form mass organizations and broaden their claims, but the more militant among them radicalized their claims into general challenges to authority as the more moderate were moving into institutional parties and unions (Lange, Irvin, and Tarrow 1989).

The breadth of these movements and their rapid diffusion seemed to threaten the established order, giving rise to countermovements, demands for law and order, sometimes for reform, but usually to more effective forms of control. In both Europe and America, the end of the cycle saw a polarization between moderates and radicals, institutionalized tactics, and organized violence. As in 1848, what began as a springtime of freedom ended in repression and disillusionment.

REVOLUTIONARY AND NONREVOLUTIONARY CYCLES[15]

Even the casual reader will have noticed that in the two preceding sections, I have dealt indifferently with a truly revolutionary cycle – 1848 – and with the 1960s, which few would today call revolutionary without seriously stretching that concept. This conflation of revolutionary and nonrevolutionary cycles is an intended provocation: for so isolated has the study of revolution become that we need to remember that revolutions are a species of contention.[16]

As we have seen here, parallels between cycles of protest and revolutionary processes abound. To see them, we need, first, a distinction between revolutionary situations and revolutionary outcomes (Tilly 1993). While revolutionary situations are moments of deep fragmentation in state power, revolutionary outcomes are effective transfers of state power to new sets of actors. A full-fledged revolution combines the two. Great revolutions typically fall into several phases: situation – outcome – new situation – outcome, and so on until some set of political actors consolidates its hold over the state and beats down the next round of challengers.

With hindsight, we can say that a revolution can occur when states have lost the capacity to maintain their basic functions, and when at least two contenders struggle for control (Tilly 1993).[17] We can see such a situation in stark outline with the outbreak of the Russian Revolution in February 1917. The czar's government had lost both control and legitimacy due to its wartime failures. When the opposition was strengthened by defections at the front, weakened by interrupted food supplies in the cities, and sapped by peasant discontent, Lenin and his Bolsheviks consolidated their support by calling for "bread, land, and peace."

But since so many potentially revolutionary situations exist in these terms, as in protest cycles we can only trace those that will produce revolutions by a careful analysis of the political process that leads from revolutionary conditions to revolutionary outcomes. In both movement cycles and revolutions, a successful challenge by one previously disadvantaged actor simultaneously (1) advertises the vulnerability of authorities, (2) provides a model for effective claim making, (3) identifies possible allies for other challengers, (4) alters the existing relations of challengers and power holders to each other, and (5) thereby threatens the interests of yet other political actors who have stakes in the status quo, thus activating them as well.

Such a situation becomes revolutionary if and when the elites in place reject all competing claims, and when some challengers with claims to sovereignty gain power, then league together to fortify their positions against new challengers, a process that eventually splits mobilized actors between regime members and outsiders, demobilizes some outsiders, and drives the remainder toward increasingly risky actions until repression, co-optation, and fragmentation terminate the cycle.

The three dynamic processes described earlier can help to distinguish such revolutionary outcomes from more ordinary cycles of contention. When elites respond to broad-ranging claims from coalitions of challengers by blind repression and refusing concessions to any of them, a sense of outrage and heightened solidarity counteracts the process of polarization and halts defections. Jack Goldstone puts it this way:

> In the case of a revolutionary movement, while it may begin as a movement to achieve certain policy or attitudinal goals, it evolves into a collaborative effort of diverse groups with diverse policy goals into a movement that aims to overthrow the state. It evolves in that direction precisely because the state adopts a repressive stance of resolute resistance: it prohibits or sharply circumscribes movement actions, strongly opposes all who ally with the movement, and may seek to eliminate the movement and its supporters. (1997: 4)

But government repression can take many forms and operate with varying effectiveness. "Where the government is able to focus its repressive measures squarely and discriminately on the movement supporters," continues Goldstone, "repression is likely to either end the movement or drive it underground." But where repression is unfocused, inconsistent, and arbitrary, or where it is limited by international or domestic pressures, "the movement is likely to attract supporters while becoming more radicalized in its goals and actions" (Goldstone 1997: 5).

Radicalization also depends on internal relations in the opposition and can follow our three dynamic processes. General repression weakens the position of the moderates (e.g., because it cuts off the possibility of compromise and makes defection useless or dangerous), while strengthening that of the radicals. Violence – even governmental violence – and factionalization give the radicals the upper hand in the competition for support within the revolutionary coalition. The same process can be triggered by external attacks, which weaken the position of the moderates and strengthen those who are more determined and prepared to squelch internal opposition. Again, we see this most clearly in the case of the

Russian Revolution, as Lenin eliminated, first, the provisional government, and then his Social Revolutionary competitors.

One other process helps to advance a revolutionary route: the defection of members of the elite to the opposition, either outraged by the government's brutal repression and lack of flexibility, or out of sympathy for the opposition's goals or the desire to advance their own values, or both. This was the great – and largely unexpected – aspect of the 1989 "revolutions" in eastern Europe, when even police associated with the dreaded German Democratic Republic held back from attacking demonstrators in Leipzig and East Berlin.

Revolutionary situations then resemble the opening of new social-movement challenges to the existing polity. One becomes the other to the extent that challenges multiply, put at risk the stakes of all existing potential actors in the system, and lead to governmental choices that both repress all opposition and unwittingly throw advantages to the regime's most determined opponents. Social movements, protest cycles, and revolutions, as Goldstone concludes,

> are not different *genera* of social phenomena . . . but neither are they simply the same phenomenon, differing only by degrees from mild to extreme. Instead, they are best thought of as a family of related phenomena, originating in a similar set of circumstances, but evolving and diverging in consequence of distinct patterns in the interplay between protest movements, state response, the broader social environment, and cultural evaluations of state and protest actions. (1997: 24)

A NOTE ON DEMOCRATIZATION

The same kind of analogical reasoning may help us to unravel the processes at work and the outcomes of another kind of cycle – democratization. Based largely on Spanish models, democratization is most often treated as a largely elite-initiated and elite-run process (O'Donnell and Schmitter 1986). But democratization has in common with revolutionary cycles struggles over the right to rule between opposing leadership groups supported by different sectors of the population. Like revolutionary cycles, it also sees defections of members of the old regime and the key role for the armed forces. But when it succeeds, it is through the play among larger numbers of intermediary positions between old rulers and new elites and less the result of violence than in successful revolutions.

The democratic revolutions of 1989 in east central Europe served to remind scholars that democratization, however peaceful, is a contentious process with family resemblances to both movement cycles and revolutionary ones. Recent work on 1989 in eastern Europe (Fish 1995; Oberschall 1996; Zdravomyslova 1996) and southern Europe and Latin America (Bermeo 1997; Collier 1997, Tarrow 1995c), and theoretical work by Markoff (1996) and Pagnucco (1996) have begun to challenge the "elite transaction" view of recent democratizations;

but we still lack the conceptual tools and empirical bases to bring democratic transitions into the family of contentious processes.[18]

THE DIVERSE ENDINGS OF CYCLES

Viewed from a distance, waves of collective action from the 1848 revolutions onward describe parabolas from institutional conflict to enthusiastic peak of contention, to ultimate collapse or – in the case of successful revolutions – the consolidation of new regimes. After gaining national attention and state response, they reach peaks of conflict that are marked by the presence of organizers who try to diffuse the insurgencies to broader publics. As participation is channeled into organization, parts of the movements take on a more political logic, engaging in implicit bargaining with authorities. As the cycle winds down, exhaustion and polarization spread and the initiative shifts to elites and parties.

But the multipolarity of the interactions in these cycles and the diverse reactions of the authorities make their endings far less similar than their beginnings. The diffusion of collective action from early risers to latecomers, the shift of political opportunities from early challengers to their allies and then to elites, the different choices governments make about whom to repress and whom to facilitate, splits within the movements between radicals and moderates: these increase the number and variety of interactions in the course of the cycles and, as in the wake of the 1848 revolutions, send them off in divergent directions.

For example, the governments that followed the wave of protests in 1968 in western Europe were different in each country. In France, a conservative coalition fundamentally revised the educational system that the students had contested in May, but reversed the salary gains made by the workers; in West Germany, a Social Democratic coalition came to power, broadened the country's welfare system, and launched an *Ostpolitik* with then Communist East Germany; while in Italy, a shifting sequence of center-left governments established a degree of working-class power in the factories that was only reversed in the 1980s but left the political system intact. The ends of protest cycles are never as uniform as their beginnings, and this takes us directly to the question of movement outcomes.

10

STRUGGLING TO REFORM

S truggling to reform: a strange phrase to use in introducing a discussion of the outcomes of social movements! For few movements seek only reform, and many reject reformism altogether. Movement activists demand fundamental social change, the recognition of new identities, entry into the polity, the destruction of their enemies, or the overthrow of a social order – seldom "reform." When, as we saw in the preceding chapter, movements cumulate in a general cycle of contention, claims become so broad and elites so besieged that profound changes are forced onto the agenda. Nevertheless, as I argue in this chapter, the structure of politics through which claims are processed in democratic states forces them into a common crucible from which cycles of reform are the most likely outcome.

THE AMBIGUITY OF POLICY OUTCOMES

For many years, analysts of social movements have bewailed our lack of knowledge of their policy outcomes (Giugni 1994, 1997; Gurr 1980; Marx and Wood 1975). In the absence of convincing information on movement outcomes, a number of taxonomies have been produced – almost as many as there are studies of the subject. The best-known typology is also the simplest and the most often used, that of William Gamson. In *The Strategy of Social Protest*, Gamson distinguished between challengers receiving new advantages and gaining acceptance (1990: ch. 1). This produced his familiar fourfold classification of "full response" and defeat, at the two extremes, and "co-optation" and "preemption" in between (ch. 3). Tom Rochon and Daniel Mazmamian added a third type of outcome – changes in social values (1993). Paul Schumaker identified five kinds of system responsiveness, ranging from "access responsiveness" to "impact responsiveness" (1975), and Paul Burstein and his collaborators added "structural impacts" to Schumaker's list of five (1991).[1]

Part of the problem is that while it is possible to correlate outcomes with movement efforts, it is not as easy to identify particular movement actions as the cause for a specific outcome. To the voices of movement activists we must add the impact of public opinion, interest groups, parties, and executives as potential causes for outcomes of interest to movements. As Paul Burstein writes in his analysis of the struggle for equal employment opportunity legislation, it was "adopted as the result of social changes that were manifested in public opinion, crystallized in the civil rights and women's movements, and transformed into public policy by political leaders" (1985: 125).

In addition, international waves of movement or opinion can generate the conviction that some changes are inevitable – even when local movements are weak or lacking. For example, the success of the women suffrage movement all over the industrialized world during roughly the same period of history was more the result of a transnational wave of opinion than the outcome of particular movement resources or tactics. The same is true of environmentalism and the creation of environmental ministries and organizations around the world (Meyer, et al. 1997).

STRIKES AND OTHER OUTCOMES

A partial exception to this complexity might be found in the results of strikes. A series of scholars beginning in the 1960s analyzed the effects of labor violence, contextual variables, group size, duration, and the nature of the demands on strike outcomes.[2] The results were not completely uniform, but for countries as different as late nineteenth-century Italy, the United States at mid-twentieth century, and Poland in the 1990s, most research converges on the finding that strikes are effective in gaining concessions from the government or employers (Osa 1998). Moreover, it seems that "the characteristics of individual strikes are more important than the contextual variables in explaining both violence and outcomes" (Giugni 1994: 6).

But strikes are somewhat special: the target is usually an employer, the demands are clearly stated, the duration of the protest is short, and the workers are usually autonomous and well organized. In contrast, in the context of the cycles of contention described in Chapter 9, movements are seldom unified, their demands are often imprecise and utopian – and may be aimed more at mobilizing internal militants than at convincing opponents. "Success," for some movements, may consist more in establishing a collective identity than in achieving policy success (Melucci 1996; Pizzorno 1978).

Moreover, when elites are faced by a multitude of relations with allies and challengers, competitors and constituents, they do not respond so much to the demands of any single movement as to the generalized conflict structure they face. In such a confrontation, they are more likely to mediate among the demands placed on them than to respond piecemeal, looking for lowest-common-denominator solutions that will defeat their enemies, impose social control, and satisfy allies and supporters.

This was even true for the massive strike wave with which the French state was hit in May 1968; it was to derail the radical student movement and get the economy back on track that the government gave in to the workers' demands. When the general threat had passed, the government deflated the economy, erasing many of the workers' gains (Salvati 1981). The outcomes of the challenges of individual movements are thus difficult to detach from the general cycles of contention in which many of them arise.

The presence of allies within the polity are particularly important factors in producing policy outcomes favorable to social movements (Jenkins and Perrow 1977; Lipsky 1968). In fact, serving as often uninvited intermediaries between challengers and power holders, allies may have a greater effect in shaping elite responses than the movements themselves. The political process gives third parties, interest groups, and movement allies and opponents a key role in shaping policy responses. As Edwin Amenta and his collaborators argue, "the political context mediates the impact of movement organization and action on its goals and sets the range of possible outcomes" (1992: 309).

That said, what are the factors that help a movement to succeed? Most students agree that the power to disrupt brings about short-term success. For example, reviewing the recurring waves of welfare reform in the United States, Piven and Cloward write that "relief arrangements are initiated or expanded during the occasional outbreaks of civil disorder produced by mass unemployment" (1993: xiii). Similarly, the Tillys concluded from their study of a century of conflict in Europe that "no major political rights came into being without readiness of some portions of those [protesting] groups to overcome the resistance of the government and other groups" (1975: 184).

Other scholars have focused heavily on openings of political opportunity in explaining movement success (Jenkins and Perrow 1977; Tarrow 1989a, 1989b). In particular, the access of new actors to the polity helps to put new issues on the agenda and tilts the power balance in favor of older ones. Thus, the enlargement of Western electorates to include the working class shifted the domestic power balance to parties of progress, who promptly passed welfare legislation, legalized strikes, and elected the first working men to office. Where suffrage movements failed – for example, as the Swiss women suffrage movement did for decades – it was precisely because "opposition parties never launched an electoral challenge that might have prodded governing parties into action," and elites closed ranks rather than tilt a carefully constructed internal consensus (Banaszak 1996: 215–16).[3]

Other scholars have pointed to the internal resources, organizations, and strategies of challengers as clues to success: for example, their forms of organization, whether centralized or decentralized; their degree of factionalization, whether their demands are far-reaching or limited; whether they have selective incentives to distribute to supporters; and whether they use violence against opponents.[4] Others have focused on environmental variables, such as the number of allies, the political environment, the movement's structure of political access, and whether it emerged in a crisis or during more ordinary times (Goldstone 1980).[5] Still others have pointed to the values and beliefs of challengers in bringing about success (Banaszak 1996).

But if so many variables appear to explain movement success or failure, how do they fare when considered together? In a multivariate analysis of Gamson's data, Steedly and Foley found that success was related, "in order of relative importance, to the nondisplacement nature of the goals, the number of alliances, the absence of factionalism, specific and limited goals, and the willingness to use sanctions against opponents" (Giugni 1994: 4). Most of these variables would have to be regarded as "internal" to a movement; but the importance of alliances in Steedly and Foley's work, as well as research on the role of periodic political crises (e.g., Goldstone, 1980; Snyder and Tilly 1972), suggests that a combination of factors – internal and external, organizational and political, structural and strategic – must be present to produce movement success.

The difficulty of finding such convergence, the shifting of opportunities within cycles of contention from challengers to elites, and the restoration of "order" when the cycle is over are what best explain the poor record of social movements in achieving policy success. And when they do achieve success, it is frequently in terms that are acceptable to influential allies who represent them in court. Moreover, while cycles of contention can produce temporary coalitions for reform, they are usually too brief, too divided, and too dependent on temporary opportunities to provide permanent support once the fear of disorder disappears (Piven and Cloward 1971, 1977). The rare successes and the frequent reversals of movements' policy outcomes are best expressed by the subtitle of Frances Fox Piven and Richard Cloward's eloquent book, *Poor People's Movements: Why They Succeed, How They Fail* (1977).

But movements do not simply fade away, leaving nothing but lassitude or repression in their wake; they have indirect and long-term effects that emerge when the initial excitement is over and disillusionment passes. Especially when movements leave lasting networks of activists behind them, they can regroup when the cycle is over and new opportunities appear. Three kinds of long-term and indirect effects of movements are important: their effect on the political socialization of the people and groups who have participated in them; the effects of their struggles on political institutions and practices; and their contribution to changes in political culture.

THE POLITICAL IS PERSONAL

"What we remember most" after the intoxication of a protest cycle, writes Aristide Zolberg, "is that moments of political enthusiasm are followed by bourgeois repression or by charismatic authoritarianism, sometimes by horror but always by the restoration of boredom" (1972: 205). Economist Albert Hirschman goes even further, citing a "rebound effect" in which individuals who have thrown themselves into public life with enthusiasm return to private life with a degree of disgust proportional to the effort they have expended (1982: 80).

The early risers in a cycle of contention often see it whirl off in directions they never imagined. When two of the founders of the American republic, John Adams and Thomas Jefferson, looked back at what their generation had wrought, they were far from happy. Instead of a republic of virtue, "America had created a huge, sprawling society that was more egalitarian, more middling, and more dominated by the interests of ordinary people than any that had ever existed" (Wood 1991: 348). Hating the business culture that was sweeping the country, Jefferson never appreciated "how much his democratic and egalitarian principles had contributed to its rise" (p. 367). "All, all dead," he wrote to a friend near the end of his life, "and ourselves left alone amidst a new generation whom we know not, and who knows not us" (p. 368).

Jefferson's disillusionment resulted, not from activism itself but from the gap between the ambitiousness of his vision for America and the revolution's actual outcomes. The same was true for many 1960s activists in both Europe and the United States, whose disillusionment was experienced in direct proportion to the utopianism of their claims. Activists in less ambitious movements – for example, like those with narrow goals in Gamson's studies (1990: ch. 4), or the "consensus movements" studied by John McCarthy and Marc Wolfson (1992) – are less likely to emerge permanently disillusioned from a protest campaign.

Moreover, disillusionment may only be short-term: the result of immediate disappointments and exhaustion. Through skills learned in struggle, the extension of their beliefs to new sectors of activity, and the survival of friendship networks formed in the movement, activism begets future activism, more polarized attitudes toward politics, and greater readiness to join other movements.

MOVEMENTS AS AN ANNEALING PROCESS

In describing his hopes for Freedom Summer, SNCC organizer Bob Moses called in 1964 for an "annealing process" in Mississippi. For movement activists, "in the 'white heat' of that Mississippi summer . . . politics became the central organizing force in their lives." From that time forward, "everything else – relationships, work, etc. – got organized around their politics" (McAdam 1988: 186–7). Other movement cycles around the world led to similar accretions of militancy and politicization. In Indonesia, for those who joined the radical Socialist Youth after World War II,

> the tidal-wave rage for politics roared on out of control. Each person felt as though he, she, could not be truly alive without being political, without

debating over politics. . . . Politics! politics! No different than rice under
the Japanese Occupation. (quoted in Anderson 1990: 38)

Movement participation is not only politicizing; it is empowering, both in
the psychological sense of increasing willingness to take risks and in the political
one of affording new skills and broadened perspectives. Describing her return
from Mississippi to the University of California in the fall of 1964, for example,
a Freedom Summer volunteer told Doug McAdam: "Freedom Summer tended
to boost you; you felt like you had been there and you knew what you were
talking about" (1988: 166). Another put it this way: "Everybody knew about
the summer project and everybody wanted to ask me what is was like and . . . I
was an authority, an instant authority on the civil rights movement" (p. 170).
As a result of their politicization, many former Freedom Summer activists would
play key roles in the Free Speech movement in Berkeley and, later on, in the
national student, antiwar, and women's movements (p. 203).

The latter movement was particularly enriched by veterans of civil rights
campaigns. Young women who had participated in civil rights activities learned
from their experience that their male counterparts were often no less sexist and
dismissive of women than their opponents. Their resentment, added to the self-
confidence they had gained in the South, was a key ingredient in the founding
of the new women's movement (Evans 1980: chs. 4 and 5). Interviewed twenty
years later, former Freedom Summer women volunteers were more often involved
in contemporary social movements than their male counterparts and more likely
to belong to political organizations (McAdam 1988: 222).

The narratives of former 1960s militants, however, tell a mixed story. For
some, the 1960s were not only the formative periods of their lives: they left
positive memories and produced an enduring activist orientation. For example,
Jack Nelson, a successful New Orleans attorney who had taken on a series of cases
for the civil rights movement in the early 1960s, used the following terms to
describe the personal impact of his activity to historian Kim Rogers:

I changed *my* life. And, rather than trying to change the world by using
this person, that organization, I probably started to change my life. . . .
And, you know, I said, wait a minute, I gotta change. And I changed, and
then everything just came naturally. (1993: 172)

But not everything came as naturally to all of Rogers's respondents as they
did to Nelson. The more radical younger generation of CORE and SNCC activists
she interviewed in New Orleans found their post-movement years disappointing.
Disillusioned with and cynical about politics, they "despaired of meaningful
change through the political process," remaining highly interested but ambiva-
lent about politics, and "often yearning for the collective intensity of their pasts"
(p. 174). Their determined assault on the white power structure, their involvement with poor rural blacks, and their subsequent failures left the CORE and

SNCC activists more deeply disappointed with the results of the movement than integrationists like Nelson.

Movement involvement not only politicizes people; it can radicalize them. Jack Blocker records this for the temperance movements of nineteenth-century America, which began with attempts at moral suasion, turned to more aggressive tactics when these tactics failed, and posed more ambitious demands of policy makers (Blocker 1989: xvi). The same is true of more recent movements; when McAdam compared the political attitudes of returning Freedom Summer volunteers to those of applicants who chose not to go to Mississippi, he found that the first group had moved leftward ideologically while the others remained more moderate. And when Carol Mershon compared the attitudes of Italian factory organizers recruited during the "Hot Autumn" with those of their peers, she found the former group to be more egalitarian and more likely to see industrial relations in stark class terms (1990: 311–15).

A myth has grown up, mainly generated from films like *The Big Chill*, that former activists routinely discard their radical ideas and turn their talents to exploiting the mainstream. But the evidence for this is based on the biographies of a few celebrities, and there is much evidence to the contrary. For example, the best predictor of radical attitudes found by Fendrich and Krauss among Japanese and American adults was activism during their student years (1978: 248). The same was true in Italy; when the attitudes of Communist activists who had been in the movements of the late 1960s were compared with those of their party comrades who had no independent movement experience, the former were more tolerant of protest and less punitive toward violence (Lange et al. 1989: 34–6).

Systematic findings on the effects of movement participation come from both France and the United States. When the late French political scientist Annick Percheron analyzed the political attitudes of former participants in the 1960s movements in France, she found that, among the supporters of the three major French political tendencies, participation in both Algerian war protests or in the Events of May reinforced the attitudes characteristic of their respective political groups (1991: 56–7). In the United States, similarly, Darren Sherkat and Jean Blocker found that typical 1960s activists were significantly different from non-activist counterparts – even controlling for the factors that predict protest participation (1997).[6]

ISOLATION AND REGRET

In the aftermath of the 1960s, there was a good deal of the metaphysical angst that Zolberg and Hirschman describe among former activists, both in the United States and in Europe. But this might have been more the result of life-course changes and shifts in the political context than of ideological reversals. As the activist culture of the 1960s gave way to the disappointments of the 1970s and the personalism of the 1980s, many activists defected and others enclosed themselves in a movement subculture. During the 1970s, writes McAdam, "the activist subculture was slowly disintegrating, leaving the volunteers who remained active more and more isolated as the decade wore on" (1988: 205).

Past activism has an effect on activists' personal lives, not always positively. For example, McAdam calculates that 47 percent of the Freedom Summer volunteers who married after that summer went through a divorce between 1970 and 1979. Among the applicants who chose not to go to Mississippi, the comparable figure was under 30 percent (1988: 208). The personal costs of activism were disproportionately high for women volunteers (pp. 220–1) – not because they preferred a celibate life, but because they were isolated by their independence and leftism from a political culture that was moving to the right.

Both in the United States and in Italy, former 1960s activists suffered occupational instability, changing jobs and suffering unemployment more than nonparticipants. Many of the Freedom Summer activists interviewed by McAdam delayed entry onto the job market in order to continue their activism, entering it only during the stagnant 1970s and never making up for lost career time (1988: 109–212). The same was true of former leaders of the Italian movement, Lotta continua, many of whom were still working on the margins of the job market when they were interviewed in the mid-1980s.[7]

Western Europe was different than the United States in one important way – in affording many members of the 1960s generation professional outlets in the mass parties of the left or the trade unions that were lacking for American activists. In contrast, former American activists found little outlet for their activism in the party system, especially after the devastating defeat of George McGovern in 1972. As for the unions, although a few activists became grass-roots organizers, the innate conservatism and secular decline of the American union movement in the 1970s and 1980s made it a poor outlet for activism.

KEEPING THE FAITH BY KEEPING IN TOUCH[8]

But neither of the polar extremes – apathy or professionalization – was the most typical outcome for the generation of the 1960s. Most entered private life but continued to be active in one or another form of social movement or political activity; others moved from direct-action SMOs into service organizations, self-help groups, and parties and interest groups with a family relation to their original movement homes (see Figure 8.1). Still others became professional movement activists.

These findings have been replicated in a number of studies in both western Europe and the United States. In America, nearly half of the former Freedom Summer volunteers McAdam interviewed were active in at least one social movement twenty years later. Former Italian activists interviewed were likely to be active in one of the country's traditional left-wing parties, in the Green party, or in a social movement (Lange et al. 1989). Fendrich and Krauss found former Japanese activists frequently active in a left-wing political party or movement (1978: 245). Among former participants in Algerian war protests and in the

1968 student movement in France who supported political parties, Percheron found a much higher level of political involvement than among other supporters of the same parties (1991: 54–5).

No doubt personal commitment counts for much in the maintenance of activism. But those 1960s activists who were still active in western Europe or the United States in the 1980s were often embedded in networks of former activists; they kept the faith by keeping in touch. Activists who lacked such networks, whether for ideological or organizational reasons, were less likely to remain active after the end of the decade (Gelb 1987: 281). Moreover, the construction of these postcycle networks often went beyond the activists' original SMO memberships. In studying the Italian environmental movement, Mario Diani found that both networks and identities often transcended the ideological and organizational ties of their initial socialization into the movement (1995).

The fierce politicization at the height of a protest cycle leaves disillusionment behind and produces defection from active involvement among many members of a protest generation. But this is logical, since most were never deeply involved in the movements of the period. Others, embittered by the failures of activism, spin off into utopianism or violence – like the militants who ended up in the Weather Underground in the United States or in the Red Brigades in Italy (della Porta 1995: ch. 6). But a high proportion of activists from the 1960s emerged empowered, transformed, and connected to informal networks of other activists. A kind of movement "social capital" was the most durable outcome of that period of contention (Diani 1997). As Debra Minkoff writes,

> National SMOs play a critical role in civil society and the production of social capital by providing an infrastructure for collective action, facilitating the development of mediated collective identities that link otherwise marginalized members of society, and shaping public discourse and debate. (1997: 606)

FAILED EXPLOSIONS AND SUCCESSFUL SPARKS

If policy success is difficult to predict for individual movements and if movement activists often exhaust their energies in the full flush of a cycle, what are the long-term effects of movements? Can their ultimate impact be predicted by the intensity of their emergence, or is it through incremental growth and generational reproduction that movements achieve long-term success? To illustrate this opposition, I compare two different movements. The first, the French student movement of 1968, was the wonder of the Western world when it broke out and – together with its labor allies – paralyzed the Fifth Republic. The second, the

American women's movement, was slow-starting, appeared only as an offshoot of the civil rights movement, and worked, for the most part, within the institutions of American politics.

FRENCH STUDENTS[9]

May 1968 in France is a near laboratory case for studying the political impact of a major wave of protest. As two of its most acute observers argue,

> despite the retreat of the movement and its rejection in the ballot box, the Events were the carriers of potentialities that, by one means or another, durably mortgaged the French political scene in a way that had to be immediately faced. (Capdevielle and Mouriaux 1988: 219, author's translation)

The protest wave of May 1968 was followed by a major educational reform, the Orientation Law for Higher Education, which attacked the sclerotic structures of higher education against which the students of May had first struck out. But as the initiative shifted from the students to reformers to educational interest groups and then to the conservative political class, the reform was scaled down and ultimately emasculated. A brief review of how this happened will silhouette how opportunities narrow and reforms are reshaped as disruption collapses and elites reconstitute their position after a cycle of contention.

In the early spring of 1968, left-wing students in the newly created University of Nanterre demonstrated on a variety of grounds against arbitrary administrative authority as well as against more global targets. Their demonstration in the courtyard of the Sorbonne in early May was met by a combination of police thuggery and governmental uncertainty. When a group of students was roughly hauled off in police vans, middle-class Parisians were incensed. And when news of the outrage was diffused to other areas of the country, every university in the country and a number of secondary schools were shut down.

Not only that: as the movement spread, to the natural self-intoxication of the students was added their leaders' desire to broaden their appeal to a wider public. As a result, the concrete issues of university governance were displaced by the demand that the system of capitalist domination be replaced and the imagination be released. Surrounded by contestation on so many sides, the authorities were placed on the defensive. When the movement spread to the working class, the government understood that it was facing a potential revolution. Joint action between workers and students was sporadic at best, but their objective coalition gave each part of the movement a force it would not have had on its own.

Resisting the temptation for brutal repression was the first task the government undertook – indeed, 1968 marked a permanent change in the practice of protest policing in France (Bruneteaux 1996; Fillieule 1997). Separating the working class from its student allies and getting the economy started was the second. In a reversal of his neoliberal policies, Prime Minister Pompidou negotiated dramatic wage increases with the unions so as to isolate the students in their university redoubts (Bridgford 1989). Frightening the middle class with the fear of revolution was the final goal, accomplished both by President de Gaulle's overture to the army and by a massive counterdemonstration by his supporters. When the parties of the left were pushed into announcing their readiness to form a government, de Gaulle had the opportunity he needed. The National Assembly was dissolved, the opposition was soundly defeated, and the Gaullists and their allies were returned to power with an overwhelming majority.

In the months following the June 1968 elections, the government, not without opposition, boiled down the jumble of demands for educational change that had erupted in May into a major reform law – the *loi d'orientation*. A new, left-leaning education minister, Edgar Faure, was appointed and given carte blanche to remake higher education around the goals of participation, multidisciplinarity, and the autonomy of the universities.[10] So major a change could not have been introduced into the hidebound structure of French education without the impulse of a major political earthquake.

But was the *loi d'orientation* a "success" for the student movement? Movements do not produce their major effects directly, but through their interaction with more conventional political forces and the elite. The French students had no plan for university reform and, by September, their influence was weakened, both by the satisfaction of working-class wage demands and by the breakdown of their solidarity (Tarrow 1993b). As the center of gravity shifted from the streets to the political arena and the threat of disorder receded, the students' leverage was sharply reduced. Like the "processing" of racial crisis in America (Lipsky and Olson 1976), a major struggle was politically processed into a modest reform.

AMERICAN WOMEN

While students were the early risers in the French cycle of 1968, if there was ever a movement that seemed dependent on the gates of opportunity opened by others, it is the American women's movement. Many of its founders gained their first political exposure in civil rights and in the New Left (Evans 1980: chs. 3–7), while others were the heirs of moderate older women's lobbies (Rupp and Taylor 1987) and of the anti–Vietnam War movement. When the new women's movement appeared on the scene in the mid-1960s, "many observers," writes Anne Costain, regarded it as "a transitory phenomenon, imitating the black civil rights movement, but without that movement's capacity to endure" (1992: 1).

But the women's movement *did* endure, and it prospered into the 1990s as much of the original élan of civil rights – not to mention the antiwar and student movements – was consumed. The signs of the women's movement's growth were both attitudinal, as more and more women declared themselves sympathetic to feminism, and organizational, with membership in major feminist organizations growing to about 250,000 by the early 1980s (Klein 1987). Even during the 1970s, when the American activist culture declined, the women's movement grew stronger, affording women "a vehicle to sustain their activism as well as a community to support a more general feminist lifestyle" (McAdam 1988: 202). The result was a spectacular growth in the number of women elected to office and of laws of interest to women passed by Congress (Costain 1992: 10–11).

The American women's movement never made the dramatic splash of the French students or other confrontational movements of the 1960s. Many of its early advocates were polite middle-class women who worked quietly in conventional politics and interest groups; others were feminist lawyers who carried out their movement work on the sidelines of busy careers; most were not organizationally active at all – or worked in organizations whose primary purposes were labor, civil rights, family issues, or public health. Moreover, the movement's progress was marked by significant defeats: the failure of the equal rights amendment in 1983; the whittling down of choice during the Reagan and Bush administrations; and the Senate's approval of the Clarence Thomas nomination to the Supreme Court in 1990.

But the signs of a dynamic movement were everywhere present in public space. Between 1965 and 1975, there was a tremendous increase in press coverage of both women's events in general (Costain 1992: 9) and of their protest actions in particular (p. 19). With the appearance of a "gender gap" in the electorate, politicians were quick to respond to women's issues (Freeman 1987: 206–8). The movement's apotheosis came with the election of 1992, when a large number of women were elected to Congress while a number of others were appointed to high levels of the Clinton administration. Born in the shadow of civil rights and the New Left, this was a movement that began slowly but grew steadily in strength and importance.

Moreover, if a sign of a movement's vitality is its capacity to "spin off" new "master frames" and other movement-linked organizations, as argued in chapters 7–9, the American women's movement was a shining success. Women, writes Nancy Whittier,

> established organizations, such as rape crisis centers, battered women's shelters, feminist bookstores, and women's studies programs, that aimed both to improve women's lives in the present and to lay the groundwork for more sweeping social transformations in the future. (1995: 1; also see Meyer and Whittier 1994)

What explains the dramatic differences between the success of the American women's movement and the failure of the French students? In terms of all four powers in movement we examined in Part II of this study – repertoires of contention, collective action frames, mobilizing structures, and changes in the balance of political opportunities and constraints – though American women had a slow start, they were far more favored than French students.

First, while the French students in 1968 used a contentious repertoire that was disruptive, theatrical, and potentially violent, recalling for supporters and opponents the most conflictual moments of French history, the American women's movement used a variety of forms of collective action – public and private – that leaned heavily toward the conventional, the discursive, and the symbolic. Although occasional boycotts, civil disobedience, and sit-ins marked high points of the movement, its combination of symbolic and cultural challenges with conventional marches and demonstrations and educational and lobbying activity placed it in the mainstream of American culture. In addition, in the interstices of American family and work groups, feminists acted out the slogan "the personal is political" (Evans 1980: ch. 9).

Second, there were major differences in the two movements' discourses and symbolism. French students employed a symbolic discourse that isolated them from the language of ordinary French citizens. "Power to the imagination!" or "The struggle continues!": these were "hot cognitions" that could engage new supporters and elicit enthusiasm on the barricades but had little resonance among consumers waiting on line for gasoline, workers unable to collect their paychecks, or peasants whose produce rotted on the way to market.

In contrast, an important aspect of the American women's movement and one of its major successes was its attention to signification. "Women" rather than "girls"; "gender" rather than "sex"; "partner" rather than "girlfriend": such changes in common language have become widespread in American popular culture as the result of women's realization that "naming" subjects goes a long way toward changing them. These changes coincided with, and helped to advance, a fundamental change in the role of women in the American economy and marketplace.

Organizational networks are a third area of contrast between the two movements. While both had in common with many contemporary movements a dedication to autonomy, decentralization, and spontaneity, the French student movement spread by instant diffusion and implicit collective identity, but without strong connective structures, and rapidly collapsed as the students went off on vacation. When they returned the next academic year, only the most militant contested the university elections provided for under the Faure plan.

In contrast, the American women's movement developed a broad, varied, and growing connective structure at both the summit and the base, ranging from informal women's collectives at the base to formal national organizations like the National Organization for Women (NOW).[11] A substantial "women's rights" network was already in place when the "new" movement of the 1960s appeared (Rupp and Taylor 1987). The new branch of the movement added an emphasis on informality and personalism that is still evident in the movement's style today and which has helped it to spread into many sectors of American society (Katzenstein 1998).

Fourth, with respect to political opportunities, we saw earlier how the movement of May First gave French educational reformers the political leverage to reform the educational system, and how their initiative was whittled down as the threat of disorder declined. With its reinforced electoral majority and control of the parliamentary agenda, the French government was able to take university reform in hand and guide it to a safe conclusion. But this political opportunity was soon consumed as moderates defected, reformers lost their marginal power, and the conservative majority determined how the reform would be implemented.

Far less based on the threat of disorder than on the promise of realignment, the American women's movement took longer to bear fruit, but eventually emerged as a major factor in American politics. The structure of the American party system – and especially of the Democratic Party – was crucial to its strategy and its success (Costain, 1992; Freeman 1987). This factor has given women a weight that they lack in any French party, making the Democratic platform a sounding board for feminist concerns. "We have gotten a lot of mileage out of this gender gap," said one lobbyist for a women's organization; "Hell, we don't want to close it . . . We want to widen it" (quoted in Costain and Costain 1987: 206).

CONCLUSIONS [12]

In his evocative article, Aristide Zolberg (1972) concluded of "moments of madness" that they bring about significant transformations in these three ways: first, through a "torrent of words" that involves an intensive learning experience whereby new ideas, formulated initially in coteries, sects, and the like, emerge as widely shared beliefs among much larger publics; second, in new networks of relationships, which are rapidly constituted during periods of intense activity; and, third, from the point of view of policy, the irreversible goals at the peak of the cycle, which are often institutionalized (p. 206). Each of these themes implies an indirect and a mediated – rather than a direct and immediate – effect of cycles of contention on political culture. This is why we need to look well past the end of cycles of contention to observe their effects, as we saw in the case of the American women's movement.

Let us turn to the first of Zolberg's hypothesized changes, the appearance of new beliefs among a broader public. Just as new ideas filter down from their originators to those who "vulgarize" and domesticate them, new forms of collective action invented in the enthusiasm of the peak of the cycle become modular. It is not simply that the same people continue to use the same forms of action; as their advantages become known and they are learned throughout society, they become conventional forms of activity for others to use – even for some who do not share their originators' goals or preferences.

Second, just as networks form at the peak of a cycle and diffuse new ideas and tactics to others, they help to maintain movements during periods of inertia and reaction. What Doug McAdam found with his former Freedom Summer participants was also true of the Czech signers of Charter '77 who emerged in 1989 at the heart of the movement to overthrow communism. To the extent that former activists remain embedded in such a political community, as McAdam concludes, "they are likely to feel some pressure to be active and also to feel more optimistic about the effectiveness of their activism" (1988: 218).

"Movements," Zolberg notes at the end of his article, "do not collapse the distance between the present and the future," as enthusiasts would like. But they sometimes "drastically shorten the distance, and in that sense they are successful miracles" (1972: 206). Merely placing of a new issue on the agenda in an expressive and a challenging way – at least in liberal democratic states – enables coalitions to form around them and for these issues to become aligned within general cultural frames. But this does not happen directly or even in a linear fashion. In fact, as their ideas are vulgarized and domesticated, the early risers in a protest cycle may disappear from the scene. But a portion of their message is distilled into "common sense" of public or private culture while the rest is ignored or discarded.

The effects of cycles of contention are indirect and to a large extent unpredictable. They work through capillary processes beneath the surface of politics, connecting the utopian dreams, the intoxicating solidarities, and the enthusiastic rhetoric of the cycle's peak to the glacial pace of social change. Few people dare to break the crust of convention. When they do, they create opportunities and provide models of thought and action for others who seek more modest goals in more institutionalized ways and are more effective at advancing them. What remains after the enthusiasm of the cycle is a residue of reform.

Such cycles have risen and fallen periodically over the past two centuries. Each time they appear, the world seems to be turning upside down. But just as regularly, the erosion of mobilization, the polarization between sectors of the movement, the splits between institutionalization and violence, and elites' selective use of incentives and repression combine to bring the cycle to an end. At its height, the power of movement is electric and seems irresistible; but it is eroded and integrated through the political process.

Much has changed as the world approaches the twenty-first century. Movements arise more easily and spread more rapidly than they used to do. The violent conflagrations of the decade since 1989 have led some to suspect that the cyclical rhythm of the past has been broken and we are moving into a stage of history in which movements will create continual disorder (Rosenau 1990). Are we living in such a turbulent world today? Or is the dynamic of cycles of contention traced in this and the preceding chapter simply taking new forms? This is the question I turn to in the next and in the final chapter.

TRANSNATIONAL
CONTENTION

On February 27, 1997, Louis Schweitzer, president of the ailing French auto firm Renault, announced the imminent closure of the company's plant in Vilvoorde, Belgium (*Le Soir*, February 28, 1997).[1] The first angry reaction to Renault's announcement came from Belgian prime minister, Jean-Luc Dehaene, and gave rise to accusations in the Flemish press of French "chauvinism" (*Le Monde*, March 5, 1997). Belgian ire rose when it became clear that the French government had been apprised of Renault's plan at least six weeks prior to its announcement and that the firm was hoping to use European Union (EU) structural funds to expand its plant in Valladolid, Spain, just as it closed Vilvoorde (*Le Monde*, March 6 and 8, 1997). The European Parliament expressed outrage at what some of its members called an "Anglo-Saxon" restructuring; even normally deadpan Commission President Jacques Santer called the decision "a serious blow to European confidence," urging the automaker's Belgian workers to sue the company for violating European labor law (*International Herald Tribune*, March 10, 1997). The unions promptly took the firm to court, both in Belgium and, for good measure, in France.

But if Belgian and EU officials were ruffled by Renault's move, that was nothing compared with the reactions of Vilvoorde's workers. Almost immediately following the announcement of the closure, they occupied the plant, "kidnapped" a large number of cars due for shipment, and began a series of public protests that would make Vilvoorde synonymous with a new term in the European political lexicon – "the Eurostrike."[2] These actions quickly crossed the border, bringing a Vilvoorde "commando" into France and French Renault workers into Belgium to demonstrate alongside their Belgian colleagues.[3] When the Belgian unions organized a mass demonstration in Brussels, they were joined by leaders of the French left and a large delegation of French Renault workers. As Schweitzer was hung in effigy and a giant wickerwork figure carried by the demonstrators made nazi salutes, Belgium's Christian Democratic union leader, Willy Peirens, told the crowd: "This is a signal of anger and indignation; a signal of solidarity against brutality" (Reuter's, March 17, 1997).

The joint pressure on the French government from Belgian politicians, the EU, and the French and Belgian demonstrators was too much for French Prime Minister Juppé; on March 20, he appeared on television to announce that 800,000 francs per worker would be disbursed for the measures of reconversion and accompaniment to the plant's closure (Le Monde, March 26, 1997).[4] By July, with a new Socialist government in place in France and both French and Belgian courts finding in their favor, the workers agreed to the compensation package Renault was offering (Le Monde, April 6–7, 1997). But there was no joy in Vilvoorde; as one poster on the day the workers voted to accept the plant closing put it: "In America, they have Clinton, Johnny Cash, and Stevie Wonder; in Belgium, we have Dehaene, but neither cash nor wonder" (L'Humanité, June 22, 1997).

For students of social movements, episodes like the "Eurostrike" raise important questions. Alongside the familiar artifacts of social movement theory were three new aspects: first, the conflict pitted the private citizens of one country against a firm based in another; second, there was cooperation across boundaries between national social actors with a common interest; and, third, a supranational institution and European law were used to advance their claims.

But was the episode a transnational social movement? Or even the start of one? The Belgian workers made common cause with their counterparts in France, using international law and institutions to do so; but was their protest – in the definition employed in this study – *a collective challenge, based on common purposes and social solidarities, in sustained interaction with elites, opponents, and authorities?* Or was it rather a brief episode of political *exchange* between French and Belgian workers and Belgian and EU officials upset by the "American" tactics used by the French firm (Pizzorno 1978)? Was this a stage in a growing spiral of transnational contention or merely an incident in the normal conflict between capital and labor that happened to cross national lines?

What can we learn from such episodes about the growth of transnational movements in parts of the world that are not – like western Europe – regulated by a network of supranational institutions? And can we apply what we have learned in this study to forms of transnational contention that are not precisely social movements (Keck and Sikkink 1998b)? "Western analysts," writes John McCarthy, "increasingly employ a common set of conceptual tools in making sense of the emergence and trajectories of social movements"; can we use these concepts to understand challengers in other parts of the world that "seek to influence transnational as well as national and sub-national authorities" (1997: 243)? These are the questions I raise in this chapter.

GLOBALIZATION AND TRANSNATIONAL SOCIAL MOVEMENTS

In northern Quebec, South America, and rural India, campaigns to stop dam construction have been mounted by coalitions of indigenous groups and non-governmental organizations from abroad; on the Mexican – United States border, Mexican and American environmental and workers' rights groups cooperate in the framework of the North American Free Trade Agreement (NAFTA); in eastern Europe before 1989, the Helsinki accords provided an international framework within which dissident groups organized; on the high seas, Greenpeace and other ecological groups oppose firms and governments that pollute the environment. However disparate, such episodes bring a transnational dimension to contentious politics.

Scholars have been quick to pick up on these events, often making generalizations based on a few spectacular – but perhaps unrepresentative – episodes. Some conclude that transnational collective action poses a challenge to the sovereignty of the national state (Cerny 1995), while others talk only of "fading states" (Rudolf 1997); some wonder if such movements are steps in the creation of a global civil society (Wapner 1995, 1996), while others write of "a plurality of transnational spaces" (Rudolf 1997: 2); some see globalization "disenfranchising societies" (Castells 1997), while others already speak of "world society" (Meyer, Boli, Thomas, & Ramirez 1996). As one scholar confidently puts it,

> Movements are changing from fairly coherent national organizations into transnational networks, with highly fragmented and specialized nodes composed of organizations and less organized mobilizations, all of which are linked through new technologies of communication. (Garner 1994: 431)

Transnational politics is of great importance at the turn of the new century (Risse 1995). But our problem in this chapter is not to recognize or celebrate it, but to sort out the short-term and ephemeral connections across borders from the lasting and profound ones and to assess the opportunities and constraints on the formation of transnational social movements. Only then can we begin to understand their implications for the future of contentious politics.

Three hypotheses surround the general thesis of transnational contention. The first is that the world economy is rapidly globalizing along with its attendant system of communications; the second that these changes open up enhanced possibilities for transnational collective action; and the third that – knit together by international institutions and transnational social movements – something resembling a transnational civil society is developing. Let us review these themes before turning to the processes of transnational contention that can be perceived today.

THE SOURCES OF GLOBALIZATION

In the most popular version of the theory of transnational social movements, sometime around the end of World War II, and assisted by the liberalization of international trade and the appearance of a new economic hegemon, a global economy began to develop. Its most basic aspect, writes Kevin Robins, was a shift to a world "in which all aspects of the economy – raw materials, labour information and transportation, finance, distribution, marketing – are integrated or interdependent on a global scale" (1995: 345).

Like that of many students of globalization, Robins's evocation of a global economy is stronger on declaration than demonstration. When Robert Wade carried out a careful statistical analysis of past and present international investment, trade, and finance, he concluded that "the world economy is more international than global":

> In the bigger national economies, more than 80 percent of production is for domestic consumption and more than 80 percent of investment by domestic investors. Companies are rooted in national home bases with national regulatory regimes. (1996: 61)

Where Robins has hit on a truly new factor in the world economy today is in pointing out that – in contrast to past periods of enhanced international exchange – economic changes occur "on an almost instantaneous basis" (1995: 345). This takes us to the second element of the globalization thesis: the appearance of public communication structures that weave core and periphery of the world system closer together. This growth is accelerated by decentralized and private communications technologies, which provide individuals and groups with independent means of communication, like fax machines, electronic mail, and camcorders (Ganley 1992).

The expansion of worldwide markets and global communications brings citizens of the north and west and those of the east and south closer together, making the former more cosmopolitan and the latter more aware of their inequality. The most spectacular expression of this cognitive and physical integration is immigration from the east and south to the west and north, with the consequence that global cities have developed into microcosms "in which to observe the growing dualism between the world's rich and poor and the encounter of global cultures" (Castells 1994; Robins 1995: 345). But it has also made it possible for Western environmentalists and human rights and women's rights advocates to move in the opposite direction: speaking the same language and working toward the same goals as their counterparts in the Third World. In support of this trend, Jackie Smith points out that a slowly increasing proportion of transnational organizations now have their offices outside the industrial democracies (Smith 1997: 49).

These structural changes have a cultural concomitant: that we live in a culturally more unified universe, one in which young people dress similarly, listen to the same music, and attend school systems built on the same models (Meyer et al. 1992). One result may be to "destroy the cultural isolation in which misunderstanding grows"; but another is to intensify perceptions of difference that "increase social antagonisms and promote social fragmentation" (O'Neil 1993: 68). A third is to create perceived chains of economic and social impact between different parts of the globe, while a fourth is the mutual discovery of similar problems on the part of indigenous groups in formerly isolated areas (Brysk 1994; Yashar 1996). Groups as diverse as Andean Indians and northern European Lapps are now in contact across national borders.

There is an institutional concomitant to increased economic and communication flows. Since World War II, a dense network of international institutions, regimes, and intergovernmental and transnational contacts has knit together different parts of the world (Meyer et al. 1997). Consider the international human rights regime with Thomas Risse and Kathryn Sikkink:

> Since World War II human rights have been increasingly regulated and specified in international regimes. The evolution of human rights regimes concentrates on the United Nations system complemented by regional arrangements. (1997)

Alongside this formal regime is an informal "liberal club" of nations that identify themselves and are identified as a category of states from which others are excluded (p. 4). These international institutions, regimes, and "clubs" are the armature around which transnational relations have grown. This takes us to the second part of the thesis – transnational collective action.

TRANSNATIONAL COLLECTIVE ACTION

In his summary of the rapidly burgeoning literature on globalization, Robins claimed only that it erodes the boundaries of national *economies*; but others have seen it eroding the power of the national state. In the age of globalization, the thesis continues, not only are images of contentious politics transmitted rapidly from country to country, triggering diffusion and imitation; so are people and their claims and conflicts. Cheap airline tickets and porous national boundaries make it possible for movement missionaries and their local allies to diffuse movements as diverse as Muslim fundamentalism and Serbian nationalism around the world (Kane 1997). Using fax machines, electronic mail, the collection of "charitable contributions" from well-meaning sympathizers, moving funds, arms, and terrorists across borders with ease, "diaspora nationalists" advance their causes in their home countries without moving from their comfortable Western havens (Anderson 1992).

In part in response to global economic trends, international organizations have proliferated in the twentieth century and especially since World War II. Many, like the World Bank, have become targets for social protest (Kowaleski 1989; Walton 1989), while others, like the United Nations and the European

Union, deliberately encourage transnational nongovernmental groups with subsidies, meetings, and opportunities for consultation. For example, the European Union's Directorate for the Environment, Nuclear Safety and Civil Protection subsidizes the European Environmental Bureau, an umbrella organization representing nearly all relevant environmental associations in the countries of the EU (Rucht 1997: 202, 206).

Where international organizations can make decisions that are binding – or even semibinding – on member states, they offer domestic challengers institutional opportunities to transcend their national arenas for consultation, collective action, and contestation at an international level (Keck 1995). Some of these efforts are bilateral and vertical: that is, between a particular domestic group and a particular international organization. But, as we have seen in Chapter 6, challengers create opportunities for other challengers; over the past decades, a host of transnational nongovernmental organizations (TNGOs) have clustered around each major international institution (J. Smith 1994, 1997). Like the national state in the eighteenth and nineteenth centuries, international organizations and institutions provide opportunities for collective action to a host of social actors. This takes us to what I call "the strong thesis" of transnational social movements.

THE STRONG TRANSNATIONAL THESIS

The strong thesis of transnational social movements, which I have aggregated from a number of sources, grows out of these observations. Its proponents make the following five claims.

First, in the age of global television, whirring fax machines, and electronic mail, the national political opportunity structures that used to be needed to mount collective action may be giving way to transnational ones (Pagnucco and Atwood 1994: 411).

Second, the national state may be losing its capacity to constrain and structure collective action. In part, this is because of the declining capacity of governments to disguise what is going on abroad from their own citizens. But, in part, it is because the integration of the international economy weakens states' capacity to cope with global economic trends (Badie 1997; Tilly 1991: 1).

Third, as the state's capacity to control global economic forces declines, individuals and groups have gained access to new kinds of resources to mount collective action across borders (Rosenau 1990), as we saw in the Vilvoorde case. These are not different in kind from the types of resources analyzed by resource mobilization theorists in domestic politics (Keck and Sikkink 1998b; McCarthy 1997), but they include travel abroad, communication with like-minded others across national boundaries, and growing expertise at using transnational communication and international institutions.

Fourth, as economies globalize, cultures universalize, and institutions proliferate, "principled ideas" are increasingly adopted as international norms (Finnemore 1996) and then become socialized into domestic understandings (Price 1997; Risse and Sikkink 1997).

Finally, growing out of a global economy and its attendant communications revolution, wound around the latticework of international organizations and institutions, drawing on the inequalities and abuses created by economic globalization and fortified by international norms, a web of new transnational organizations and movements is being formed.

Although the parameters she uses to identify transnational social movements (TSMOs) are broader than ours are (see subsequent discussion), Jackie Smith's compendium of TSMOs illustrates the tremendous growth in these organizations.[5] Smith found that "the transnational social movement sector is quite large and diverse and that it has grown dramatically in recent years – from just over 300 in 1983 to about 600 in 1993" (1997: 47). "Sixty-five percent of all TSMOs active in 1993," she writes, "were formed after 1970, and their average age declined over the two decades from 33 to 25 years" (p. 46). There is a growing potential for contentious politics beyond the borders of national states as the world enters the twenty-first century. But how new is this new phenomenon? And how contentious is it likely to be?

WHAT HISTORY TEACHES

Before proposing a thesis that is not quite as strong as the one previously sketched – but which seems to fit better with many emerging trends in the world today – it is important to provide some historical background to the claim that it is new technologies and new forms of communication that are creating a world of transnational movements. In the course of this study – and long before the advent of the airplane, the fax machine, and electronic media – we have encountered the diffusion of a number of movements across national boundaries.

For example, as Susanne Rudolf reminds us, the fluidity of religion across political boundaries is very old, both from West to East and from East to West (1997: 2). The most dramatic example was perhaps the transfer of organized Catholicism to Latin America on the swords of Spanish and Portuguese colonialism. In the eighteenth century, there was a close connection between the American Revolution, the Dutch Patriot movement, and the French Revolution (Markoff 1996). Soon after, a relationship developed among antislavery advocates in Britain, the United States, and western Europe. The first modern slave rebellion – that of Haiti – was a direct response to the French Revolution (Drescher 1987: ch. 2).

In the nineteenth century, as we saw in the case of the 1848 revolutions, every major revolution and many minor ones had reverberations in other countries. By the 1880s the loose ties that had linked the working-class movement across Europe crystallized into the Second International, whose parties built similar organizations and at least claimed to be working toward the same international goal. European strike waves and protest cycles responded to broad international trends too (Mikkelson 1996). Transnational advocates of antislavery, nationalism, and women's emancipation were able to win converts and make modest progress against traditional or colonial governments (Hanagan 1998; Keck and Sikkink 1998a: ch.2).

History also teaches that transnational contention takes many forms – not all of them easy to catalog as social movements. Although most of the campaigns studied by Margaret Keck and Kathryn Sikkink from the nineteenth century were based on religious belief, some, like the antifemale circumcision campaign in Kenya, involved only missionaries (Keck and Sikkink 1998a: 66–72); others, like the campaign against Chinese foot binding, involved missionaries and secular nationalists (60–6); still others, like antislavery, "built linkages largely on the basis of corresponding religious organizations" (41–51). Of Keck and Sikkink's cases, only women's suffrage involved dedicated international movement organizations (51–8).

Moreover, although the initial impetus for many movements came from the diffusion of advocacy across national boundaries, they often depended on the power of hegemonic states – like the British use of its powerful navy to impede the slave trade – and took root differently in different soils. Where they did so successfully, they produced increasingly differentiated national movements, parties, and unions. As Keck and Sikkink observe, "Advocacy campaigns take place in organizational contexts; not only must their ideas resonate and create allies, their organizations must also overcome opposition" (1998a: 74).

Consider the differences that grew up within the national parties of the Second International: under a common umbrella of internationalism, each was invested in different national cultures – cultures that became active forces for division when, in 1914, almost every socialist party in Europe supported its national government's "capitalist war." As John McCarthy points out, "national political opportunity structures affect the variable likelihood of transnational activism" (1997: 256).

History also casts a skeptical eye on the assumption that international norms can be socialized into domestic norms without concrete mechanisms to effect such transformations. In the more abstract formulations, civil society "generates" international norms, which somehow shape and redefine state interests (Price 1997). But although new definitions of interest and identity are constantly being proposed by concrete actors, history provides few that are transformed into international norms and even fewer that are successfully socialized into domestic societies without the exercise of agency. Consider the spread of antislavery around the world; it had as much to do with the British navy protecting the economies of former British slave colonies as it did with the "norm" of human rights (Markoff 1996: ch. 2). As Margaret Keck puts it, there are "limits to social construction" (1995: 420–1).

In summary, history not only teaches that transnational contention is nothing new under the sun; it shows that it takes a number of forms and integrates differently within domestic societies; and that it requires special conjunctures of incentives and opportunities to be mounted and transmit new norms and identities. Before concluding that the world is fast becoming a global civil society, we should examine these forms and levels of integration and ask where they are leading and which ones are likely to produce new norms and identities.

A TYPOLOGY OF TRANSNATIONAL CONTENTION

Two empirical observations drawn from these brief historical examples can help us to unravel the complex strands in transnational politics in the world today. First, many of the phenomena that must have seemed structurally transnational at the time turned out to be part of processes that ended when political conditions changed. Second, many of the examples of transnational contention lacked solid bases in domestic social networks. Turned into analytical dimensions and inter-sected, these two observations help us to differentiate and describe the broad range of transnational contention that we see in the world today. This intersection is represented graphically in the typology in Figure 11.1. In what follows, I define each of these forms, provide a few examples from the literature on both social movements and transnational politics, and then speculate briefly about their major properties and dynamics.

TRANSNATIONAL SOCIAL MOVEMENTS

By transnational social movements, I intend *sustained contentious interactions with opponents – national or nonnational – by connected networks of challengers organized across national boundaries.* The targets of transnational movements can change from time to time; they may be either international or national, private or public. What is important in our definition is that the challengers themselves be both rooted in domestic social networks and connected to one another more than episodically through common ways of seeing the world, or through informal or organizational ties, and that their challenges be contentious in deed as well as in word. Such a definition is tight enough to exclude some kinds of transnational interactions but broad enough to include those which – in terms of the typology in Figure 11.1 – combine duration in time and integration within the domestic structures of more than one society.

Our definition is restrictive, but not so restrictive that it would be impossible to find real-world phenomena that match it. For example, Greenpeace is a trans-national movement organization with the properties proposed in the foregoing definition. It claims millions of members in a number of countries, connected in

TIME FRAME	INTEGRATION IN DOMESTIC SOCIAL NETWORKS	
	Nonintegrated	Integrated
Temporary	Diffusion	Political Exchange
Sustained	Transnational Issue Networks	Transnational Social Movements

Figure 11.1. A Typology of Transnational Collective Action

a hierarchical way by a transnational organization; its members share a common world view; and it engages in confrontational actions with both governments and private firms that pollute or threaten to pollute the environment (Wapner 1995, 1996). Greenpeace has also developed an action repertoire that allows it to oppose projects and opponents outside national boundaries – for example, in its opposition to French nuclear testing in the Pacific or against Shell Oil's plan to sink an oil platform in the North Sea, or against the overkill of ocean stocks by French and British trawlers (Imig and Tarrow 1996).

The European and American peace movement of the 1980s was a second transnational movement, albeit one that lacked a single hierarchical organization (Rochon 1988). Islamic fundamentalism is a third, even if it appears to take different forms in different parts of the world, from the Afghanistani Taliban to Iranian nationalism to the Algerian Islamic Salvation Front (Eickelman 1997; Kane 1997). The former movement was able to mobilize hundreds of thousands of demonstrators against nuclear missiles in the early 1980s, while the latter has seriously challenged or undermined numerous governments since the Iranian Revolution in 1979.[6]

The conditions necessary to produce a sustained social movement that is, at once, integrated within several societies, unified in its goals and organization, and capable of mounting contention against a variety of targets are hard to fulfill. Greenpeace grew out of a congeries of domestic movements that were similarly motivated and had a few highly visible targets whose activities crossed national boundaries. The peace movement of the 1980s was a response to an international issue that combined threat and opportunity – the policies of an American president who appeared to be threatening the planet with his administration's arms buildup. And Islamic fundamentalism grew up within one of the oldest transnational institutions in the world, with autonomous religious schools, mosques, and sects all over the world in which to root itself. These conditions are not reproduced each time a transnational interaction occurs among nongovernmental actors and, as Margaret Keck observes, "the international attention span is, after all, short" (1995: 421). Far more common are the conditions that permit the rapid cross-border diffusion of domestic contention.

CROSS-BORDER DIFFUSION

By cross-border diffusion, I mean the communication of movement ideas, forms of organization, or challenges to similar targets from one center of contention to another. Such interaction can lead to strong movements – but not necessarily to movements with strong connective tissue in more than one society. Since it is uncontrolled by strong connective tissue across boundaries, diffusion leaves great scope for domestic opportunities and constraints to affect how challenges are transformed in their new settings (Ernst 1997). Diffusion is a transnational phenomenon that is both temporary and unrooted as such in domestic social networks.

Diffusion is perhaps the oldest form of transnational politics we know of. We saw it first in the Reformation, when Calvinist "saints," Puritan immigrants, and exiled Catholic priests carried religious ideas and contentious practices from one country to another. We saw it again in the diffusion of the ideas of the American and French revolutions – although the movement of soldiers from Paris to the rest of Europe was one important vehicle for diffusion. By the nineteenth century social movements were less dependent on the movement of arms. We saw in Chapter 9 how particular forms of collective action, like the barricade and the mass demonstration, were adopted in virtually every country touched by the 1848 revolutions. By the second half of the century, eastern and southern European immigrants were building workers' movements in the New World, from the lower east side of Manhattan to Chile and Argentina.[7] But once established, each national movement that struck indigenous roots and encountered local opportunity structures became largely independent of the others.

Contemporary collective action is diffused more rapidly than these nineteenth-century movements and is assisted in its diffusion both by the internationalization of the world economy and by mass communications. Consider the tactics linking the series of "fishing wars" that spread from the Bay of Biscay to the Grand Banks to the offshore North American salmon fisheries. In 1994, Spanish tuna fishermen sequestered a French trawler, accusing both British and French fishermen of using illegal nets to bag more than their share of tuna stocks. When the French government responded by taking one of the Spanish ships in tow, the Spaniards blocked the port of Hendaye. It took complicated negotiations among the three states and a decision by the European Union to resolve the dispute (Tarrow 1998a).

Six months later a different group of Spanish fishermen was in the news – this time, taking fish from the Grand Banks that Canadian fishermen thought were rightly theirs. The Canadian navy sequestered a Spanish trawler and towed it into the harbor of St. Johns, to the jeers and thrown tomatoes of the fishing port's citizens (Tarrow 1998a). The Canadian government resolved the issue, but only after the European Union intervened on behalf of the Spaniards. Finally, in 1997, it was Canadian and American sailors who were locked in conflict on the Pacific coast, when over a hundred Canadian salmon boats blocked an American ferry in the port of Prince Rupert in retaliation for the Americans' taking of Canadian salmon from international waters (*New York Times*, July 23, 1997; *Toronto Globe and Mail*, July 18, 1997). Six thousand miles apart, similar issues gave rise to a similar form of action and brought social actors and governments from five countries into international contention.

The diffusion of the tactics of the "fishing wars" was the result of unconnected emulation. But diffusion can also occur at the hands of purposive agents. The spread of nationalism in east central Europe after 1989 was, as Mark Beissinger shows, no automatic transfer of ideas from one country to another but a set of purposive events depending on opportunities, interests, and threats, real and anticipated, advanced by movement entrepreneurs, some of them in power and others seeking power in the vacuum created by the fall of communism (1996).

The eastern European nationalism studied by Beissinger was triggered by international opportunities but created *national* movements. Can *trans*national movements result from diffusion? Claire Ernst's work on French Act-Up suggests it can. She tells of how both emulation and informal contacts in New York led to the creation of an Act-Up branch in Paris, struggling to defend the interests of AIDS victims there (1997). But after showing how closely French activists emulated the tactics and the slogans of their New York friends, Ernst examines how the specifics of French politics affected the outcome of the movement – in particular, the French republican tradition that demands integration in place of difference (pp. 22–3).

TRANSNATIONAL POLITICAL EXCHANGE

By transnational political exchange, I refer to temporary forms of cooperation among essentially national actors that identify a common interest or set of values in a particular political configuration. Like transnational diffusion, political exchange across boundaries generally involves actors from different countries with ideological affinities, each of whom has something to gain from the relationship and offers something to the other. Unlike diffusion, the actors on both sides of the exchange have a stable existence in their respective countries prior to the episode that brings them together, but their interaction is the product of a particular national and international conjuncture.

Needless to say, the terms "gains" and "losses" should not be interpreted narrowly and materially. For example, in the 1980s, a number of northern environmental organizations, based partly on contacts made through anthropologists with experience in the area, formed alliances with the representatives of Brazilian rubber tappers (Keck 1995: 415–16). The original issue had been one of economic gains and losses, due to the hectic land rush in northeastern Brazil in the late 1970s. The environmental core group based in Washington, D.C., linked the tappers' plight to the World Bank's Polonoroeste project in Rondónia and interested the American Congress in the case, giving Brazilian activists the leverage on the Brazilian government to create reserves for the tappers' activities. It was the combination of labor union and church pressure domestically and environmental pressure internationally that tipped the scales in favor of the tappers. As Margaret Keck concludes, "foreign environmentalists and representatives of the rubber tappers' movement in Acre finally met and established a relationship that filled important needs and provided important political resources for all of them" (1995: 415).

These were not permanent arrangements. Although the northern groups involved had strong ideological beliefs in both the environment and the rights of indigenous peoples, the alliances were organized around a specific issue, and when that issue was resolved or became irrelevant, the campaign ended. Because political exchange is issue-based and is not lodged in a permanent organization, it is hardly more stable than the diffusion of collective action across national boundaries. But it can create networks that survive after a particular issue is resolved.

TRANSNATIONAL ADVOCACY NETWORKS

This takes us to the hundreds of nongovernmental associations that link citizens across the world in environmental, human rights, women's, peace, and indigenous peoples' networks. Do they not qualify for inclusion in the concept of "transnational social movements"? My answer is that, although they are the most rapidly growing sector of transnational politics today, we do not advance understanding by assimilating them to social movements. It seems more accurate to classify them, with Margaret Keck and Kathryn Sikkink, as parts of "transnational advocacy networks." To quote Keck and Sikkink, "a transnational advocacy network includes those relevant actors working internationally on an issue, who are bound together by shared values, a common discourse, and dense exchanges of information and services" (1998a: 2). Such networks, they continue, "are most prevalent in issue areas characterized by high value content and informational uncertainty" (p. 2). They involve actors from nongovernmental, governmental, and intergovernmental organizations, and are increasingly present in such issue areas as human rights, women's rights, and the environment (also see Keck and Sikkink 1998b).

How do these networks differ from social movements and why are they often confused with them? Part of the confusion results from two different uses of the term "network": connective structures and the social networks that are the building blocks for social movements and a number of other kinds of contentious politics. In the usage suggested in Chapter 8, advocacy networks are connective structures that cross national boundaries, whereas social networks are the bases for contentious politics within domestic societies. While some scholars are coming to believe that electronic communications are providing groups with the resources to form social networks across wide bands of space (Wellman and Gulia 1998), there is a clear difference between Keck and Sikkink's concept of *advocacy* networks and the interpersonal *social* networks that social movement researchers have detected at the foundation of domestic social movements.[8]

Keck and Sikkink's advocacy networks are primarily communicative in content; they are "distinguishable largely by the centrality of principled ideas or values in motivating their formation"; and "at the core of the relationship [among their components] is information exchange." "They mobilize information strategically so as to gain leverage over much more powerful organizations and governments" (Keck and Sikkink 1995: 1). And, it should be added, they profit from financial support from international agencies and northern governments interested in the norms they try to advance (Risse and Sikkink 1997).

Advocacy networks lack the categorical basis, the sustained interpersonal relations, and the exposure to similar opportunities and constraints that social movement scholars have found in domestic social networks. But they have working for them the enormous increase in the density of transnational communication and in the involvement of northern governments, foundations, and public interest groups in issues of equality, human rights, and the environment in other parts of the world. "Minding other people's business" is becoming an important spur to social and political change in the world today.

NETWORKING FOR CHANGE

Are transnational advocacy networks therefore *un*important, compared with what we know of transnational social movements? Certainly, because of their frequent dependency on foundation funding and the support of northern governments, they lack the drama, the deliberate contentiousness, and the broad goals of such transnational movements as Greenpeace, the 1980s peace movements, and fundamentalist Islam. But although transnational advocacy networks are analytically distinct from social movements, they are a powerful force for change in the world today, and this for at least three reasons. First, many of them are *biographically* and *thematically* in the debt of social movements. Second, given the undemocratic or semiauthoritarian conditions of many parts of the world today, they provide a second-best but a safer alternative to social movements for millions of people. Third, their most important role may be to provide a mechanism for the diffusion of collective action frames to resource-poor domestic actors that can help them construct their own social movements. Each of these arguments could be elaborated at great length and supported with numerous examples. But since Margaret Keck and Kathryn Sikkink have done exactly this in their recent book, *Activists beyond Borders* (1998a), we can content ourselves with brief summaries of their arguments.[9]

MOVEMENT SOURCES OF NETWORK RECRUITMENT

In the fields of human rights, women's rights, and ecology, transnational advocacy networks do not resemble social movements, but recruit supporters whose domestic experience in movements provides skills and models of activism. Such movement activists may join transnational networks through casual contacts with activists like themselves from other countries; through experiences with Western foundations or international organizations; and in part because, as they get older, their willingness to engage in vigorous and possibly dangerous movement actions gives way to a desire for more routine activities.

One such area of activism involves the international conferences that have been held periodically for women activists under the auspices of the United Nations since the mid-1970s. They provide a venue in which personal and foundation contacts are made and ideas and experiences exchanged, and activists may find themselves invited to foreign countries. While continuing to think of themselves as movement activists, many become increasingly involved in such transnational networks, at times losing their contacts with the grass roots, but bringing much needed resources to where they can do the most good.

In western Europe, a similar process of transnational exchange and funding has seen a European environmental network created with the encouragement of the Environmental Directorate of the European Union. Russell Dalton's study of this "green network" demonstrates clearly how important networking at the European level has become for many of its members through membership in the transnational European Environmental Bureau (1994). But such external sources of support and networking also have a negative implication: in tending to attract the more moderate environmental groups, they can deepen the cleavage between them and the more radical ecological movement, stretching the bonds of the "green networks" that give activists their power in domestic politics.

The same danger appears in the women's movement in Third World countries. It appears increasingly divided between (largely urban and well-educated) former militants linked into transnational networks through their ties with foundations, northern governments, and "big sister" organizations in the North, and grass-roots activists struggling against female exploitation, abuse, and legal inequality on the ground. Without strong domestic connective structures, the women's movement of the South risks a split very similar to the gap between its internationally oriented export sector and its domestic economies.

DOMESTIC BLOCKAGES AND TRANSNATIONAL OPPORTUNITIES

"Advocacy networks," write Keck and Sikkink, "have been the most visible in situations where domestic access of claimants is blocked, or where those making claims are too weak politically for their voices to be heard" (1998b). In such cases, international or foreign venues may be the only ones in which claims can be legitimately or safely presented. By shifting venues, activists try to involve new and more sympathetic actors to their cause, hoping in this way to tilt the domestic power balance that has been skewed against them in their favor. This is what Keck and Sikkink mean by what they call "the boomerang effect" (1998a: 12–13): "attempting to produce it is one of the most common strategies of advocacy networks."

Keck and Sikkink use the human rights and indigenous rights networks activities in Latin America to illustrate the strategy of venue shopping (1998a: 18). They argue that, although stable domestic structures help to determine the outcome of transnational politics (Risse and Schmitz 1995), domestic structures do not tell enough of the story. Like the domestic movements we have encountered in many parts of this book, it is more often "purely conjunctural, and sometimes even accidental aspects of political opportunity for which transnational networkers . . . watch ceaselessly" (Keck and Sikkink 1998b).

NETWORK SOURCES OF DOMESTIC MOVEMENTS

So much of the attention of scholars of transnational contention has been taken up with the image of a global civil society that a crucial implication of transnational advocacy is often forgotten – the socialization of new movements within national states (McAdam 1998; Risse and Sikkink 1997). We saw in Chapter 7 how building new collective action frames is an essential part of movements' work; in this respect, transnational advocacy networks resemble movements in their attempts to both place new issues on the agenda and make them resonant with indigenous cultural understandings (Keck and Sikkink 1998b). But there is a special problem in doing so: "unlike domestic movements," observe Keck and Sikkink, "different parts of advocacy networks need to appeal to belief systems, lifeworlds, and stories, myths and folk tales in many different countries and cultures."

Two dangers result: first, the search for transnational common denominators that will resonate at some level with many cultures and traditions; second, following a variety of issues that take root in particular places, which can produce ideological divergence within the same transnational network, as activists adapt them to "their" cultures.

A good example of the former is the attempt to reproduce the success of such movements as the Brazilian rubber tappers in places, such as Sarawak, where the same conditions do not obtain. "Although the stories that make social problems resonate in the experience of people far from their situation can legitimately be said to have a life of their own," writes Margaret Keck, the tappers of Northeastern Brazil had a strong tradition of labor organization, the support of domestic church and labor organizations, and the particular political opportunity of a democratizing government (Keck 1995: 420–1).

On the other hand, with no overarching themes or organization, transnational networks can divide along ideological or political lines. This was clearly the case for the 1980s peace movements in western Europe and the United States, the former calling for complete nuclear disarmament and the latter for no more than a "nuclear freeze" (Meyer 1990). It is no wonder that transnational movement organizations like Greenpeace maintain rigid control over the kinds of issues their militants become involved in.

In summary, the effects of transnational activism within domestic politics may be their most important function. Transnational advocacy networks can help resource-poor actors construct new *domestic* movements out of combinations of indigenous and imported materials. If nothing else, they can help to create "imagined commonalities" which provide otherwise isolated activists with the impression that they are part of broader, more cosmopolitan movements.

Skeptics may point out that the creation of such imagined commonalities is nothing new. After all, what else did Marx and Engels mean by the phrase "workers of the world, unite"? No doubt thousands of working-class militants struggled toward an imaginary goal because they were convinced that unseen hundreds of thousands like themselves were working toward the same goal around the world. What seems to be qualitatively new is that, unlike the international working-class movement of the past, transnational advocacy networks are not locked teleologically into a fixed social movement; their geographic mobility, loose organizational models, and access to communications provide the capacity to shift their campaigns and resources to venues in which they have the strongest chance to succeed; and they can draw upon the elements of common cultural framing that economic globalization and the communications revolution have brought to many corners of the world.

If this hypothesis is correct, rather than focusing on the abstraction of a global civil society and regarding every incident of transnational activism as evidence of its coming, we will learn more by seeing transnational networks as external actors providing resources and opportunities for domestic movements in formation. These movements may identify themselves ideologically – and financially – with their transnational collaborators; but unless we focus empirically on what happens within national political struggles, we may miss the true significance of transnational contention.

For example, when Doug Imig and the author began to investigate collective action surrounding the decisions of the European Union, our assumption was that a neat dividing line would separate national from transnational contention, with the latter taking the cross-border forms illustrated in the conflict that introduced this chapter (1996). But even a brief exposure to a large population of cases of European collective action showed that social actors aggrieved by European decisions are most likely to turn to the institutions with which they have the most familiarity, and which implement EU decisions – their own national states. Rather than the transnationalization of contention, Europeans may be creating a Europeanization *within* domestic conflict structures (Imig and Tarrow 1997).

IS THERE A TRANSNATIONAL DYNAMIC?

The next research task in plotting the progress and the process of transnational contention is to look more closely at the *kinds* of linkages that are developing across national boundaries. Are they cumulative and dynamic or distinct and differentiating? And do they construct the most durable new realities at the transnational or at the domestic levels?

Consider, first, the spread of indigenous rights campaigns in Latin America and elsewhere over the past decade or so. Assisted by transnational advocacy networks and drawing on ecological activism, the emergence of Indian organizations in Ecuador, Bolivia, Colombia, Guatemala, and Mexico at roughly the same time may relate to a particular political moment – what Deborah Yashar calls "the twin emergence of delegative democracies and neo-liberal reforms" (1996: 87). If Yashar is right, then the co-occurrence of indigenous rights movements in so many countries at the same time is not due to anything so grand or world-systemic as "globalization" and may subside with the next phase of Latin American political struggle.

Next, consider the expanding web of e-mail networks that are traversing the world today, and which excite the attention of those with easy access to computers. They have an obvious capacity to reduce transaction costs and transmit information across national lines, as could be seen in their role in diffusing information about the dramatic Chiapas rebellion in Mexico around the world. They put those with access to computers into contact with others like themselves rapidly and with a sense of participation lacking in less personal forms of communication (Bob 1997). But do such contacts promise the same crystallization of collective trust as, say, the lived experience of mounting a barricade in Parisian neighborhoods studied by Roger Gould (1995) or Mark Traugott (1995)? Or the creation of cross-organizational collective identities woven out of the coalitional campaigns of the Italian environmental organizations studied by Mario Diani (1995)? As anyone who has caught the internet virus can attest, virtual activism may serve as a *substitute* – and not as a spur – to activism in the real world.

On the other hand, the trends that some have seen creating a world of transnational movements are only in their infancy and may be cumulative. As in the past, some forms of transnational exchange and diffusion may ultimately produce true transnational movements, but – as was more often true in the past – these processes may also generate separate national movements or dissipate in the face of indifference or repression. So I close this chapter not with a conclusion, but with five questions that we will need to confront about the dynamics of transnational contention.

First, is the new technology of global communication changing the forms of the diffusion of collective challenges or only the speed of their transmission? Before concluding that the world is entering an unprecedented age of global movements, we will need to follow some of the recent campaigns that have been assisted by electronic communication to find out whether it increases the movement's power or merely changes how it frames its message.

Second, can integrated social movements span continents in the absence of an integrated interpersonal community at both ends of the transnational chain? And, to question an even stronger claim, can such transnational communities be *created* with resources borrowed from abroad? Those who are convinced of the strong thesis will need to show that impersonal cyberspace networks or cheap air travel not only stimulate new national movements but can also maintain the transnational tie as part of their underlying connective structures. Evidence like that of Margaret Keck's about the rubber tapper's movement underscores the advantages of organization and opportunity that preceded their alliance with transnational activists (1995: 420).

Third, will the new forms of transnational exchange lead to benevolent forms of "people's power," as writers like O'Neil seem to think (1993: ch. 4)? Or will they lead to the violent forms that Anderson and others have seen in the potential of "long distance nationalism" (1992)? The most powerful global movement of the early 1990s was not made up of Western environmentalists or human rights activists linked benevolently to indigenous people's movements, but radical Islamic fundamentalists who slit the throats of folk singers and beat up women who dare to go unveiled.

Fourth, is there a cumulative movement from the two temporary forms of transnational politics sketched here – diffusion and political exchange – to the two stronger ones, and particularly toward true transnational movements? Although it might seem logical that transnational advocacy networks will evolve into unified transnational movements, they are actually seen as alternatives for many activists who come out of the risky world of domestic movements, and see transnational activism as an alternative to mobilization.

Finally, what of the role of the national state in all of this? Modern states developed in a strategic dialogue with social movements, ceding to them the autonomy and opportunity to organize when they had to and reclaiming that territory whenever these movements faded or became too dangerous. Why would states be any more supine today when faced by transnational diffusion, exchange, advocacy networks, or even social movements than they were against domestic movements in the late nineteenth or early twentieth centuries?

Some states play a role transnationally today that they seldom could in the past: intervening peacefully and publicly on behalf of domestic movements or groups in other countries whose claims are brought to their attention by groups in their own countries. For understandable reasons, transnational groups claim credit for such intervention – and often play a key role in publicizing the claims of their allies to governments in other countries. Trying to understand this relationship without reference to state power is just as deceptive, in its way, as the attempt to understand international politics as a world made up only of states.

Many states are evolving transnational strategies and creating transnational organizations responsive to their interests. States encourage some movements – like the European environmental movement – to take their claims to transnational institutions like the European Union, while inhibiting these institutions from dealing with others, such as the less welcome antinuclear movement. In the mid-nineteenth century, states like Austria, Russia, and Britain intervened in contentious episodes with cannon fire and bayonets; in the late twentieth century, states make more than war; they make transnational organizations and institutions to combat and pacify social movements. If this is the case, then both the national state and the national social movement will be with us for a long time to come.

CONCLUSION:
THE FUTURE OF
SOCIAL MOVEMENTS

In 1789, as word of France's revolution reached England, abolitionist Thomas Clarkson crossed the Channel to urge his French colleagues to join his country's antislavery movement. Clarkson took the same route again in 1814, following a second wave of British agitation. But "twice," writes the leading American student of antislavery, "he failed utterly" (Drescher 1994).

Two hundred years later, as the French were commemorating the revolution that brought Clarkson to Paris,[1] a new wave of revolution swept over the Communist world. Diffused by word of mouth, by printed page, and, especially, by radio and television, contention spread across the internal boundaries of the collapsing Soviet bloc, enjoying a brief, tragic echo in China, and giving way to savage confrontations in Romania, in the Caucasus, and ultimately in Yugoslavia. Within a year, the state system that had dominated fifty years of European conflict was gone. By 1991, even the Soviet Union, heartland of proletarian internationalism, had imploded, giving way to a galaxy of semidemocratic, semimarket, deeply conflictual societies.

When we compare the rapid diffusion of the movements of 1989 to Clarkson's inability to bring abolitionism across thirty miles of water to a France in full flood of revolution, we can begin to understand the progress made by the social movement over the past two hundred years. For not only did eastern Europeans, Baltic ethnics, and Chinese students rebel en masse: they did so against similar targets, at virtually the same time, and in the name of goals that varied only in their details. In 1789, antislavery advocates had difficulty bringing their movement across thirty miles of water; but in 1989, the democracy movement spread from Berlin to Beijing in a matter of weeks, unleashing a wave of movements both benign and malignant across the world.

The significance of this change for democracy is uncertain, as we saw when the former Yugoslavia imploded in 1992. But its implications for the future of social movements are profound. For not only did these changes close the door on marxism-leninism, the most important revolutionary movement of the twentieth century; by the end of 1989, the movement against state socialism became general and its modalities modular.[2] Both there and elsewhere, it had become easy for ordinary people to advance collective claims against powerful opponents. It is to understanding the implications of these changes that this chapter is addressed. I briefly summarize some of our main findings, before examining some current problems that face social movement scholars.

TWO DISCLAIMERS AND A CALL
FOR SYNTHESIS

But before turning to those issues, it is worth underscoring what this study has *not* attempted to do – to provide a single model showing the common properties of all contentious politics everywhere and anywhere since the beginning of time. Instead, I have tried to identify the processes through which contention arises in different milieux and how its intersection with different forms of mobilization, identity creation, organization, and opportunities and constraints creates social movements and major cycles of contention. Two alternative approaches make broader claims.

RATIONALIZING CONTENTION

Thirty years ago, political scientists and sociologists interested in movements began to look at their subject, not from the standpoint of actions taken but from the puzzle that collective action is difficult to bring about. They were properly reacting to earlier models that held that the identification of common interests was sufficient to bring about collective action. Economist Mancur Olson and his followers forced many scholars – some of them imbued with movement causes – to see that collective action does not follow automatically from grievances but requires individual *decisions* to participate. Because of the tendency to "free-ride" on the activism of others, Olson saw a serious collective action problem dogging the lives of those who would organize them.

Two things followed from this – the first one fortunate and the second less so. First, the causal chain from the identification of grievances to the decision to act was recognized to pass through calculations of perceived opportunity, constraint, and incentive. But second, this concentration on the individual's decision to participate neglected the broader social processes in which it was embedded. Moreover, Olson's "collective action problem" was only a puzzle – and not a sociological law – because in so many situations and against so many odds, collective action *does* occur, often instigated by people with few resources and little inherent power.

The "solution" to that puzzle was first sought in Olson's idea that "large groups" mobilize members through selective incentives and constraints (1965). But while the Olsonian theory worked well for interest groups, it was inadequate for movements, for the simple reason that, apart from contention, they have few incentives or constraints to employ. From this there follows the need to find out how people interact with others, are influenced by traditions of collective action, and are facilitated or discouraged by institutions, networks, and identities. People will rise in contention under the most discouraging circumstances, as long as they recognize collective interests, join others like themselves, and think there is a chance their protests will succeed.

In recent years, scholars beginning from an Olsonian perspective have gone beyond Olson's market model to recognize the variety of incentives that people bring to collective action (Chong 1991; Golden 1997; Hardin 1995; Lichbach 1995, 1997). Mark Lichbach, for example, recognizes four main models of collective action: marketlike, contractual, communal, and hierarchical. In his *Rebel's Dilemma* (1995), he goes further than any other rationalist in recognizing the variety of situations that structure contention, offering middle-range theories of the origins, operations, and outcomes of dissident entrepreneurship and of the patronage of dissident groups. But most rationalists leave unspecified what Tilly calls the "downstream" connections and consequences of such decisions. In particular, they make it hard to decide:

- How to characterize and explain relations among interest-oriented decisions, actual implementations of those decisions by the decision makers in concrete actions, and outcomes of the actions involved.
- How to explain and place incremental effects, delayed effects, indirect effects, environmentally mediated effects, and effects unnoticed by their agents.
- How to explain and trace interdependence among situations of individual decisions and decision makers, either simultaneously or over time (Tilly 1997b).

In this study, I go part way with the rationalists – particularly in emphasizing how changes in opportunities and constraints either spur people to action or caution them to inactivity. I also argue that cycles of contention have something of the logic of economic cycles, with competition among challengers for a pool of supporters helping to explain the dynamics of a cycle. But I could provide no good accounts of movement emergence, dynamics, or outcomes without grounding my observations in specific historical and institutional settings. An opposing perspective to rational choice takes specificity much further.

CULTURE AND CONTENTION

In the past few years, culturally oriented scholars like John Foran (1993), Hank Johnston (1995), and most recently Eric Selbin (1997) have offered a competing set of answers to the collective action question. In contrast to the methodological

individualism and theoretical monism of the rationalists, theirs is a phenome-
nological individualism and theoretical syncretism that places great emphasis on
narrative, on how actors define their situations, and on social construction. Selbin
in particular appeals for a richly encultured approach, one that will be sensitive
to the uniqueness of individual experience, to different forms of contention, and
to the "messiness" of human interactions (1997).

In this study, I drew on the insights of the culturalists in several ways,
particularly with the concept of the repertoire, the notion of framing, and the
attention paid to collective identity and diffusion within cycles. But I drew back
before the lure of reading all contention as struggles over meaning. The appeal –
but also the danger – of social constructionism is that it diverts attention from
the contexts of meaning construction, away from social networks and connective
structures, and apart from the important links between imagined and lived experiences (Castells 1997: 29). Like Beissinger studying nationalism (1996), I
focused on the events that make meaning manifest; like Sewell studying the
taking of the Bastille (1996), I argued that culture must be embedded in structural change; like Katzenstein studying the women's movement in the church
(1998), I tried to show how political opportunities trigger discursive responses;
and like Tilly studying contentious gatherings (1995a, 1995b), I focused on what
people choose to *do* when they act collectively.

Reality is indeed "messy" – as Eric Selbin rightly claims and as many rational
choice theorists deny. My argument with the latter is that replacing messiness
with theorems of generic reach leads to so high a level of abstraction as to produce
little of enduring use, while my unease with the former is that accepting messiness and embracing phenomenology leads to rich but unconnected narratives
and can easily substitute the interpretations of the observer for those of the subject.

The assumption of this study has been that we can best reduce the messiness,
neither by proposing general laws for contention wherever or whenever it occurs,
nor by celebrating particularity, but by examining the powers in movement
whose development we traced historically in Part I and analyzed in Parts II and
III. We learned most by seeking a middle space between the ungrounded formulations of rational choice theory and the all-too-grounded interpretations of
culturalism. I have tried to do so by using a limited set of concepts – opportunities and constraints, repertoires, frames and mobilizing structures, cycles and
institutional response. Let us begin by summarizing the findings that this approach has produced before turning to some final issues and questions.

OPPORTUNITIES, CONSTRAINTS, AND RESOURCES

Enough has been said about changes in political opportunities and constraints in
this study to make it necessary only to repeat that, while they do not on their

own "explain" social movements, they play the strongest role in triggering general episodes of contention in which elites reveal their vulnerability, new social actors and forms of conflict appear, alliances are struck, and repression becomes sluggish or inconsistent. Some sectors of society respond more rapidly to changes of opportunity than others, but this is no more than saying that grievances, capacities, and threats vary and combine in manifold ways. Some dimensions of opportunity, like state strength or repressiveness, are more permanent than others, but the outbreak of episodes of contention is not based on stable structures alone.

If we were to elevate political opportunity structure into a general covering law, we would always find movements it cannot "explain" and those that arise as opportunities are closing. But that has not been the claim of this study. Instead, I have tried to show how movements develop as specific interactions within general phases of contention, depending on the forms of mobilization they employ, their meanings and identities, and the social networks and connective structures on which they build. We have traced this process first historically, through the structural and cultural changes of the last two centuries, and then analytically, by employing the concepts of contentious repertoires, frames, and mobilizing structures. A brief review of these will take us to some current problems in the study of movements.

THE OLD AND THE NEW REPERTOIRES

Long before the appearance of the modern social movement, contention took manifold forms, including uprisings, revolts, revolutions, and civil and religious wars. The structure of early modern society made it possible to war over religion or dynastic succession, but inhibited seekers of bread, belief, land, and freedom from state oppression from aggregating their interests. These inhibitions were reflected in the nature of claim making, which remained for the most part direct, parochial, and segmented.

The societies that formed around consolidating states in the past two centuries provided more translocal connections, more rapid communications, denser associational networks and – especially – targets and arenas for groups that felt their interests were impaired. But these processes did not stop with the availability of opportunities created by state building. In order to form a social movement, it took organizers – either coming from preexisting associations or emerging from within a struggle – to create focal points for movements. The social movement was not an automatic outcome of modernization but emerged from the long, tormented, but ultimately interactive process of state formation and citizenship and from the diffusion of these forms of interaction over time and across territory.

REPERTOIRES, MOBILIZING STRUCTURES, AND FRAMES

Once opportunities open and constraints contract, the main kinds of resources that organizers use are three: the forms of contention that arise out of – and innovate upon – culturally familiar repertoires; the informal networks and connective structures that people live within and build; and the cultural frames they find in their societies and create in struggle. Movements use different forms of collective action singly and in combination to link people to one another and to opponents, supporters, and third parties. They both take advantage of the cultural familiarity of these forms of action and innovate around their edges to inspire the imagination of supporters and create fear among opponents. Collective action is best seen not as a simple cost, but as both cost and benefit for social movements, for it is a means of communication and mobilization as well as a message and a challenge to opponents.

The balance between the costs and benefits of collective action helps to determine the dynamics of the movement. As the benefits of a particular form of collective action wane and people weary of contention, organizers have incentives to develop new ones, appeal to new participants, or radicalize their interaction with opponents. The conflicts and defections we often see within movements, as well as their increased confrontations with the state, result in part from the attempt to maintain momentum through the use of new and more daring forms of collective action and in part from the changing balance of moderates and radicals within their circle of activists.

In the formation of a social movement, there is more than a "pull" toward particular forms of collective action; there must also be a "push" of solidarity and collective identity. Solidarity has much to do with interest, but it produces a sustained movement only when consensus is built around common meanings and identities. These meanings and identities are partly inherited and partly constructed in the act of confronting opponents. They are also constituted by the interactions within movements. One of the main factors distinguishing successful movements from failures is their capacity to link inherited understandings to the imperative for activism.

Collective action is often led by organizations, but these are sometimes beneficiaries, sometimes inciters, and at other times destroyers of popular politics. The recurring controversy about whether organizations produce movements or suppress them can be resolved only if we examine the less formal structures they draw upon – the social networks at the base of society and the connective structures that link them to one another. Sustaining a movement is the result of a delicate balance between throttling the power in movement by providing too much organization and leaving followers to spin off into the tyranny of decentralization.

OPPORTUNITIES, CYCLES, AND THE CONSUMPTION OF MOVEMENT

Collective action repertoires, cultural frames, and mobilizing structures are only potential sources of power; they can be employed just as easily for social control as for insurgency. The recurring cycles of contention that were described in Chapter 9 are the products of a wider diffusion of political opportunities that transform the potential for mobilization into action. In these crucibles of conflict and innovation, challengers and their opponents not only take advantage of available opportunities; they create them for others by producing new forms of action, hammering out new "master frames," and making coalitions that force the state to respond to the disorder around it.

The response to cycles of contention is often repressive, but even repression is often mixed with reform. Particularly when elites within the system see the opportunity to aggrandize themselves in alliance with challengers, rulers are placed in a vulnerable position to which reformism is a frequent response. As conflict collapses and militants retire to lick their wounds, many of their gains are reversed, but they often leave behind incremental expansions in participation, changes in popular culture, and residual movement networks. Cycles of contention are a season for sowing, but the reaping is often done in the periods of demobilization that follow, by latecomers to the cause, by elites and authorities.

If cycles are opened by expanding opportunities, how do they decline, as they inevitably do? Is it simply because people tire of agitation, because enervating factional struggles develop, because organizations become oppressive; or because elites repress and placate challengers? All these are contributory causes of cyclical decline but there is a more systemic cause as well: since the power in movement depends on the mobilization of external opportunities, when opportunities expand from initial challengers to other groups and shift to elites and authorities, movements lose their primary source of power. For brief periods the power in movement seems irresistible; but it disperses rapidly and passes inexorably into more institutional forms. Clever power holders exploit these opportunities by selectively facilitating some movements and repressing or ignoring others.

NEW MOVEMENTS, CHANGING PROBLEMS

The contentions of the years since 1989 have helped to consolidate many of the findings summarized here. But they also brought a wave of new challenges – not only to states but to the image of movements formed in the shadow of the relatively peaceful movements of the 1960s and 1970s. Some of these challenges to movement theory, such as the so-called new social movement school, have paled as these movements went through life cycles much like their predecessors' (Calhoun 1995; Offe 1990). But others remain on the agenda of both international politics and social movement theory. The most disturbing are the "warring movements" and identity politics of the 1990s; less threatening, but equally important are the trends to contained contention and differentiating activism in Western democracies. Underlying these are the general question of whether the world is entering a period of general turbulence or, rather, institutionalizing movements. These are the final issues in this concluding chapter.

WARRING MOVEMENTS

As the former Soviet empire collapsed, violent social movements were flourishing. In the Middle East and North Africa, a series of militant Islamic movements, taking their inspiration from the Iranian Revolution of 1979, challenged both secular regimes like Egypt and royal theocracies like Saudi Arabia. In North Africa, one such movement took control of the Sudan, while another fought to the death against the Algerian government. Nowhere was their triumph more electric than in Afghanistan, where, following a fight over the spoils of the defunct socialist regime, fundamentalist militias clashed in internal war.

Fundamentalism was not alone in creating turbulence in the mid-1990s. In central Africa, a genocidal war in Rwanda in 1994 produced a mass migration into neighboring states and fed a devastating civil war in Zaire, whose corrupt leadership was overthrown in 1997. Across the world in Southeast Asia, both the Burmese and Indonesian dictatorships were challenged by democracy movements. In Latin America, in 1994, a rebellion in Chiapas held the world's attention, while, in 1997, a desperate guerrilla movement was able to hold hundreds hostage in the Japanese embassy in Peru.

Scholars of social movements have been stunned by these events, some applying mechanically past models of mobilization to new challenges and others rejecting the heritage of social movement theory altogether. Was the wave of ethnic and religious conflict and the guerrilla and civil wars of the 1990s a peripheral reflex of the crises of liberal capitalism and state socialism? There are disturbing signs that the postwar synthesis of social peace and economic expansion was ending at the heart of the capitalist core as well. In western Europe, the running sore of Catholic nationalism in Northern Ireland, right-wing parties like the French National Front, the Flemish Vlamsblok, and the Austrian Freedom Party, and skinhead violence were gaining support from those suffering from rising unemployment and antiimmigrant phobia.

The United States has not been bereft of such "ugly movements" either. While the peace, women's, and ecology movements of the previous decade were less in evidence, new – and less pacific – movements were organizing in America. Close to the Republican Party, but never actually merging with it, the Christian Coalition was able to influence that party's platform and affect its nominating process (Usher 1997). In the states of the West and Southwest, militant antigovernmental movements and armed militias defied the federal government, attacking both churches and Jewish institutions. In Waco, Texas, the members of a religious sect were incinerated when federal officials tried to eject them from a ranch complex. And in Oklahoma City, a bomb intended to strike a blow against the state destroyed a federal building and took the lives of hundreds of citizens.

Even within Western civil politics, the rise of a spectrum of "identity movements" has had a mixed heritage for popular politics. In place of the universalist goals of the American civil rights movement, its identitarian heirs answer to the god of "difference" – which has the obvious advantage of soldering solidarities but the defects of squandering alliances and distancing opponents. Looking inward rather than outward, building redoubts in friendly spaces rather than venturing into contested places, movements that privilege identity ignore opportunities, engage in sterile "purer than thou" exercises, and often end up – in Todd Gitlin's poignant epigram – "marching on the English Department while the right takes the White House" (1995: ch. 5).

The spread and dramatic successes in the 1990s of violent, sectarian, and self-enclosed identity movements reflect the powers of movement that I have described in this book. But they also raise troubling questions for social movement theory: about the increase of violence, the recrudescence of ethnic conflict, the decline of civility, and the internationalization of conflict; and about the extent to which we have allowed the examples of Western civic movements from the 1960s to shape our models (McAdam, Tarrow, and Tilly 1997). Some students of nationalism, ethnic conflict, and terrorism have concluded that these models are simply irrelevant in the post-1989 world. But if our theories are any good, they ought to provide hints about the causal dynamics of different types of movement. Besides, as the world approaches a new century, other trends are more familiar.

CONTAINED CONTENTION[3]

In his fine textbook on citizen politics, Russell Dalton writes of the survey results he found in four liberal democracies of the West (the United States, Britain, Germany, and France):

> In every nation, unconventional political activities are more common at the end of the survey period [1974–1990] than at the first time point. . . .
> Protest is becoming a more common political activity in advanced industrial democracies. (1996: 75)

These changes were not linear or equal for all countries. But in places as different as peaceful Switzerland and turbulent Italy, the end of the protest cycle of the late 1960s left a higher magnitude of contention than at its beginnings (Kriesi 1985; Tarrow 1989a). And when Kriesi and his collaborators examined the trend of "new" social movements of the 1970s and 1980s in western European countries, three of these countries described protest cycles similar in shape to what we saw in the 1960s. At the end of the 1980s, Germany, Holland, and Switzerland experienced a larger number of protests by new social movements than in the mid-1970s (Kriesi et al. 1995: 74).[4]

In addition to being more frequent, contentious politics appears to be employed today by a wider variety of organizations and by a broader range of people than was the case thirty years ago. Particularly in the United States, but also in western Europe, there has been a dramatic increase in the establishment of interest organizations that claim to support "distant issues," excluded constituencies, or "the public interest." Such organizations often combine institutional advocacy with more contentious activities (Minkoff 1994; Walker 1991). Even older ones – like staid conservation groups in the United States or the once compliant unions in Germany – have experienced an increase in protest activity.

New social actors have been increasingly visible in protest activities since the 1960s. Middle-class Britons protesting against new highways or the barbarism of the hunt, truckdrivers blocking the roads for early retirement in France, Catholic priests and Protestant ministers demonstrating for peace in the Netherlands, shopkeepers protesting against stricter tax collection in Italy: alongside traditional protesting groups of students, peasants, and workers, these were familiar figures in the contentious politics of the 1990s.

The most striking shift was in gender. Although men still protest more than women, "there is evidence," writes Dalton, "that this pattern is changing with a narrowing of gender roles" (1996: 78). Consider the most dramatic protests in the United States in the last two decades: from Phyllis Schlafly's Anti-ERA campaign and Mothers against Drunk Driving in the 1980s to the antiabortion blockades and the Gay and Lesbian March on Washington in 1993, women have been more visible and increasingly found in leadership roles. In Latin America, some of the most visible protests against military rule, torture, and disappearances were mounted by mothers' groups, while in Britain, the Greenham Common protest against nuclear armaments was organized exclusively by women.

CONVENTION AND CONTENTION

But as we reach a new century, contention is becoming more complicated than a quantitative increase in magnitude or an extension to new actors. First, in most Western countries, the increases in reported protest participation between the 1970s and the 1990s were greatest for the *least* contentious forms of collective action – petitions and peaceful demonstrations – while more contentious ones (e.g., building occupations and political violence) increased only slightly (Dalton 1996: 76). In the United States, the use of political violence fell dramatically between the early 1970s and the late 1980s (Gurr 1989), making the occasional dramatic incident, like the Oklahoma City bombing, all the more shocking. Of the countries for which we have comparable information, only in West Germany did the more contentious forms of action appear to increase between the 1960s and the late 1980s – and this was only true for "new" movements like the peace movement.[5]

Moreover, the general public's "acceptance" of the legitimacy of protest is confined to a narrow range of protest activities and has declined for most of the countries Dalton analyzed (cf. Crozat 1998). The one Western country in which the approval of more confrontational actions has increased since the 1960s is Germany, whereas in Italy it was dramatically reversed (compare Crozat 1998 with Rucht 1998b). In general, the evidence from both Europe and the United States suggests that the amount of strongly contentious forms accepted and actually used by Western citizens seems to be more circumscribed than it was two decades ago. What has been increasing both relatively and absolutely are the peaceful forms associated with what we called "the conventional repertoire" in Chapter 6 – especially petitions and peaceful demonstrations.

Finally, even as protest use has spread into new sectors of the population, militancy – by which I mean regular activism in social movement organizations – has declined. This may be part of a more general trend to privatization, described by Robert Putnam as a decline of "social capital" in countries like the United States (1995). But it is even found in France, where protest activity is – if anything – increasing (Ion 1997). So herein lies a puzzle for the future of social movements: how can we reconcile the increase and diffusion of protest activity, however mild and conventional, with this decline of militancy? Here is one hypothesis.

DIFFERENTIATING ACTIVISM

Declining mass militancy does not mean a decline of the classical social movement; but it does seem to reflect a decline in the traditional movement *organization* and a differentiation into the other movement forms described in Chapter 8. As mass movement organizations decline in numbers and militancy, self-help groups, intentional communities, service organizations, and parties and interest groups with a movement vocation have become more prominent. Although each new cycle of contention revives mass movement organizations, these soon prove unstable and subject to fission, and eventually fractionate in a variety of directions.

Soon after the 1960s in America and somewhat later in western Europe, there was a widespread development of public interest groups and parties with a movement vocation. If the public interest group is more typical in the United States, while parties like the Greens are more central to western Europe, that is probably the result of differences in electoral systems. The two subtypes share many features: a professionalization of leadership, a dominant orientation toward public authorities, and, at best, passive forms of mass participation from their supporters.

The importance of public interest groups should not be sneered at by seekers after "pure" movement forms. Often providing training grounds for future activists, they serve as "movement halfway houses" and sources of expertise, information, and communication for protest campaigns that more militant groups could not mount on their own. Especially in periods of doldrums between cycles of contention, they help to keep alive the themes that movements place on the agenda and provide expertise and resources for movement allies.

At the same time, a variety of forms of action turn away from participation in the political process and toward activism in society. One strand involves direct participation and seeks, among other things, the personal development of constituents. These range all the way from the communal movement in the United States, through a wide spectrum of self-help and support groups, to home schooling and consciousness raising. Though not aimed directly at mobilization (indeed, they are often seen as an alternative to mobilization), such groups can maintain consensus around movement goals, as well as providing services and opportunities for self-development. In institutions as diverse as the American Catholic Church and western European trade unions, "collectives" and consciousness-raising groups help to keep activism alive during periods of low mobilization.

Other movement-linked forms of organization, like the autonomous sector that grew out of the movements of 1968 in Germany, provide professional services to larger publics. On an international level, a loose archipelago of support groups and solidarity associations provides health services, technical advice, and solidarity to Third World populations – sometimes working closely with their governments and sometimes with internal groups. In the West, a green and solidarity-oriented consumption movement is gaining ground to distribute the products of Third World peasantries and craftspeople without the intermediation of profit-taking middlemen.

Finally, the mass movements of the past have not disappeared but have adapted their shape to the changes in society. In the past two decades, we have seen the development of loose, decentralized networks of activists and leaders who organize coalitions around particular campaigns and make claims on political authorities. Even as they put forward ideologies of spontaneity, the core of most of these movements is highly professional. They are not mass parties or bureaucratic mass movement organizations but take the form of coalitional campaigns led by small cadres of organizers mobilizing a much larger penumbra of sporadically active citizens.

What is "new" about these movements is not that they are "spontaneous" whereas their predecessors were "organized," or that they put forward "identity claims" in contrast to the supposedly "instrumental" claims of "old" social movements, or even that they routinely use unconventional forms of action (in fact, they mainly use conventional petitions and peaceful demonstrations). What *is* new is that they have greater discretionary resources, enjoy easier access to the media, have cheaper and faster geographic mobility and cultural interaction, and can call upon the collaboration of different types of movement-linked organizations for rapidly organized issue campaigns. In this sense, the decline of the old centralized mass movement was a benefit, rather than a cost, to the social movement. Here is a specific innovation that depends on these resources.

TRANSNATIONAL CONTENTION

For most of the periods of history from which this study was drawn, national social movements dominated contentious politics. This was due to the growing predominance of the consolidated national state, both vis-à-vis the state forms that had preceded it and the smaller territorial units it enveloped. But sometime around the middle of the twentieth century, national states began to be challenged – by state-based empires linked by ideology and military power, by sub-state mobilized identities, and by transnational entities like multinational corporations.

Are television, cheap air travel, and electronic communication accelerating the process of state disintegration? In places as widespread as eastern Europe and Beijing in 1989, Chiapas in 1994, and the campaigns on the high seas by Greenpeace, electronic communication and transnationally mobile teams of activists play a critical role in challenging state autonomy. About their future as social movements, the record is still unclear; but these recent changes have certainly sped up the processes of transnational diffusion and given organizers new weapons of mobilization. This was the question raised in the previous chapter, one that – at this stage of world history – it would be foolish to try to answer, since it involves nothing less than the institution of the sovereign national state.

MOVEMENTS AND INSTITUTIONS

At various points in this study, we have seen how closely movements interact with institutions. This is not simply a question of challenging institutions – although that is the central image the social movement cultivates – but also of collaborating with institutional actors and, at various times, gaining support from institutions. When we compared the failure of the French student movement of 1968 with the success of the American women's movement in Chapter 10, the latter movement certainly profited from institutional collaboration and participation.

But institutional participation is, as we have seen, a double-edged sword. Social movements that are too alienated from institutions risk isolation and sectarianism; but those which collaborate too closely with institutions and take up institutional routines can become imbued with their logic and values. This is one danger we have observed in the case of transnational advocacy networks, which often take the name of "movement" while enjoying financial succor from foundations, national states, and international organizations. Whether they will invigorate weak domestic movements or remain free-floating elite networks is a major question that scholars of social movements as well as the states they target will have to carefully watch.

Some types of institutions seem to facilitate movements more than others. Repeatedly, we have seen how centralized states tend to structure protest at the national level, whereas federal ones provide alternative sites for movement activity and "venue shopping." While authoritarian states try to suppress protest, they also radicalize it and thus put themselves in greater danger than democratic states when opportunities open and constraints collapse, as we saw in the cases of the former Soviet Union and east central Europe since 1989. And while democratic states facilitate challengers, the very ease of mobilization – increased by reforms in police practice since the 1960s – takes the sting out of movements' capacity to disrupt.

Movements in democratic states have learned to combine institutional and extrainstitutional action. Consider as disruptive a group as Act-Up: alongside the "zaps" that harass movement opponents, and the theatrical "die-ins" staged in public places on behalf of AIDS victims, Act-Up activists maintain specialized committees, groups to run their day-to-day affairs, lobbying committees, and coordinating committees (Ernst 1997: 17). Whether such movements' spanning of institutional and noninstitutional practices is leading to a more turbulent society or to the domestication of movements is the major question for scholars of social movements today.

Over the past two hundred years, there has been a slow, ragged but inexorable civilizing trend in the nature of contention and in the state's means of controlling it. As modular repertoires linked social movements to the state, violent and direct forms of attack were increasingly replaced by the power of numbers, by solidarity, and by an informal dialogue between states and movements. With its low level of violence and its employment of nonviolent action, the cycle of the 1960s was the apotheosis of this trend. But the guerrilla wars, the hostage takings, the bombings, and the ethnic conflicts of the past two decades must make us wonder whether the trend to a peaceful repertoire was no more than a parochial parenthesis and is being reversed.

Much of the violence takes place in the impoverished "South," but citizens of Western countries cannot feel superior when they contemplate the violent developments in the non-Western world. The puritanical beliefs, if not the violent methods, of militant Islam or integral nationalism bear a striking resemblance to recent trends in Western culture: to politicized ministers who preach intolerance on Sunday morning television shows; to the "rescuers" of unborn fetuses who refuse to recognize women's right to reproductive freedom; to orthodox attacks on secular values in education and personal life; and to identitarian movements that claim the superiority of their nations or races. The methods are far different, but how far are movements like the French National Front or the American militias from the fanatics of the Party of God?

The citizens of modern states have lived through such "moments of madness" before. It is enough to remember that severed heads were paraded around Paris on pikes during the great French democratic revolution to find parallels for the violence and intolerance that have emerged in the 1990s. The concern raised by these more recent outbreaks is that – if a "movement society" is developing out of the social, economic, and cultural changes of the late twentieth century – it will have a broader cultural valence and more rapid global diffusion than the movements that broke out in Boston in 1765, in Paris in 1789 and 1848, and in the nonviolent protests of the 1960s.

Is the new world order that was supposed to result from the liberation of 1989 turning instead into permanent violence and disorder? Have the resources for violent contention become so widely accessible, integralist identities so widespread, and militants so freed of national constraints that a permanent and violent movement society is resulting? Or will the current wave of ethnic and religious movements be partially outgrown, partially domesticated, and partially mediated by the political process, as in previous cycles of contention?

The violence and intolerance at century's end constitute a frightening trend. But this is not the first great wave of movement in history nor will it be the last. If its dynamic comes to resemble the contentious politics that we have encountered in this book, then its power will at first be ferocious, uncontrolled, and widely diffused, but ultimately ephemeral and institutionalized. If so, like previous waves of movement, it will disperse "like a flood tide which loosens up much of the soil but leaves alluvial deposits in its wake" (Zolberg 1972: 206).

NOTES

INTRODUCTION

1. For this argument with illustrative syntheses, see McAdam, Tarrow, and Tilly 1996, 1997.

2. In other words, I cannot agree with Russell Hardin when he writes, in his book *Collective Action*, that "there is no reason to parcel the theory [of collective action] according to the boundaries of substantive problems." Generalizing the explanation of participation would only lead to greater theoretical power if, as Hardin claims, the resources and problems of coordination of the actors were comparable in all of these substantive realms (pp. xiii–xiv).

3. The indifference of scholars of ethnic nationalism to social movement theory is cordially reciprocated by most social movement scholars. Perusing the table of contents of several texts on movements shows much interest in the relatively "civil" movements of liberal democracies and little attention to the "bad" movements that have emerged in the past decade.

4. Charles Tilly writes: "Authorities and thoughtless historians commonly describe popular contention as disorderly. . . . But the more closely we look at that same contention, the more we discover order. We discover order created by the rooting of collective action in the routines and organization of everyday social life, and by its involvement in a continuous process of signaling, negotiation, and struggle with other parties whose interests the collective action touches." See his *The Contentious French*, p. 4.

5. Such movements have been characterized as "discursive" by political scientist Mary Katzenstein, who studies the movement of radical Catholic women in America in her *Protest inside Institutions.* I return to the relations between discourse and collective action in Chapter 7.

6. Some students of social movements take the criterion of common consciousness to an extreme. Rudolf Heberle, for example, thought a movement had to have a well-worked-out ideology. See his *Social Movements: An Introduction to Political So-*

ciology. But others, like Alberto Melucci, think that movements purposefully "construct" collective identities through constant negotiation. See Melucci's "Getting Involved: Identity and Mobilization in Social Movements."

1. CONTENTIOUS POLITICS AND SOCIAL MOVEMENTS

1. For an account of theorists who focus on civil violence as the antithesis of normal social processes, see James Rule's *Theories of Civil Violence*, ch. 3.
2. Lenin criticized the theory, then current in some socialist circles, that revolutionary leadership must *necessarily* fall mainly upon the shoulders of an extremely small intellectual force. "It need not 'necessarily' be so. It is because we [in Russia] are backward." *What Is to Be Done?*, pp. 123–4.
3. In 1924, Gramsci wrote, "The error of the party has been to have accorded priority in an abstract fashion to the problem of organization, which in practice has simply meant creating an apparatus of functionaries who could be depended on for their orthodoxy towards the official view." See Antonio Gramsci, *Selections from the Prison Notebooks*, p. lxii, where this passage is translated.
4. This was a special danger on the periphery of the working-class party, among the middle class and the peasantry. See Stephen Hellman, "The PCI's Alliance Strategy and the Case of the Middle Classes," and Sidney Tarrow, *Peasant Communism in Southern Italy*.
5. I do not attempt to summarize this school here but refer the reader to Doug McAdam's magisterial synthesis in *The Political Process and the Development of Black Insurgency*, ch. 1.
6. The problem of the size of the group has exercised a great fascination among scholars in both the public goods and game theoretic tradition. See John Chamberlin, "Provision of Collective Goods as a Function of Group Size"; Russell Hardin, *Collective Action,* ch. 3; and Gerald Marwell and Pam Oliver, *The Critical Mass in Collective Action: A Micro-Social Theory,* ch. 3, which demonstrates theoretically that the size of the group is not the critical variable that Olson thought it was.
7. Thus General Motors has enough of an interest in the collective good of American auto production to take on the leadership of all domestic car producers, including those who are too small to take action on their own. If enough members of the group take a free ride, then the leaders' efforts are not only to no avail – their efforts themselves will induce free-riding.
8. Zald's dissertation and first book (1970), unsurprisingly, dealt with the formation, transformation, and politics of the YMCA.
9. In the United States, Thompson's cultural language and his emphasis on meaning were appropriated by an anthropologically gifted political scientist, James Scott (1976), who used them to study the reaction of subsistence peasants to the strains of commercialization. Scott, also influenced by Gramsci's concept of hegemony, went on to apply his thinking to peasant resistance in general, in his *Weapons of the Weak* (1985), before turning away from collective action to the formulation of what he called "hidden transcripts" (1990).
10. In the field of comparative revolution, culturally sensitive work was offered by

John Foran's *Fragile Resistance: Social Transformation in Iran from 1500 to the Revolution* and Mark Selbin's *Modern Latin American Revolutions*, which is an attempt to bring agency centrally into the study of revolution.

11. See Eisinger 1973, Kitschelt 1986, McAdam 1982, Piven and Cloward 1977, Tarrow 1988, and Tilly 1978 and 1986 for some of the main historical benchmarks in the development and use of this concept.

12. Tilly's theory of collective action has gone through several permutations since then, some of which are examined later in this volume. For an outline of his fundamental contributions to this field, see my review article, "The People's Two Rhythms."

13. For a sensitive critique, see Gamson and Meyer, "The Framing of Political Opportunity."

14. Some of the critiques assumed that opportunity structures could be identified that affected individual social movements. In fact, few political process theorists took such a view; for example, Goldstone (1980), McAdam (1982), and Tarrow (1989a, 1996b) argue that opportunity structures tend to widen for constellations of groups, and that early risers make opportunities for others (see Chapter 9).

15. The concept first appears in Tilly's *From Mobilization to Revolution*, ch. 6, again in "Speaking Your Mind without Elections, Surveys, or Social Movements," and then in *The Contentious French*, ch. 1. Chapter 2 takes up the theory in more detail and offers an important modification.

16. Some of the main sources are collected in Bert Klandermans, Hanspeter Kriesi, and Sidney Tarrow, eds., *From Structure to Action*, and in Aldon Morris and Carol Mueller, eds., *Frontiers in Social Movement Research*. For an ingenious use of frame analysis to examine the ideas of ordinary American citizens, see William Gamson's *Talking Politics*.

17. Experimental researchers were also learning about the importance of social incentives to cooperation. In an ingenious piece of research, William Gamson and his collaborators showed that a supportive group environment was essential to triggering individuals' willingness to speak out against unjust authority – authority that they might well tolerate if they faced it on their own (Gamson, Fireman, and Rytina 1982). Similarly, when Robyn Dawes and his associates carried out a series of experiments on collective choice, they found that neither egoistic motives nor internalized norms were as powerful in producing collective action as "the parochial one of contributing to one's group of fellow humans" (Dawes, Van de Kragt, and Orbell 1988: 96). In social dilemma situations, they argue in their article "Not Me or Thee but We," "people immediately start discussing what 'we' should do, and spend a great deal of time and effort to persuade others in their own group to cooperate (or defect!), even in situations where these others' behavior is irrelevant to the speaker's own payoffs" (p. 94).

18. At the same time, European scholars like Hanspeter Kriesi (1985) were finding that movement subcultures were the reservoirs in which collective action took shape. This dovetailed with what sociologist Alberto Melucci (1988; 1996: ch. 4) was learning about the role of movement networks in defining the collective identity of the movements he studied in Italy.

19. Hardin hints at this when he points out that "a convention covering the behavior of a very large class of people, none of whom interacts personally with more than

a fraction of the class, can be built up out of smaller subgroup interactions in a large class of situations"; see *Collective Action*, p. 186.

20. As Gerald Marwell and Pam Oliver put it, in their study, *The Critical Mass*, "Olson's 'large group' problem is often resolved by a 'small group' solution" (1993: 54).

2. MODULAR COLLECTIVE ACTION

Parts of this chapter were published in my "Modular Collective Action and the Rise of the Social Movement: Why the French Revolution Was Not Enough," in *Politics and Society* 21 (1993): 69–90.

1. The trials, including the one summarized here, have been most thoroughly studied by Hans-Jürgen Lusebrink in his "L'imaginaire social et ses focalisations en France et en Allemagne à la fin du XVIII siècle" and in Sarah Maza's *Private Lives and Public Affairs*.

2. Pathbreaking work on the barricades is in progress by Marc Traugott who is investigating their evolution and changing functions. See his article "Barricades as Repertoire: Continuities and Discontinuities in the History of Nineteenth Century France." I am grateful to Traugott for his helpful comments on an earlier version of this section.

3. In his "Speaking Your Mind without Elections, Surveys, or Social Movements," Tilly describes the "sacking routine" as common in the eighteenth century, observing that it was frequently used to punish tavern or brothel keepers who cheated their customers or public officials who had passed the bounds of legitimacy. Its use to punish a venal householder who had abused a servant seems to have been an innovation of the prerevolutionary period. It continues to appear throughout the French Revolution, most dramatically in the Reveillon riots of May 1789. On the latter, see Simon Schama's vivid reconstruction in *Citizens*, pp. 326–32.

4. For example, Godechot, in his inventory of the 1848 revolutions, lists at least nine different claims for which barricades were used in France alone. See Godechot's *Les révolutions de 1848*. The analysis of how the barricade was used in 1848 is reported in Sarah Soule and Sidney Tarrow, "Acting Collectively, 1847–1849: How the Repertoire of Collective Action Changed and Where It Happened."

5. Tilly's contributions to the field of collective action and social movements are so massive as to make them difficult to summarize. For a brief bibliography and critical analysis, see William Sewell Jr., "Collective Violence and Collective Loyalties in France: Why the French Revolution Made a Difference," and Sidney Tarrow, "The People's Two Rhythms: Charles Tilly and the Study of Contentious Politics."

6. The concept was not new to Tilly's work. In his 1978 text, *From Mobilization to Revolution*, p. 151, he wrote: "At any point in time, the repertoire of collective actions available to a population is surprisingly limited. Surprisingly, given the innumerable ways in which people could, in principle, deploy their resources in

pursuit of common ends. Surprisingly, given the many ways real groups have pursued their own common ends at one time or another."

7. This replaces my earlier term, "protest cycles," which now seems to me to be too narrowly constrained by its associations with the contemporary term "protest."

8. "Because similar groups generally have similar repertoires," writes Tilly, "we can speak more loosely of a general repertoire that is available for contention to the population of a time and place." *The Contentious French*, p. 2.

9. Like all sweeping historical schemes, the concept of the repertoire can be criticized for overly privileging "anonymous sociological processes" and underestimating the importance of great events (Sewell 1990: 548). It can also be charged with insensitivity to the meanings of collective action for those who use it (pp. 540–5). The role of "great events" – and of the movement cycles with which they are often associated – are dealt with in Chapter 9; that of the "framing" of contention appears in Chapter 7.

10. The following paragraphs are based closely on Tilly's "Food Supply and Public Order in Modern Europe" and draw on Steven Lawrence Kaplan's *Provisioning Paris*.

11. Natalie Davis in "The Rites of Violence" has given us the most vivid evocation of the brutally mimetic qualities of early modern religious conflicts in France.

12. In France, the first rural movement to resemble the modern social movement in its use of assemblies – the Croquants – was an outgrowth of the wars of religion. See Yves-Marie Bercé's deceptively titled *History of Peasant Revolts*, actually a brilliant case study of the Croquants, part 2. (The French edition was accurately titled *Histoire des croquants*.)

13. For examples of the reevocation of these historical memories in peasant land seizures in southern Europe, see Eric Hobsbawm, *Primitive Rebels: Studies in Archaic Forms of Social Movement in the 19th and 20th Centuries*; Julian Pitt-Rivers, *People of the Sierra*; and Sidney Tarrow, *Peasant Communism in Southern Italy*. For similar reenactments in Latin America, see Hobsbawm's "Peasant Land Occupations."

14. Focusing on the protests of agricultural laborers in England, Andrew Charlesworth in *An Atlas of Rural Protest in Britain* finds that it was only in the agrarian revolt of 1816 that "men from many different occupations over the whole of a rural area made common cause by each responding to the protests and demonstrations of their fellow workers" (p. 146).

15. The funeral protest became a major form of mobilization in South Africa in the 1980s. Each time the police would shoot demonstrators, a major funeral demonstration followed.

16. Note that the practice existed long before the term "boycott" existed, the colonists using the term "nonimportation." The modern terminology dates only from 1880 – and in Ireland – when the practice was used against a certain Captain Boycott. It quickly spread across the West, as indicated by the French term *boycotter*.

17. Indeed, it was only to enforce a general boycott that was succeeding elsewhere that a coalition of Boston merchants and publicists employed the older routine of destroying imported tea. See Richard D. Brown, *Revolutionary Politics in Massachusetts*.

18. I am grateful to Seymour Drescher for his comments on an earlier version of this section, which leans heavily on his *Capitalism and Antislavery*. Also see Drescher's articles "Public Opinion and the Destruction of British Colonial Slavery" and "British Way, French Way: Opinion Building and Revolution in the Second French Slave Emancipation," as well as Leo d'Anjou's *Social Movements and Cultural Change: The First Abolitionist Campaign Revisited*.

19. With revolution breaking out all over Europe and anarchy threatening in Ireland, this was too much for the government, which mobilized 150,000 "voluntary" constables to stop the presentation of the Chartists' petition on Kennington Common. See Dorothy Thompson, *The Chartists*, ch. 3, on the use of the mass petition by the Chartists. On the unsuccessful Kennington Common demonstration, see Raymond Postgate, *The Story of a Year: 1848*, p. 117.

20. But see William Sewell Jr.'s persuasive argument that it was only with the taking of the Bastille in July 1789 that the urban insurrection was linked normatively to the concept of popular sovereignty in his "Historical Events as Transformation of Structures."

21. The events leading up to the Day of the Tiles and why it brought together so broad a coalition are summarized by Schama in *Citizens*, pp. 272–87. The reactions of the provincial aristocrats and parliaments to the edicts are summarized by Jean Egret in *The French Pre-revolution, 1787–88*, pp. 170–7.

22. See the discussion by Traugott in his "Barricades as Repertoire," pp. 43–56. Also see his "Neighborhoods in Insurrection: The Parisian Quartier in the February Revolution of 1848." It is not clear how much use was made of barricades during the first French Revolution. Hobsbawm is of the opinion that they were never used at all (see his *The Age of Revolution: 1789–1848*, p. 146).

23. Even in our century, Danielle Tartakowsky found evidence of the construction of thirty-one different barricades in France between 1919 and 1968 (1997).

24. From a letter of April 21, 1848, to his librettist, Piave, quoted in Open University, *Music and Revolution: Verdi*, p. 42.

25. I have made this argument in a more technical form in "Studying Contentious Politics: From Event-ful History to Movement Cycles," in Dieter Rucht, Ruud Koopmans, and Friedhelm Neidhardt, eds., *Acts of Dissent: The Study of Protest in Contemporary Democracies*.

3. PRINT AND ASSOCIATION

1. Antoine de Baecque analyzes the political pornographic pamphlet from 1787 on in his "Pamphlets: Libel and Political Mythology." Also see the description of "Body Politics" in Schama's *Citizens*, pp. 203–27 and the libels of Marie-Antoinette that he refers to. Schama writes, "It was her [Marie-Antoinette's] transformation in France to the 'Austrian whore' . . . that damaged the legitimacy of the monarchy to an incalculable degree" (p. 205). Lynn Hunt, in her *Family Romance of the French Revolution*, takes the subject up in exhaustive detail.

2. The title of this section is the same as that of the excellent collection edited by Robert Darnton and Daniel Roche on the role of the press in France before and during the revolutionary period. I am also grateful to Benedict Anderson's *Imag-*

ined Communities: Reflections on the Origin and Spread of Nationalism, ch. 3, for the origin of some of the ideas taken up and expanded in this section.

3. See the collection edited by Jack Goody, *Literacy in Traditional Societies*, for a good introduction to this subject. Lawrence Stone's "Literacy and Education in England, 1640–1900," Kenneth Lockridge's *Literacy in Colonial New England*, and Roger Chartier's *The Cultural Uses of Print in Early Modern France,* have added to the literature, respectively, for England, the American colonies, and France. Alvin Gouldner, in his "Prologue to a Theory of Revolutionary Intellectuals," goes furthest in linking literacy to rebellion by arguing that modern radicalism is centrally rooted in written modes of discourse. My own thinking has been profoundly influenced by the work of my colleague, Benedict Anderson.

4. Even the forms of rebellion that appeared in the French Revolution varied in line with the presence or absence of literacy. For example, in *The Abolition of Feudalism*, pp. 382–3, John Markoff found that rural collective action in different regions varied with the strength or weakness of a primitive indicator of literacy.

5. Readers will note the use of the term "invisible" in place of Anderson's "imagined" communities (1991). The merchants and shippers who launched the stamp boycott in 1765 on behalf of their commercial interests might not yet have recognized themselves as "Americans," but they would have been surprised to learn that their interests were "imagined."

6. See Elizabeth Eisenstein's "Revolution and the Printed Word," p. 195. For a history of book production and reading between the sixteenth and eighteenth centuries in France, see Roger Chartier's *The Cultural Uses of Print in Early Modern France*. Robert Darnton's work is required reading for understanding the importance of prohibited books and pamphlets leading up to the French Revolution. See his *The Business of Enlightenment* and *The Literary Underground of the Old Regime*.

7. When French booksellers asked for works of philosophy from the Société Typographique de Neuchâtel, the Swiss publisher responded: "We don't carry any, but we know where to find them and can supply them when we are asked to." Quoted in Darnton's "Philosophy under the Cloak," in Darnton and Daniel Roche's *Revolution in Print*, p. 31. Note that the term "philosophical works" was a code name for a wide range of censored subjects ranging from pure philosophy through political tracts to more or less pure pornography.

8. He was, as Hobsbawm notes, "the only member of the French Convention who fought openly against the death sentence on Louis XVI." See Hobsbawm's *Labouring Men*, pp. 1–4. For an evocative and penetrating treatment of Paine's importance, see Isaac Kramnick, *Republicanism and Bourgeois Radicalism*.

9. Hobsbawm, *Labouring Men*, p. 2. Paine's language resembled that of the Bible much more than that of the more learned essayists who penned political pamphlets up until his time. For example, he used biblical parallels to convince his Bible-reading public that kingship causes wars and that, for the ancient Hebrews, "it was held sinful to acknowledge any being under that title but the Lord of Hosts." *Common Sense*, ed. Kuklick, pp. 8–9.

10. Bailyn reports that there were thirty-eight American newspapers in 1775, "crowded with columns of arguments and counter-arguments appearing as letters, official documents, extracts of speeches, and sermons." Broadsides appeared everywhere, and even almanacs "carried, in odd corners and occasional columns,

a considerable freight of political comment. Above all, there were pamphlets."
See his *Ideological Origins of the American Revolution*, pp. 1–2.

11. The same was soon true back in Britain; when the reaction began against the French Revolution in 1792, repressing Paine's *Rights of Man*, part II, and his *Address to the Addressers* was one of the first tasks that the magistrates set for themselves. See Albert Goodwin's *The Friends of Liberty*, ch. 8.

12. The 1848 figure for Paris is from Jacques Godechot, *Les révolutions de 1848*. For the developments of the working-class press in Germany and Italy in 1848, see Godechot, ed. *La presse ouvrière*. On the explosion of new journals in Florence, see Clementina Rotondi, *Bibliografia dei periodici toscani, 1847–1852*.

13. "In this small world" (of English upper-class Catholics), writes Antonia Fraser, "which for security's sake perpetuated itself by intermarriage, it is perhaps simplest to state that almost everyone was related to almost everyone else." See her *The Gunpowder Plot*, and especially the chart of the conspirators' relationships and the map of their residences in the Midlands. The quotation is from p. 35.

14. The major published sources, in addition to Maier's *From Resistance to Revolution*, are Richard Ryerson, *The Revolution Is Now Begun,* for Philadelphia; Edward Countryman, *A People in Revolution*, for New York; Richard D. Brown, *Revolutionary Politics in Massachusetts*, for Boston and its hinterland; and Richard W. Walsh, *Charleston's Sons of Liberty*, for the South Carolina city.

15. As Richard D. Brown, in his *Knowledge Is Power*, writes: "The diffusion of information regarding the Battles of Lexington and Concord was at once contagious, spreading spontaneously from person-to-person and place-to-place, and prearranged and channeled through patriot networks. As a result, word of the bloody conflict moved with a rapidity, social penetration, and territorial reach never before witnessed in colonial America" (p. 247).

16. For example, Johnson shows how the sabbatarian movement in Rochester was organized by an organization of Protestant laymen from several local churches. See his *Shopkeeper's Millennium*, p. 109.

17. For some typical patterns of diffusion, see Donald G. Mathews, "The Second Great Awakening as an Organizing Process, 1780–1830." On the role of religion in producing movements for civic morality, see Clifford S. Griffin, *Their Brothers' Keeper;* Ian R. Tyrrell, *Sobering Up*; and Ronald G. Walters, *American Reformers, 1815–1860*. The relationship between religion and antislavery is dealt with by Walters in *The Antislavery Appeal*. A study that emphasizes class, gender, and political – as well as religious – origins of abolitionism is Herbert Aptheker's *Abolitionism: A Revolutionary Movement*.

18. This was less true of the middle class, for although French legislation prohibited the discussion of politics in associations, by the 1830s there were scores of cultural and musical groups, sporting associations, and "gentlemen's clubs" in the capital alone – *pace* Tocqueville (Harrison 1996: 42).

19. For example, Hobsbawm and Rudé report a number of cases in which networks of Swing agitators were organized along family lines. See *Captain Swing*, pp. 205–6.

20. See Eisenstein's "Revolution and the Printed Word," p. 197. Also see Darnton's *The Literary Underground of the Old Regime* and Jack R. Censer and Jeremy O. Popkin, eds., *Press and Politics in Pre-Revolutionary France*.

21. Georges Lefebvre, *The Coming of the French Revolution*, p. 54. At the same time,

an amnesty was granted to booksellers and merchants who had been arrested for distributing tracts critical of the government, as Eisenstein points out in her "Revolution and the Printed Word," p. 199.

4. STATE BUILDING AND SOCIAL MOVEMENTS

1. On the imbrication between state consolidation and citizenship in France, see Simon Schama's *Citizens,* part 1. On the general relation between state consolidation and citizenship, see Charles Tilly, *Coercion, Capital, and European States, 990–1990,* ch. 4. On the different national patterns leading to national citizenship, see Wayne te Brake, *Shaping History: Ordinary People in European Politics, 1500–1700.*

2. Both Tocqueville's image of the old regime and that of the governments that followed were painted with too broad a brush. With respect to the old regime, we know now that he exaggerated both its strength and how thoroughly it had eviscerated France's intermediate bodies.

3. Alexis de Tocqueville, *Recollections,* pp. 61–8. Tocqueville's most direct recent interpreter is Michel Crozier, who adumbrates the strong thesis of centralization and disorder into the language of organizational sociology. See Crozier's *The Bureaucratic Phenomenon*, especially ch. 8. Also see Stanley Hoffmann's essay, "The Ruled," pp. 111–44, on how state centralization and civil society atomization have produced a characteristic French style of protest behavior.

4. For evidence on the first point, see my " 'The Very Excess of Democracy': State Building and Contentious Politics in America." On the "stateless" quality of antebellum America, see Steven Skowronek's *Building a New American State.*

5. Exceptions were temperance societies, which he found quaint, and the nullification movement, which he thought dangerous. For a more detailed treatment based on Tocqueville's journals, see my " 'The Very Excess of Democracy': State Building and Contentious Politics in America."

6. Samuel Finer reports that, while the number of French troops used against Spain in 1635 was 155,000, Napoleon mustered 700,000 for the Russian campaign in 1812. And while the Prussians assembled 160,000 men for the Seven Years' War, as many as 300,000 were recruited in 1814. For England, the numbers were always smaller, but growth was proportional: from the 75,000 troops assembled in 1712 to the 250,000 called up at the peak of the Napoleonic campaigns. See Finer's "State- and Nation-Building in Europe: The Role of the Military," p. 101.

7. Finer notes that "as late as the third quarter of the eighteenth century, from one-half to one-third of the troops of any state would have been foreigners." See his "State- and Nation-Building in Europe: The Role of the Military," pp. 101–2.

8. Donald Read writes in his *The English Provinces* that it called for "opposition to that mercenary phalanx" that ruled the country, through the formation of "associations in the several districts of the kingdom, acting by their respective Committees, and by general deputation from the Associated Bodies" (p. 12).

9. The administrator was Bertier de Sauvigny, whose unpublished manuscript from the Bibliothèque Nationale, "Observations sur le commerce des grains," is quoted by Steven Lawrence Kaplan in his *Provisioning Paris,* p. 23.

10. Primary responsibility for assuring the capital's food supply was divided among a number of agencies and inspectors. See Kaplan's *Provisioning Paris*, pp. 36–7, for the architecture of food regulation in Paris.

11. According to Gabriel Ardant, in his essay "Financial Policy and Economic Infrastructure of Modern States and Nations," pp. 202–3, between 1736 and 1738, English domestic revenues, on average, came from taxes on land, 17.5%; on windows, annuities, and functions, 2.4%; customs duties, 24.6%; excise taxes, 52.8%; and stamp taxes, 2.6%.

12. For example, New York's expenses were met from an import duty, an excise on various commodities, and a license fee paid by hawkers and peddlers. As in England, land was taxed only in times of war, leaving large landholders bearing a slim portion of the colonies' expenses and cities like New York and Albany bearing disproportionate amounts of the tax. See Edward Countryman's *A People in Revolution,* p. 83, for New York's revenue structure.

13. For example, in New York, writes Countryman, "the Sugar Act, the Stamp Act, and the Townshend Acts all threatened the assembly's control over provincial finance. The revamping of the customs service introduced an alien bureaucracy, and the stationing of British troops was intended to give that bureaucracy the strength to enforce its will." See his *A People in Revolution,* p. 85.

14. The *départements* created during the French Revolution were an archetypical example. Constructed out of mapmakers' calculations and named for whatever river happened to flow through them, the departments were designed to break up old provincial loyalties, especially in areas of late integration that had been indirectly governed by the monarchy. But in reaction to the state's territorial and fiscal policies, they eventually gave rise to administrative and then to political identities.

15. The sequence took until 1928 to complete. Robert Peel (thus, the "bobbies"), who had served the government in Ireland before becoming prime minister, created the predecessors of the English civilian police there under the trying circumstances of colonial government. Like the Indian civil service whose lessons were later transferred to Britain, the Irish colony was an experimenting ground for later metropolitan innovations in state building.

16. On this development, see Roger Geary, *Policing Industrial Disputes, 1893–1895*; and Jane Morgan, *Conflict and Order: The Police and Labor Disputes in England and Wales, 1900–1939.*

17. For example, the banquets that marked the republicans' determination to widen the suffrage and set off the 1848 revolution were replays on a larger scale of those that had marked the transition to the Orléanist regime in 1830. On neither occasion could the authorities curb Frenchmen's natural propensity to dine together and socialize (Corbin 1994; Tocqueville 1987).

5. POLITICAL OPPORTUNITIES AND CONSTRAINTS

This chapter has profited greatly from the comments of Val Bunce, David Meyer, and Charles Tilly.

1. Jack Goldstone and Charles Tilly are preparing a paper on the problem of "threat" and social movements in the framework of a collective volume in preparation by the Mellon research group on contentious politics.

2. Readers who have followed international debates on the relations between American and European approaches will recognize the approach taken here as the one put forward in Bert Klandermans's and my essay "Mobilization into Social Movements: Synthesizing European and American Approaches."

3. There is a long and somewhat technical literature on the relations between economic conditions and strikes. The most thorough summary and assessment is found in John Kennan's "The Economics of Strikes," in Orley Ashenfelter and Richard Layard, eds., *Handbook of Labor Economics*, vol. 2.

4. The most synthetic interpretation of the economic sources of the wage explosions of the late 1960s is David Soskice, "Strike Waves and Wage Explosions, 1968–1970: An Economic Interpretation," in Crouch and Pizzorno, eds., *The Resurgence of Class Conflict in Western Europe since 1968*, vol. 2.

5. The ultimate, but not always recognized, source of political opportunity theory was Charles Tilly's *From Mobilization to Revolution,* ch. 4. Also see the article by David Snyder and Charles Tilly, "Hardship and Collective Violence in France." Explicit building blocks in the United States were Doug McAdam, *The Political Process and the Development of Black Insurgency*; Anne Costain, *Inviting Women's Rebellion*; Suzanne Staggenborg, *The Pro-Choice Movement*; and David Meyer, *A Winter of Discontent: The Nuclear Freeze and American Politics.* Explicitly comparative use of the concept was made by Charles Brockett, "The Structure of Political Opportunities and Peasant Mobilization in Central America"; by Mary Katzenstein and Carol Mueller in their edited volume, *The Women's Movements of the United States and Western Europe*; by Herbert Kitschelt in his "Political Opportunity Structures and Political Protest"; and by Tarrow, *Struggle, Politics and Reform.*

6. Among others, by this author, in the first edition of this study (1994), and by Peter Eisinger (1973) and Herbert Kitschelt (1986). The use of the term "structure" may have created the misinterpretation among some critics that these authors assumed that opportunities did not need to be perceived in order to act as incentives to action.

7. Eisinger's claim was based on more than a tocquevillian hunch. Operationalizing opportunity structure in American cities through the differences in the formal and informal political structures of local government, he studied the behavior of urban protest groups in a sample of fifty-three cities during the turbulent 1960s. He found that the level of activism of these groups was highest not where access was either open or closed but at intermediate levels of political opportunity.

8. The major published source is Peter Evans, Dietrich Reuschmeyer, and Theda Skocpol, eds., *Bringing the State Back In.* Also see Richard Valelly's "Party, Coercion and Inclusion," which compares American state structures and party systems over time.

9. For example, Herbert Kitschelt traces differences in the environmental movements of France, Germany, Sweden, and the United States to such institutional differences in state structure. See his article, "Political Opportunity Structures and Political Protest."

10. Note that Kriesi et al. (1995) find a lower level of mobilization for France only

for the so-called new social movements; traditional class-based movements are more vigorous. These findings are contested by the enormous level of street protests found by Olivier Fillieule in his recent book *Stratégies de la rue*, based on close examination of French police files on protests.

11. See Open University, *Music and Revolution: Verdi* (1976). On rock music as an expression of dissent in the Soviet Union before 1989, see Sabrina Ramet's *The Soviet Rock Scene* (1987). Rock began to play a similar role in authoritarian Indonesia during the 1980s.

6. ACTING CONTENTIOUSLY

1. For the most balanced and well-informed background study of the Balkan conflicts in the early to mid-1990s, see John Lampe's *Yugoslavia as History* and V. P. Gagnon's "Serbia's Road to War." The narrative and approximate participation figures in Figure 6.1 are based on Reuter's press releases. For a lively narrative after the fact, see Timothy Garton Ash's "In the Serbian Soup."

2. There were provincial demonstrations in many Serbian towns and cities; international press coverage can only be considered accurate for Belgrade. Even so, the numbers of demonstrators in Figure 6.1 can only be regarded as the crudest of estimates.

3. See the collection of articles edited by Marc Traugott, *Repertoires and Cycles of Collective Action,* for a good representation of recent work on repertoires. Also see Dieter Rucht, Ruud Koopmans, and Friedhelm Neidhardt, eds., *Acts of Dissent*, for a more technical collection of essays.

4. Della Porta shows that the rise of violent politics in Italy and France in the 1970s led to a polarization between a "law-and-order coalition" and a "civil rights" coalition. See her *Social Movements, Political Violence, and the State*, p. 192.

5. Gene Sharp, in *The Politics of Nonviolent Action*, finds nonviolence as far back as the Roman plebeians who, rather than attack the consuls, withdrew from Rome to a hill later called "the Sacred Mount" (p. 75). He also finds examples of it in the American Revolution, in Hungarian resistance against Austrian rule in the nineteenth century, and in the general strike and shutdown of governmental functions that defeated the Kapp putsch in Weimar Germany (pp. 76–80).

6. The movement's effectiveness was demonstrated by the increasing unwillingness of American doctors or hospitals to perform abortions during the 1980s and by the shame and guilt induced in women who were forced to go through with unwanted pregnancies. The antiabortion movement is dealt with sensitively by Suzanne Staggenborg in her *The Pro-Choice Movement,* part 3. Some organizational and tactical aspects are analyzed by John McCarthy in his article, "Pro-Life and Pro-Choice Mobilization."

7. Flemming Mikkelson points out that from a small gathering of fifteen hundred participants in the town of Alborg, this form of passive resistance spread to other provincial towns and eventually to Copenhagen, "reaching a crescendo on September 1, 1940, when c. 740,000 people gathered all over the country singing their national anthems" (1996: 8–9).

8. For example, the practice of assembling in a public place, even for subversive practices, was familiar from parish meetings, guilds, and penitent orders in early

modern Europe. See Bercé, *History of Peasant Revolts*, pp. 23–5. When the first Croquants began to organize at the end of the Wars of Religion, their basic form of collective action was the assembly, organized at the level of the parish (p. 7).

9. As late as the 1872 French census, writes Ronald Aminzade, though artisans in both handicraft and industrial production "constituted only 21.9% of the labor force and 29.5% of the working class, handicraft artisans alone accounted for 72% of the strikes during the years from 1830 to 1879." See his *Class, Politics, and Early Industrial Capitalism*, pp. 77–8.

10. An early example: the English weavers who convened at Spitalfields in 1765 marched to London by three different routes to petition for relief against the importation of French silk. See Gene Sharp's *The Politics of Nonviolent Action*, p. 152, for this and other early examples.

11. Pierre Favre, in *La manifestation,* defines the demonstration as "a collective movement organized in a public space with the goal of producing a political outcome through the peaceful expression of an opinion or a demand" (p. 5) (my translation). But note that it was not until later in the nineteenth century that French dictionaries recognized the *manifestation* as a simple noun – long after the practice had become general.

12. "In taking arms against the government," writes historian Ted Margadant, "they appeared to engage in an intrinsically violent form of collective action. . . . But as an instrument of military force," he continues, "it was hopelessly outclassed by the French army." See Margadant's *French Peasants in Revolt*, p. 267.

13. This section summarizes the author's "Cycles of Collective Action: Between Moments of Madness and the Repertoire of Contention," in Traugott, ed., *Repertoires and Cycles of Collective Action*.

14. The following argument is developed in greater length in the author's " 'The Very Excess of Democracy': State Building and Contentious Politics in America."

7. FRAMING CONTENTION

I am grateful to Ron Aminzade, Ben Anderson, David Blatt, Stuart Blumin, John Borneman, Bill Gamson, Lynn Hunt, Mary Katzenstein, David Kertzer, Roman Laba, David Laitin, George Mosse, David Snow, Dan Thomas, and my late friend Aaron Wildavsky for comments on earlier versions of this chapter.

1. Archives Nationales, III Isère 9, Correspondance, 1791–1853, "Adresse du Commissaire du pouvoir exécutif près l'administration centrale du département de l'Isère." Quoted by Lynn Hunt in her *Politics, Culture, and Class in the French Revolution*, p. 52.

2. The most thorough treatment of the festivals of the French Revolution is Mona Ozouf's *Festivals and the French Revolution*. The symbol of Marianne, goddess of liberty and the Republic, has been magnificently studied by Maurice Agulhon in his *Marianne au combat*. The importance of symbolism for the future of mass politics was first signaled by George Mosse, in his 1975 book, *The Nationalization of the Masses*.

3. Recent versions of this "constructivist" perspective are Ron Eyerman and Andrew Jamison's *Social Movements: A Cognitive Approach*, William Gamson's *Talking Pol-*

itics, Bert Klandermans's *The Social Psychology of Protest*, and Alberto Melucci's *Challenging Codes*, in addition to the work by Robert Benford and David Snow, which will be discussed at greater length below. An application of the constructivist perspective to nationalism is Benedict Anderson's *Imagined Communities*. For a longer review and some problems in the constructivist approach, see my "Mentalities, Political Cultures and Collective Action Frames."

4. Among others, see Eyerman and Jamison, *Social Movements: A Cognitive Approach;* Laraña, Johnston, and Gusfield, eds., *New Social Movements;* Johnston and Klandermans, eds., *Social Movements and Culture;* and Morris and Mueller, eds., *Frontiers in Social Movement Theory.*

5. For their most important theoretical contributions, see Snow, Rochford, Worden, and Benford, "Frame Alignment Processes"; Snow and Benford, "Ideology, Frame Resonance, and Participant Mobilization," and "Master Frames and Cycles of Protest"; Robert Benford, "Frame Disputes within the Disarmament Movement"; and Benford and Hunt, "Dramaturgy and Social Movements."

6. I am grateful for these observations to Arthur Kleinman, speaking at a meeting of the "contentious politics research group" at the Center for Advanced Study in the Behavioral Sciences in June 1997.

7. For example, movements against antiimmigration laws in France often reevoke the memory of the deportation by marching from the Gare de l'Est from which Jews and others were sent to the gas furnaces by the Vichy regime.

8. See, in particular, Leila Rupp's " 'Imagine My Surprise' " and Barbara Ryan's *Feminism and the Women's Movement.*

9. I am grateful to Sarah Soule for her help in assembling the materials on which the following section is based.

10. In many ways the apotheosis of the blending of religious and sports symbolism is the "Promise Keepers," the male-only fundamentalist movement that has grown by leaps and bounds in the United States in the 1990s. For a report, see Conason, Ross, and Kokorinos, "The Promise Keepers Are Coming."

11. I am grateful to Bill Gamson for this insight, at a meeting of the "contentious politics research group" at the Center for Advanced Study in the Behavioral Sciences in June 1997. See his "Social Psychology of Collective Action" and *Talking Politics.*

12. Media coverage can also favor one branch of a movement over another in forming the public image of a movement. For example, Liesbet van Zoonen found that a series of public events mounted by the Dutch women's movement provided three main issue elements that almost all the media sources featured. These "framing elements" formed the building blocks for the future public identity of the movement (1992: 13).

13. But contrary to what some scholars of American contention think, this is hardly an American monopoly: for a suggestive discussion of "rights consciousness" in rural China, see Li and O'Brien's "Villagers and Popular Resistance in Contemporary China."

14. The locus classicus of collective identity theory is found in Alberto Melucci's *Challenging Codes: Collective Action in the Information Age.* Issues of identity formation in social movements are central to several major collections in the social movement field: Johnston and Klandermans's *Social Movements and Culture;* Lar-

ana, Johnston, and Gusfield's *New Social Movements*; and Morris and Mueller's *Frontiers in Social Movement Theory*.

15. It is significant that, in August 1980, at the Lenin shipyard gate, above the wooden cross, the portraits of the pope, a picture of the Black Madonna of Czestochowa and the crowned White Eagle of Poland, there flew a banner saying "Workers of all factories, unite!" Laba, *Roots of Solidarity*, p. 130.

8. MOBILIZING STRUCTURES AND CONTENTIOUS POLITICS

1. For a comparison of Hobsbawm's and Piven and Cloward's approaches, see Hobsbawm's interesting review of Piven and Cloward's work, "The Left and the Crisis of Organization," and the response of Piven and Cloward to their critics in the preface to the 1979 edition of *Poor People's Movements*.

2. The section that follows is much in debt to the work of Ted Margadant, whose *French Peasants in Revolt: The Insurrection of 1851* is a model of theoretically informed social and political history.

3. The insurgents attacking Béziers proclaimed: "In the name of the French People! The President of the Republic has violated the Constitution, so the People reclaim their rights." Margadant, *French Peasants,* p. 5.

4. On the formation of the Socialist Workers Party (SAP), see Donald Blake, "Swedish Trade Unions and the Social Democratic Party: The Formative Years." On the Austrian party and its relation to the German model, see Vincent Knapp, *Austrian Social Democracy, 1889–1914*, ch. 1. On the influence of German Marxism on the development of Russian social democracy, see John Plamenatz, *German Marxism and Russian Communism*, pp. 317–29.

5. Basic materials on this poorly understood movement will be found in Daniel Guérin, *Anarchism: From Theory to Practice*; Irving Louis Horowitz, ed., *The Anarchists*; and James Joll, *The Anarchists*.

6. In England, where revolutionary impulses were pretty much dead by the 1870s, the major tendency was toward a sturdy form of "guild" socialism. Where anarchism gave way to syndicalism, as it did in France, the result was a mentality of sterile *ouvrièrisme* – the conviction that revolution would emerge from the healthy instincts of the working class.

7. The fastest-growing types, however, are the most centralized: federations of religious congregations. Linked nationally by well-organized "networks," "faith-based community organizations are significantly more effective in gaining organizational power, imparting skills and a sense of efficacy to members and building cross-race coalitions than other types of community organizations" (Swarts 1997: 2).

8. Note that Jenkins and Eckert, in their "Channelling Black Insurgency," find that foundation support did not coincide with the most insurgent phase of the civil rights movement but with the more institutionalized, more moderate phase in the late 1960s and early 1970s.

9. Evidence suggesting that new movement organizations have smaller memberships today than in the past comes from Hanspeter Kriesi's work on new social

movement organizations in four European democracies (1996). Kriesi finds that, with the exception of Greenpeace, the organizations created since 1965 had much smaller memberships than those created before that date (p. 172).

10. The core of Putnam's empirical work, however, has been in Italy, where he and his collaborators, Robert Leonardi and Raffaella Nanetti, published a massive study based on the concept of social capital, *Making Democracy Work*.

11. I am grateful to Hanspeter Kriesi for this observation.

12. For example, the Dutch Committee against Cruise Missiles brought together at least ten major peace organizations, in addition to the largest trade union federations and the leading left-wing parties in a series of national peace demonstrations. See Rochon, *Mobilizing for Peace*, pp. 79–80, and Schennink, "From Peace Week to Peace Work." Also see Robert Kleidman's "Organizations and Coalitions in the Cycles of the American Peace Movement," and his book, *Organizing for Peace: Neutrality, the Test-Ban and the Freeze*.

13. The National Front had called its national congress for the city of Strasbourg, where a socialist mayor joined with a coalition of organizations from all over the country behind a massive antifascist demonstration. See *Le Monde*, March 31, 1997. I am grateful to Jonathan Lawrence for the data on this demonstration.

9. CYCLES OF CONTENTION

This chapter profited from the comments of both Jack Goldstone and Charles Tilly. The chapter is also much in debt to the stimulating article by Doug McAdam, " 'Initiator' and 'Spin-off' Movements: Diffusion Processes in Protest Cycles."

1. For an initial statement of a program for applying the method of "causal analogical reasoning," see Charles Tilly, "Kings in Beggar's Raiment." For a path-dependent approach, see Jack Goldstone, "Social Movements and Revolutions: On the Evolution and Forms of Collective Action." I am grateful to Goldstone for permission to cite his as-yet-unpublished paper and for comments on a draft of this chapter.

2. Jack Goldstone argues that "Where the existing regime and policies are widely viewed as undesirable, the environment for protest is highly supportive. Under such conditions, the emergence of a protest movement, and its mild handling by the state, is likely to encourage others. . . . this sequence tends to build to form a society-wide cycle of protest" (1997: 21). My view is similar to Goldstone's, except for the ambiguity in the term "mild handling by the state." The handling may be mild, but what distinguishes the onset of a cycle is the assimilation of movement demands to those of others – which is frequently the result of refusal to consider the movement's demands.

3. The outline in the text reflects experience in western Europe and the United States since the 1960s and has been expanded in the light of the recent experiences of eastern Europe and the former Soviet Union. It will be for other scholars to determine whether and in what ways the picture resembles waves of collective action in other systems and other periods of history. For a set of empirical investigations linked to the concepts developed here, see Marc Traugott, ed., *Repertoires and Cycles of Collective Action*.

4. Jack Goldstone points to another example: the English Revolution of 1640, in which a largely united Parliament and gentry split into royalist and parliamentary factions over whether to take extreme measures against the king.

5. This account is based on Craig Calhoun, *Neither Gods nor Emperors*, ch. 2 and pp. 183–85.

6. But more rigid authoritarianisms, like that of the shah of Iran, were doomed by a pattern of repression that was "indiscriminately aimed at economic, religious, and technical elites, thus creating a national cross-class coalition against him" (Goldstone 1997: 20).

7. The following section summarizes parts of the analysis in Soule and Tarrow, "Acting Collectively, 1847–1849: How the Repertoire of Collective Action Changed and Where It Happened." I am grateful to Sarah Soule for her collaboration in analyzing the data on which this section is based and for her helpful comments on a draft of this chapter.

8. For a survey of the main background causes of the revolutions in the various European countries, see Roger Price, *The Revolutions of 1848,* and the excellent basic bibliography he provides.

9. Generally speaking, religious cleavages were dominant in Switzerland, ethnic and nationalist ones in the Hapsburg Empire outside of Austria, and issues of political representation in France, Germany, and Austria itself. Although the national question came to dominate the Italian *quarantotto*, it began with agitations for liberal reform in Rome and the Kingdom of the Two Sicilies; only as it moved northward to areas controlled by the Hapsburgs did it take on a nationalist coloration. In France and Germany, although food riots occurred in the early stages of the conflagration, the major axes of conflict were over representative institutions and workers' rights.

10. Marx writes in his *Eighteenth Brumaire*: "Bourgeois revolutions, like those of the eighteenth century, storm swiftly from success to success . . . soon they have attained their zenith and a long crapulent depression lays hold of society. . . . proletarian revolutions . . . criticize themselves constantly, interrupt themselves continually in their own course, come back to the apparently accomplished in order to begin it afresh" (1963: 19).

11. No information is provided by Godechot for Scandinavia (except for the brief war between Denmark and Prussia over Schleswig-Holstein); none for Greece and Portugal; and none for the European parts of the Ottoman Empire. For a more detailed analysis of his data and of some of the problems that they present, see Soule and Tarrow, "Acting Collectively."

12. Here we must be cautious, since Godechot's term *manifestation* may lack the specificity of the form of collective action that we now call by that term, which Pierre Favre, in *La manifestation*, defines as "a collective movement organized in public space with the goal of producing a political outcome by the peaceful expression of an opinion or a demand" (p. 15, my translation).

13. On the French "Events," the most detached treatment is by Jacques Capdevielle and René Mouriaux, *Mai 68: L'entre-deux de la modernité*. For a recent compendium of reflections, see Mouriaux, ed., *1968: Exploration du Mai français*. On the Italian *sessantotto*, see Peppino Ortoleva, *Saggio sui movimenti del 1968 in Europa e in America*, and Sidney Tarrow, *Democracy and Disorder*, ch. 6. An excellent comparison of the outcomes of the two cases in terms of economic policy is Michele

Salvati, "May 1968 and the Hot Autumn of 1969: The Responses of Two Ruling Classes."

14. For the United States, the most pungent reflections on this period are found in Todd Gitlin's *The Sixties* and James Miller's *Democracy Is in the Streets*.

15. Part of the section that follows draws heavily from an essay by Doug McAdam, Sidney Tarrow, and Charles Tilly, "Towards an Integrated Perspective on Social Movements and Revolution."

16. But see Goldstone 1997 for an important challenge to the tradition of separating the analysis of revolutions from social movements.

17. Tilly specifies this as more than one contender for power, each of which has substantial support from within the population. When some regimes fall apart, however, they turn out to have little support from any substantial group within society – as when the apparently powerful shah of Iran fled ignominiously because he turned out to have little support. I am grateful to Jack Goldstone for pointing this out to me.

18. For a first effort, see McAdam, Tarrow, and Tilly, "Towards an Integrated Perspective on Social Movements and Revolution."

10. STRUGGLING TO REFORM

1. When we add nonpolicy goals like personal transformation and movement stabilization to the list, the dimensions of success become even larger and it is clear why Marx and Wood concluded that "the systematic study of social movement consequences is much less developed than that of the prior conditions that give rise to movements." See their "Strands of Theory and Research in Collective Behavior," p. 405.

2. See Taft and Ross 1969; Snyder and Kelly 1976; Shorter and Tilly 1971; and Conell 1978, as well as the summary of their findings in Giugni 1994.

3. In a comparative study of the Swiss and American women suffrage movements, Lee Ann Banaszak insists on the primacy of values and beliefs in explaining the differential success and failure of the two movements (1996) and is skeptical of the weight of opportunities (she has little to say about constraints). "We must," she argues, "move beyond the political opportunity structure and examine theories about how collective values and beliefs play a role in the processing of information and how perceptions, especially those affecting action, are developed" (p. 32). But if Swiss women's values and perceptions "largely determined whether and how the movement acted" (p. 217), perhaps what they perceived was an opportunity structure that – by Banaszak's own evidence – was fairly bleak.

4. William Gamson's *Strategy of Social Protest* is the required starting point for the analysis of the internal facets of movements that conduce to their success. A number of works followed the publication of Gamson's research, some supporting his findings, while others came up with different results. For a thorough review on the replications and criticisms following the publication of Gamson's study, see Marco G. Giugni's "Outcomes of Social Movements: A Review of the Literature" (1994).

5. These findings and their replications and modifications in later work are summarized in Giugni 1994: 9–13.

6. Specifically, Sherkat and Blocker found that former protesters hold "more liberal political orientations and are more aligned with liberal parties and actions; select occupations in the 'new class'; are more educated; hold less traditional religious orientations and are less attached to religious organizations; marry later; and are less likely to have children" (1997: 1050).

7. Tarrow, *Democracy and Disorder*, ch. 11. This observation is based on too few cases to present statistically, but occupational marginality was true of most of the former leaders interviewed.

8. The first part of the subtitle is the same as one of McAdam's, in *Freedom Summer* (pp. 213–19), but it was too good a title not to appropriate.

9. The following section summarizes my article, "Social Protest and Policy Reform: May 1968 and the Loi d'Orientation in France."

10. See Jacques F. Fomerand's "Policy Formulation and Change in Gaullist France: The 1968 Orientation Act of Higher Education," the best analysis of the policy process surrounding the Orientation Act and its policy outcomes.

11. Organization has been the weak point of studies of the women's movement, with more feminist scholars focusing on consciousness – perhaps reflecting the movement's own emphasis on discourse and collective identity. However, studies that analyze organization, and especially informal movement networks, are beginning to multiply. For example, see Anne Costain's *Inviting Women's Rebellion*, ch. 3; Myra Marx Ferree and Patricia Yancey Martin, eds., *Feminist Organization: Harvest of the New Women's Movement*; Mary Katzenstein's "Feminism within American Institutions"; Jane Mansbridge's *Why We Lost the ERA*, chs. 12–13; and Suzanne Staggenborg's *The Pro-Choice Movement*.

12. This section draws on my "Cycles of Collective Action: Between Moments of Madness and the Repertoire of Contention" in Traugott, ed., *Repertoires and Cycles of Collective Action*.

11. TRANSNATIONAL CONTENTION

An earlier version of this chapter is to be published in M. Hanagan, L. Page Moch, and W. te Brake, eds., *Challenging Authority: The Historical Study of Contentious Politics* (1998), ch. 15. Thanks to Matt Evangelista, Doug Imig, Margaret Keck, and John Meyer for comments on a draft of this chapter.

1. For a more detailed analysis of the strike, see Imig and Tarrow, "From Strike to Eurostrike: The Europeanization of Social Movements and the Development of a EuroPolity."

2. Just who coined the term "Eurostrike" remains to be investigated. In our present state of knowledge, it first appeared in the French newspaper, *Le Monde*, March 10, 1997, p. 24 ("L'Eurogrève a mobilisée les salariés de Renault contre la fermature du site de Vilvorde"). The term does not appear in Reuter's dispatches, but on March 11, 1997, Reuter's quoted a French union spokesman who called the demonstration that day a "pan-European demonstration."

3. When Schweitzer announced that he would meet with the Renault Works Council

at the firm's Paris headquarters, a convoy of eighty buses transported three thousand workers in their red and green union jackets to Paris, where they called for solidarity strikes (Reuters, March 11, 1997; *Le Monde,* March 13, 1997). The Belgian workers followed with a surprise "commando action" on March 13 across the border at the Renault plant in Douai.

4. These figures turned out to combine both "social measures" and the loss of value due to the abandonment of Renault's investment in the plant, but Juppé's tactic was enough to disarm the unionists.

5. Smith drew her analysis from the *Yearbook of International Organizations,* which uses "UN records on NGO's, self-reports, referrals, and the media to identify organizations." In her "Characteristics of the Modern-Transnational Movement Sector," in Smith, Chatfield, and Pagnucco, eds., *Transnational Social Movements and World Politics* (1997: 45-6), she coded "every nongovernmental organization whose primary aims included some form of social change (broadly defined)."

6. While we have a number of good studies of the Western peace movement (see Kleidman 1993, Meyer 1990, Rochon 1988, and Meyer and Rochon 1997), less work has been done on religion as a transnational movement. But see the impressive collection of work edited by Susanne Rudolf and James Piscatori, *Transnational Religion and Fading States,* and especially the contributions by Eickelman, Kane, and Levine and Stoll.

7. Three classic studies trace the transfer of the eastern European labor movement experience to the New World: for the United States, see Isaac Hourwich's *Immigration and Labor* (1969); for the influence of immigrants on the Argentinean labor movement see del Campo 1973; on the immigrant origins of the Chilean labor movement, see Ansell 1972.

8. I believe that this is so even though Keck and Sikkink derive their definition of the term "network" from the work of J. Clyde Mitchell, who was writing about domestic networks (1973: 23). For an excellent adaptation of social network analysis to the study of social movements, see Mario Diani, *Green Networks,* and his 1997 paper, "Social Movements and Social Capital: A Network Perspective on Social Movement Outcomes."

9. I am grateful to Professors Keck and Sikkink for allowing me to consult their book prior to its publication, as well as for Keck's comments on this and several previous papers on a subject they know far better than I do.

CONCLUSION: THE FUTURE OF SOCIAL MOVEMENTS

1. Even as they celebrated it, the French were interring 1789. See Kaplan's *Adieu 1789,* which treats the bicentennial as a celebratory rite for the funeral of the French Revolution, with François Mitterrand as king president and historian François Furet as majordomo.

2. Even in Italy – so far from the periphery of world communism that its Communist Party was barely recognizable by 1989 – party leaders rejected the hammer and sickle and changed their name to the Democratic Party of the Left. On this change, see Stephen Hellman, "Italian Communism in the First Republic."

3. Much of the reasoning in this and the next section, and some of the data reported,

are drawn from the introduction to David Meyer and Sidney Tarrow, eds., *A Movement Society? Contentious Politics for a New Century*

4. The exception was France, both because the "cycle" of new social movement activity came earlier in Kriesi's fifteen-year period and because the co-option of a number of movement organizations by the Socialist-led government in the early 1980s saw an overall reduction of protest during the mid-1980s. For a more detailed study based on the same data, see Jan Willem Duyvendak, *Le Poids du politique.*

5. These findings come from the results of a study directed by Dieter Rucht at the Wissenschaftszentrum-Berlin. For a first report, see his "The Structure and Culture of Collective Protest," in which he finds an increase in demonstrative, confrontational, and violent forms of protest for the West German peace movement between the 1950s and the 1980s (see his table 5).

SOURCES

Ackerman, Peter, and Christopher Kruegler (1994). *Strategic Nonviolent Conflict: The Dynamics of People Power in the Twentieth Century.* Westport, Conn.: Praeger.

Agnew, John, ed. (1997). *Political Geography: A Reader.* London: Arnold.

Agulhon, Maurice (1979). *Marianne au combat: L'imagerie et la symbolique républicaines de 1789 à 1880.* Paris: Flammarion.

    (1982). *The Republic in the Village: The People of the Var from the French Revolution to the Second Republic.* Translated by Janet Lloyd. Cambridge: Cambridge University Press.

Alinsky, Saul (1971). *Rules for Radicals.* New York: Vintage.

Allardt, Erik (1962). "Community Activity, Leisure Use and Social Structure," *Acta Sociologica* 6:67–82.

Amenta, Edwin, Bruce G. Caruthers, and Yvonne Zylan (1992). "A Hero for the Aged? The Townsend Movement, the Political Mediation Model, and U.S. Old-Age Policy, 1934–1950," *American Journal of Sociology* 98:308–39.

Aminzade, Ronald (1981). *Class, Politics, and Early Industrial Capitalism: A Study of Mid-Nineteenth-Century Toulouse, France.* Albany: State University of New York.

    (1993a). *Ballots and Barricades: Class Formation and Republican Politics in France, 1830–1871.* Princeton: Princeton University Press.

    (1993). "Capitalist Development, Class Formation, and the Consequences of Political Repression," *Political Power and Social Theory* 8:79–106.

Anderson, Benedict (1990). "Language, Fantasy, Revolution: Java, 1900–1945," *Prisma* 50:25–39.

    (1991). *Imagined Communities: Reflections on the Origin and Spread of Nationalism.* 2nd rev. ed. London: Verso.

    (1992). "Long-Distance Nationalism. World Capitalism and the Rise of Identity Politics," Center for Asian Studies, Amsterdam, Netherlands.

Anderson, Eugene N., and Pauline R. Anderson (1967). *Political Institutions and Social*

Change in Continental Europe in the Nineteenth Century. Berkeley: University of California Press.

Ansell, Alan (1972). *Politics and the Labour Movement in Chile*. New York: Oxford University Press.

Apter, David E., ed. (1964). *Ideology and Discontent*. Glencoe, Ill.: Free Press.

Aptheker, Herbert (1989). *Abolitionism: A Revolutionary Movement*. Boston: Twayne Publishers.

Ardant, Gabriel (1975). "Financial Policy and Economic Infrastructure of Modern States and Nations," in Charles Tilly, ed., *The Formation of National States in Western Europe*. Princeton: Princeton University Press, pp. 164–242.

Badie, Bertrand (1976). *Stratégie de la Grève*. Paris: Presses de la Fondation Nationale des Sciences Politiques.

  (1997). "Le jeu triangulaire," in Pierre Birnbaum, ed., *Sociologie des nationalismes*. Paris: Presses Universitaires de France, pp. 447–62.

Bailyn, Bernard (1967). *The Ideological Origins of the American Revolution*. Cambridge, Mass.: Harvard University Press.

Banaszak, Lee Ann (1996). *Why Movements Succeed or Fail: Opportunity, Culture, and the Struggle for Woman Suffrage*. Princeton: Princeton University Press.

Barkan, Steven E. (1984). "Legal Control of the Southern Civil Rights Movement," *American Sociological Review* 49:552–65.

Beissinger, Mark (1996). "How Nationalism Spread: Eastern Europe Adrift," *Social Research* 63:97–145.

  (1998). "Event Analysis in Transitional Societies: Protest Mobilization in the Former Soviet Union," in Dieter Rucht, Ruud Koopmans, and Friedhelm Neidhardt, eds., *Acts of Dissent: The Study of Protest in Contemporary Democracies*. Berlin: Sigma.

Beloff, Max (1963). *Public Order and Popular Disturbances, 1660–1714*. New York: Barnes and Noble.

Benford, Robert D. (1993). "Frame Disputes within the Disarmament Movement," *Social Forces* 71:677–701.

Benford, Robert D., and Scott A. Hunt (1992). "Dramaturgy and Social Movements: The Social Construction and Communication of Power," *Sociological Inquiry* 62:36–55.

Bensel, Richard (1990). *Yankee Leviathan: The Origins of Central State Authority in America, 1859–1877*. Cambridge: Cambridge University Press.

Bercé, Yves-Marie (1990). *History of Peasant Revolts: The Social Origins of Rebellion in Early Modern France*. Ithaca, N.Y.: Cornell University Press.

Berejikian, Jeffrey (1992). "Revolutionary Collective Action and the Agent-Structure Problem," *American Political Science Review* 86:649–57.

Bermeo, Nancy (1997). "Myths of Moderation. Confrontation and Conflict during Democratic Transitions," *Comparative Politics* 27:305–22.

Bevilacqua, Piero (1980). *Campagne del mezzogriorno tra fascismo e dopoguerra*. Turin: G. Einaudi.

Blake, Donald (1960). "Swedish Trade Unions and the Social Democratic Party: The Formative Years," *Scandinavian Economic History Review* 8:19–44.

Bloch, Marc (1931). *Les caractères originaux de l'histoire rurale française*. Paris: Armand Colin.

Blocker, Jack S., Jr. (1989). *American Temperance Movements: Cycles of Reform.* Boston: Twayne Publishers.

Blom Amélie (1997). "Mobilisation et mondialisation des communications: La protestation contre *Les versets sataniques,*" unpublished paper, Paris.

Bob, Clifford (1997). "The Marketing of Rebellion in Global Civil Society: Political Insurgencies, International Media, and the Growth of Transnational Support." Ph.D. dissertation, Massachusetts Institute of Technology.

Bobbio, Luigi (1979). *Lotta continua: Storia di una organizzazione rivoluzionaria.* Roma: Savelli.

Bonnell, Victoria (1983). *Roots of Rebellion: Workers' Politics and Organizations in St. Petersburg and Moscow, 1900–1914.* Berkeley: University of California Press.

Boudreau, Vincent (1996). "Northern Theory, Southern Protest: Opportunity Structure Analysis in a Cross-National Perspective," *Mobilization* 1:175–89.

Boyte, Harry C. (1980). *The Backyard Revolution.* Philadelphia: Temple University Press.

Brand, Karl-Werner (1990). "Cyclical Aspects of New Social Movements: Waves of Cultural Criticism and Mobilization Cycles of New Middle-class Radicalism," in Russell Dalton and Manfred Kuechler, eds., *Challenging the Political Order.* Oxford: Oxford University Press, pp. 23–42.

Brewer, John (1976). *Party Ideology and Popular Politics at the Accession of George III.* Cambridge: Cambridge University Press.

(1989). *The Sinews of Power: War, Money and the English State, 1688–1783.* New York: Knopf.

Bridges, Amy (1986). "Becoming American: The Working Classes in the United States before the Civil War," in Ira Katznelson and Aristide R. Zolberg, eds., *Working Class Formation: Nineteenth Century Patterns in Western Europe and the United States.* Princeton: Princeton University Press, pp. 157–96.

Bridgford, Jeff (1989). "The Events of May: Consequences for Industrial Relations in France," in D. L. Hanley and A. P. Kerr, eds., *May '68: Coming of Age.* London: Macmillan, pp. 100–16.

Bright, Charles C. (1984). "The State in the United States during the Nineteenth Century," in Charles Bright and Susan Harding, eds., *Statemaking and Social Movements: Essays in History and Theory,* Ann Arbor: University of Michigan Press, pp. 121–58.

Bright, Charles, and Susan Harding, eds. (1984). *Statemaking and Social Movements: Essays in History and Theory.* Ann Arbor: University of Michigan Press.

Brinton, Crane (1965). *The Anatomy of Revolution.* New York: Vintage.

Brockett, Charles D. (1991). "The Structure of Political Opportunities and Peasant Mobilization in Central America," *Comparative Politics* 23:253–74.

(1995). "A Protest-Cycle Resolution of the Repression/Popular-Protest Paradox," in Mark Traugott, ed., *Repertoires and Cycles of Collective Action.* Durham, N.C.: Duke University Press, pp. 117–44.

Brown, Richard D. (1970). *Revolutionary Politics in Massachusetts: The Boston Committee of Correspondence and the Towns, 1772–1774.* Cambridge, Mass.: Harvard University Press.

(1989). *Knowledge Is Power: The Diffusion of Information in Early America.* New York: Oxford.

Bruneteaux, Patrick (1996). *Maintenir l'ordre. Les transformations de la violence d'Etat en régime democratique.* Paris: Presses de la Fondation Nationale des Sciences Politiques.

Brysk, Alison (1994). "Acting Globally: Indian Rights and International Politics in Latin America," in Donna Lee Van Cott, ed., *Indigenous Peoples and Democracy in Latin America.* New York: St. Martin's, pp. 29–51.

Buechler, Steven M. (1986). *The Transformation of the Woman Suffrage Movement: The Case of Illinois, 1850–1920.* New Brunswick, N.J.: Rutgers University Press.

Bunce, Valerie (1984–5). "The Empire Stikes Back: The Transformation of Eastern Europe from a Soviet Asset to a Soviet Liability," *International Organization* 39: 1–46.

  (1991). "Democracy, Stalinism and the Management of Uncertainty," in Gyorgy Szoboszlai, ed., *Democracy and Political Transformation.* Budapest: Hungarian Political Science Association, pp. 138–64.

  (forthcoming). *Subversive Institutions: The Design and the Destruction of Socialism and the State.* Cambridge: Cambridge University Press.

Burstein, Paul (1985). *Discrimination, Jobs, and Politics: The Struggle for Equal Opportunity in the United States.* Chicago: University of Chicago Press.

  (1998). "Interest Organizations and the Study of Democratic Politics," in Anne Costain and Andrew McFarland, eds., *Social Movements and American Political Institutions.* Boulder, Colo.: Rowland and Littlefield, ch. 3.

Burstein, Paul, Rachel L. Einwohner, and Jocelyn A. Hollander (1991). "The Success of Political Movements: A Bargaining Perspective," unpublished paper, University of Washington, Department of Sociology.

Bushnell, John (1990). *Moscow Graffiti: Language and Subculture.* Boston: Unwin Hyman.

Calhoun, Craig (1982). *The Question of Class Struggle: Social Foundations of Popular Radicalism during the Industrial Revolution.* Chicago: University of Chicago Press.

  (1994a). *Neither Gods nor Emperors: Students and the Struggle for Democracy in China.* Berkeley: University of California Press.

  (1994b). "Social Theory and the Politics of Identity," in C. Calhoun, ed., *Social Theory and the Politics of Identity.* Oxford: Blackwell, pp. 9–36.

  (1995). "New Social Movements of the Early Nineteenth Century," in Mark Traugott, ed., *Repertoires and Cycles of Collective Action.* Durham, N.C.: Duke University Press, pp. 173–216.

Calvino, Italo (1985). *Il barone rampante.* Milan: Garzanti.

Capdevielle, Jacques, and René Mouriaux (1988). *Mai 68: L'entre-deux de la modernité.* Paris: Presses de la Fondation Nationale des Sciences Politiques.

Cardon, Dominique, and Jean-Philippe Huertin (1991). " 'Tenir les rangs.' Les services d'encadrement des manifestations ouvrières (1909–1936)," in Pierre Favre, ed., *La manifestation.* Paris: Presses de la Fondation Nationale des Sciences Politiques, pp. 123–55.

Castells, Manuel (1994). "European Cities, the Informational Society, and the Global Economy," *New Left Review*, 204:18–32.

  (1997). *The Information Age: Economy, Society, and Culture.* Vol. 2, *The Power of Identity.* Oxford: Blackwell.

Censer, Jack R., and Jeremy D. Popkin, eds. (1987). *Press and Politics in Pre-Revolutionary France*. Berkeley: University of California Press.

Cerny, Philip (1995). "Globalization and the Changing Logic of Collective Action." *International Organization* 49: 595.

Chamberlin, John (1974). "Provision of Collective Goods as a Function of Group Size," *American Political Science Review* 68:707–16.

Champagne, Patrick (1996). *Maintenir l'ordre: Les transformations de la violence d'Etat en régime démocratique*. Paris: Presses de la Fondation Nationale des Sciences Politiques.

Charlesworth, Andrew (1983). *An Atlas of Rural Protest in Britain, 1548–1900*. Philadelphia: University of Pennsylvania Press.

Chartier, Roger (1987). *The Cultural Uses of Print in Early Modern France*. Princeton: Princeton University Press.

  (1991). *The Cultural Origins of the French Revolution*. Durham, N.C.: Duke University Press.

Chong, Dennis (1991). *Collective Action and the Civil Rights Movement*. Chicago: University of Chicago Press.

Christie, Ian (1982). *Wilkes, Wyvill and Reform: The Parliamentary Reform Movement in British Politics, 1760–1785*. London: Macmillan.

Collier, Ruth (1997). "Between Elite Negotiation and Working-Class Triumph: Labor and Democratization in Western Europe and Latin America," unpublished book manuscript.

Conason, Joe, Alfred Ross, and Lee Cokorinos (1996). "The Promise Keepers Are Coming: The Third Wave of the Religious Right," *Nation*, October 7, pp. 11–19.

Conell, Carol (1978). "Was Holding Out the Key to Winning Strikes? Massachusetts, 1881–1894," Center for Research on Social Organization Working Paper No. 187. Ann Arbor, Mich.

Corbin, Alain (1994). "L'impossible présence du roi: Fêtes politiques et mises en scène du pouvoir sous la Monarchie de Juillet," in A. Corbin, N. Gérôme, and D. Tartakowsky, eds., *Les usages politiques des fêtes aux XIX–XX siècles*. Paris: Publications de la Sorbonne, pp. 77–116.

Corbin, Alain, N. Gérôme, and D. Tartakowsky, eds. (1994). *Les usages politiques des fêtes aux XIX–XX siècles*. Paris: Publications de la Sorbonne.

Cortright, David, and Ron Pagnucco (1997). "Limits to Transnationalism: The 1980s Freeze Campaign," in Jackie Smith, Charles Chatfield, and Ron Pagnucco, eds., *Transnational Social Movements and World Politics: Solidarity beyond the State*. Syracuse: Syracuse University Press, ch. 9.

Costain, Anne N. (1992). *Inviting Women's Rebellion: A Political Process Interpretation of the Women's Movement*. Baltimore: Johns Hopkins University Press.

Costain, Anne N., and W. Douglas Costain (1987). "Strategy and Tactics of the Women's Movement in the United States: The Role of Political Parties," in Mary F. Katzenstein and Carol McClurg Mueller, eds., *The Women's Movements of the United States and Western Europe: Consciousness, Political Opportunity and Public Policy*. Philadelphia: Temple University Press, pp. 196–214.

Costain, Anne N., and Andrew McFarland, eds. (1998). *Social Movements and American Political Institutions*. Boulder, Colo.: Rowman and Littlefield.

Cott, Nancy (1977). *The Bonds of Womanhood*. New Haven: Yale University Press.

Countryman, Edward (1981). *A People in Revolution: The American Revolution and Political Society in New York, 1760–1790.* Baltimore: Johns Hopkins University Press.

Courty, Guillaume (1993). "Barrer, filtrer, encombrer: Les routiers et l'art de retenir ses semblables," *Projet,* no. 235 (fall): 143–68.

Cross, Whitney R. (1982). *The Burned-Over District: The Social and Intellectual History of Enthusiastic Religion in Western New York, 1800–1850.* Ithaca, N.Y.: Cornell University Press.

Crozat, Matthew (1998). "Are the Times A-Changing? Assessing the Acceptance of Protest in Western Democracies," in David Meyer and Sidney Tarrow, eds., *The Social Movement Society: Contentious Politics for a New Century.* Boulder, Colo.: Rowman and Littlefield, ch. 2.

Crozier, Michel (1967). *The Bureaucratic Phenomenon.* Chicago: University of Chicago Press.

(1970). *The Stalled Society.* New York: Viking.

d'Anieri, Paul, Claire Ernst, and Elizabeth Kier (1990). "New Social Movements in Historical Perspective," *Comparative Politics* 22:445–58.

Dalton, Russell (1994). *The Green Rainbow: Environmental Groups in Western Europe.* New Haven: Yale University Press.

(1996). *Citizen Politics in Western Democracies.* 2nd rev. ed. Chatham, N.J.: Chatham House.

d'Anjou, Leo (1996). *Social Movements and Cultural Change: The First Abolition Campaign Revisited.* New York: Aldine de Gruyter.

Darnton, Robert (1979). *The Business of Enlightenment: A Publishing History of the Encyclopédie, 1775–1800.* Cambridge, Mass.: Harvard University Press.

(1982). *The Literary Underground of the Old Regime.* Cambridge, Mass.: Harvard University Press.

(1989). "Philosophy under the Cloak," in Robert Darnton and Daniel Roche, eds., *Revolution in Print: The Press in France, 1775–1800.* Berkeley: University of California Press, pp. 27–49.

Davis, John A. (1988). *Conflict and Control: Law and Order in Nineteenth-Century Italy.* Atlantic Highlands, N.J.: Humanities Press International.

Davis, Natalie (1973). "The Rites of Violence: Religious Riot in Sixteenth-Century France," *Past and Present* 59: 51–91.

Dawes, Robyn M., Anthony J. C. Van de Kragt, and John M. Orbell (1988). "Not Me or Thee but We: The Importance of Group Identity in Eliciting Cooperation in Dilemma Situations: Experimental Manipulations," *Acta Psychologica* 68: 83–97.

de Baecque, Antoine (1989). "Pamphlets: Libel and Political Mythology," in Robert Darnton and Daniel Roche, eds., *Revolution in Print: The Press in France, 1775–1800.* Berkeley: University of California Press, pp. 165–76.

del Campo, Hugo (1973). *Los orígenes del movimiento obrero argentino, Historia del movimiento obrero* 25. Buenos Aires: Centro Editor de America Latina.

della Porta, Donatella (1990). *Organizzazioni politiche clandestine. Il terrorismo di sinistra in Italia durante gli anni Sessanta.* Bologna: Il Mulino.

(1995). *Social Movements, Political Violence, and the State: A Comparative Analysis of Italy and Germany.* Cambridge: Cambridge University Press.

(1996). "Social Movements and the State: Thoughts on the Policing of Protest," in Doug McAdam, John D. McCarthy, and Mayer N. Zald, eds., *Comparative Perspectives on Social Movements: Political Opportunities, Mobilizing Structures, and Cultural Framings*. Cambridge: Cambridge University Press, pp. 62–92.

della Porta, Donatella, Olivier Fillieule, and Herbert Rieter (1998). "Policing Protest in France and Italy: From Intimidation to Cooperation?" in David Meyer and Sidney Tarrow, eds., *The Social Movement Society: Contentious Politics for a New Century*. Boulder, Colo.: Rowman and Littlefield, ch. 5.

della Porta, Donatella, and Herbert Rieter, eds. (1997). *Policing Protest: The Control of Mass Demonstrations in Contemporary Democracies*. Minneapolis: University of Minnesota Press.

della Porta, Donatella, and Sidney Tarrow (1986). "Unwanted Children: Political Violence and the Cycle of Protest in Italy, 1966–1973," *European Journal of Political Research* 14: 607–32.

d'Emilio, John (1992). *Making Trouble: Essays on Gay History, Politics and the University*. New York: Routledge.

Diamanti, Ilvo (1993). *La Lega: Geografia, storia e sociologia di un nuovo soggetto politico*. Rome: Donzelli.

Diani, Mario (1995). *Green Networks: A Structural Analysis of the Italian Environmental Movement*. Edinburgh: Edinburgh University Press.

(1996). "Linking Mobilization Frames and Political Opportunities: Insights from Regional Populism in Italy," *American Sociological Review* 61:1053–69.

(1997). "Social Movements and Social Capital: A Network Perspective on Social Movement Outcomes," unpublished paper, University of Strathclyde, Glasgow.

Drescher, Seymour (1982). "Public Opinion and the Destruction of British Colonial Slavery," in James Walvin, ed., *Slavery and British Society, 1776–1846*. Baton Rouge: Louisiana State University Press, pp. 22–48.

(1987). *Capitalism and Antislavery: British Mobilization in Comparative Perspective*. New York: Oxford University Press.

(1991). "British Way, French Way: Opinion Building and Revolution in the Second French Slave Emancipation," *American Historical Review* 96:709–34.

(1994). "Whose Abolition? Popular Pressure and the Ending of the British Slave Trade," *Past and Present*, no. 143: 136–66.

Durkheim, Emile (1951). *Suicide: A Study in Sociological Interpretation*. Glencoe, Ill.: Free Press.

Duyvendak, Jan Willem (1994). *Le poids du politique: Nouveaux mouvements sociaux en France*. Paris: L'Harmattan.

Egret, Jean (1977). *The French Pre-revolution, 1787–88*. Chicago: University of Chicago Press.

Eikelman, Dale F. (1997). "Trans-state Islam and Security," in Susanne Rudolf and James Piscatori, eds., *Transnational Religion and Fading States*. Boulder, Colo.: Westview, pp. 27–46.

Eisenstein, Elizabeth (1986). "Revolution and the Printed Word," in Roy Porter and Mikulas Teich, eds., *Revolution in History*. Cambridge: Cambridge University Press, pp. 186–205.

Eisenstein, Zillah (1996). *Hatreds: Racialized and Sexualized Conflicts in the 21st Century*. New York: Routledge.

Eisinger, Peter K. (1973). "The Conditions of Protest Behavior in American Cities," *American Political Science Review* 67:11–28.

Elias, Norbert (1994). *The Civilizing Process. Vol. 2, State Formation and Civilization.* Oxford: Blackwell.

Ernst, Claire (1997). "Americans in Paris. Act Up – Paris and Identity Politics," *French Politics and Society*, in preparation.

Esherick, Joseph W., and Jeffrey N. Wasserstrom (1990). "Acting Out Democracy," *Journal of Asian Studies* 49: 835–65.

Evans, Peter B., Dietrich Rueschemeyer, and Theda Skocpol, eds. (1985). *Bringing the State Back In.* Cambridge: Cambridge University Press.

Evans, Sara M. (1980). *Personal Politics: The Roots of Women's Liberation in the Civil Rights Movement and the New Left.* New York: Vintage.

Evans, Sara M. and Harry C. Boyte (1992). *Free Spaces: The Sources of Democratic Change in America.* Chicago: University of Chicago Press.

Eyerman, Ron, and Andrew Jamison (1991). *Social Movements: A Cognitive Approach.* University Park: Pennsylvania University Press.

Fantasia, Rick (1988). *Cultures of Solidarity: Consciousness, Action, and Contemporary American Workers.* Berkeley: University of California Press.

Favre, Pierre, ed. (1990). *La manifestation.* Paris: Presses de la Fondation Nationale des Sciences Politiques.

Fendrich, James M., and Ellis S. Krauss (1978). "Student Activism and Adult Left-wing Politics: A Causal Model of Political Socialization for Black, White and Japanese Students of the 1960s Generation," in L. Kriesberg, ed., *Research in Social Movements, Conflicts and Change,* vol. 1. Greenwich, Conn.: JAI, pp. 231–55.

Ferree, Myra Marx, and Patricia Yancey Martin, eds. (1995). *Feminist Organization: Harvest of the New Women's Movement.* Philadelphia: Temple University Press.

Fillieule, Olivier (1997). *Stratégies de la rue: Les manifestations en France.* Paris: Presses de la Fondation Nationale des Sciences Politiques.

Finer, Samuel E. (1975). "State- and Nation-Building in Europe: The Role of the Military," in Charles Tilly, ed., *The Formation of National States in Western Europe.* Princeton: Princeton University Press, pp. 84–163.

Finnemore, Martha (1996). "Norms, Culture, and World Politics: Insights from Sociology's Institutionalism," *International Organization* 47:565–98.

Fireman, Bruce, and William A. Gamson (1979). "Utilitarian Logic in the Resource Mobilization Perspective," in Mayer N. Zald and John D. McCarthy, eds., *The Dynamics of Social Movements: Resource Mobilization, Social Control and Tactics.* Cambridge, Mass.: Winthrop, pp. 8–44.

Fish, M. Steven (1995). *Democracy from Scratch: Opposition and Regime in the New Russian Revolution.* Princeton: Princeton University Press.

Fomerand, Jacques (1975). "Policy Formulation and Change in Gaullist France. The 1968 Orientation Act of Higher Education," *Comparative Politics* 8:59–89.

Foran, John (1993). *Fragile Resistance: Social Transformation in Iran from 1500 to the Revolution.* Boulder, Colo: Westview.

Foucault, Jacques (1972). *The Archeology of Knowledge.* New York: Pantheon.
      (1980). *Power/Knowledge: Selected Interviews and Other Writings, 1972–1977.* Edited by Colin Gordon. New York: Pantheon.

Franzosi, Roberto (1989). "From Words to Numbers: A Generalized and Linguistics-

Based Coding Procedure for Collective Event-Data from Newspapers," *Sociological Methodology* 19:263–98.

Fraser, Antonia (1996). *The Gunpowder Plot: Terror and Faith in 1605.* London: Weidenfeld and Nicolson.

Freeman, Jo (1987). "Whom You Know versus Whom You Represent: Feminist Politics in the United States," in Mary Fainsod Katzenstein and Carol McClurg Mueller, eds., *The Women's Movements of the United States and Western Europe: Consciousness, Political Opportunity and Public Policy.* Philadelphia: Temple University Press, pp. 215–44.

Furet, François (1981). *Interpreting the French Revolution.* Cambridge: Cambridge University Press.

Gagnon, V. P. (1994). "Serbia's Road to War," in L. Diamond and M. Platterner, eds., *Nationalism, Ethnic Conflict, and Democracy.* Baltimore: Johns Hopkins University Press, pp. 117–31.

Gamson, William (1988). "Political Discourse and Collective Action," in Bert Klandermans, Hanspeter Kriesi, and Sidney Tarrow, eds., *From Structure to Action: Comparing Social Movement Research across Cultures.* International Social Movement Research, vol. 1. Greenwich, Conn.: JAI, pp. 219–44.

(1990). *The Strategy of Social Protest.* 2nd rev. ed. Belmont, Calif.: Wadsworth.

(1992a). "The Social Psychology of Collective Action," in Aldon D. Morris and Carol McClurg Mueller, eds., *Frontiers in Social Movement Theory.* New Haven: Yale University Press, pp. 53–76.

(1992b). *Talking Politics.* Cambridge: Cambridge University Press.

Gamson, William, Bruce Fireman, and Steven Rytina (1982). *Encounters with Unjust Authority.* Homewood, Ill.: Dorsey Press.

Gamson, William, and David Meyer (1996). "The Framing of Political Opportunity," in Doug McAdam, John D. McCarthy, and Mayer N. Zald, eds., *Comparative Perspectives on Social Movements: Political Opportunities, Mobilizing Structures, and Cultural Framings.* Cambridge: Cambridge University Press, pp. 275–90.

Ganley, Gladys (1992). *The Exploding Political Power of Personal Media.* Norwood, N.J.: Ablex.

Gans, Herbert (1979). *Deciding What's News: A Study of the CBS Evening News, NBC Nightly News, Newsweek and Time.* New York: Pantheon.

Garner, Roberta Ash (1994). "Transnational Movements in Postmodern Society," *Peace Review* 6: 427–33.

Garner, Roberta Ash, and Mayer N. Zald (1985). "The Political Economy of Social Movement Sectors," in Gerald Suttles and Mayer N. Zald, eds., *The Challenge of Social Control: Citizenship and Institution Building in Modern Society. Essays in Honor of Morris Janowitz.* Norwood, N.J.: Ablex, pp. 119–45.

Garton Ash, Timothy (1984). *The Polish Revolution.* New York: Scribner.

(1990). *The Magic Lantern: The Revolution of '89 Witnessed in Warsaw, Budapest, Berlin and Prague.* New York: Random House.

(1997). "In the Serbian Soup," *New York Review of Books*, April 24, pp. 25–30.

Geary, Roger (1985). *Policing Industrial Disputes: 1893–1895.* Cambridge: Cambridge University Press.

Geertz, Clifford (1973). *The Interpretation of Cultures: Selected Essays.* New York: Basic Books.

Gelb, Joyce (1987). "Social Movement Success: A Comparative Analysis of Feminism in the United States and the United Kingdom," in Mary F. Katzenstein and Carol McClurg Mueller, eds., *The Women's Movements of the United States and the Western Europe: Consciousness, Political Opportunity and Public Policy.* Philadelphia: Temple University Press, pp. 267–89.

Gerhards, Jürgen, and Dieter Rucht (1992). "Mesomobilization: Organizing and Framing in Two Protest Campaigns in West Germany," *American Journal of Sociology* 98:555–96.

Gerlach, Luther P., and Virginia H. Hine (1970). *People, Power, Change: Movements of Social Transformation.* Indianapolis: Bobbs-Merrill.

Gitlin, Todd (1980). *The Whole World Is Watching: Mass Media in the Making and Unmaking of the New Left.* Berkeley: University of California Press.

    (1987). *The Sixties: Years of Hope, Days of Rage.* New York: Bantam Books.

    (1995). *The Twilight of Common Dreams: Why America Is Wracked by Culture Wars.* New York: Metropolitan Books.

Giugni, Marco G. (1994). "The Outcomes of Social Movements: A Review of the Literature," Center for Studies of Social Change Working Paper No. 197. New York: New School for Social Research.

    (1997). "Was It Worth the Effort: The Outcomes and Consequences of Social Movements," unpublished paper, Studies of Social Change, New School for Social Research.

Giugni, Marco, Doug McAdam, and Charles Tilly, eds. (1998). *How Movements Matter.* Minneapolis: University of Minnesota Press.

Glenn, John K., III (1997). "Citizens in Theatres: Framing Competition and the Velvet Revolution in Czechoslovakia, 1989," unpublished paper, Harvard University, Department of Sociology.

Godechot, Jacques (1971). *Les révolutions de 1848.* Paris: Albin Michel.

    ed. (1966). *La presse ouvrière, 1819–1850.* Paris: Bibliothèque de la Révolution de 1848.

Goffman, Erving (1974). *Frame Analysis: An Essay on the Organization of Experience.* Cambridge, Mass.: Harvard University Press.

Golden, Miriam A. (1997). *Heroic Defeats: The Politics of Job Loss.* Cambridge: Cambridge University Press.

Goldstone, Jack A. (1980). "The Weakness of Organization: A New Look at Gamson's *The Strategy of Social Protest,*" *American Journal of Sociology* 85: 1017–42.

    (1991). *Revolution and Rebellion in the Modern World.* Berkeley: University of California Press.

    (1997). "Social Movements and Revolutions: On the Evolution and Forms of Collective Action," unpublished paper, University of California at Davis.

Goldstone, Jack A., Ted R. Gurr, and Farrokh Moshiri, eds. (1991). *Revolutions of the Late Twentieth Century.* Boulder, Colo.: Westview.

Goodwin, Albert (1979). *The Friends of Liberty: The English Democratic Movement in the Age of the French Revolution.* Cambridge, Mass.: Harvard University Press.

Goody, Jack, ed. (1968). *Literacy in Traditional Societies.* Cambridge: Cambridge University Press.

Gould, Roger (1995). *Insurgent Identities: Class, Community, and Protest in Paris from 1848 to the Commune.* Chicago: University of Chicago Press.

Gouldner, Alvin W. (1975–6). "Prologue to a Theory of Revolutionary Intellectuals," *Telos* 26:3–36.

Gramsci, Antonio (1971). *Selections from the Prison Notebooks*. Edited and translated by Quintin Hoare and Geoffrey Nowell Smith. New York: International.

Granovetter, Mark (1973). "The Strength of Weak Ties," *American Journal of Sociology* 78:1360–80.

Green, John C. (1995). "The Christian Right and the 1994 Election: A View from the States," *PS: Political Science and Politics* 28:5–8.

Grew, Raymond (1984). "The Nineteenth-Century European State," in Charles Bright and Susan Harding, eds., *Statemaking and Social Movements: Essays in History and Theory*. Ann Arbor: University of Michigan Press, pp. 83–120.

Griffin, Clifford S. (1960). *Their Brothers' Keepers: Moral Stewardship in the United States, 1800–1865*. New Brunswick, N.J.: Rutgers University Press.

Guérin, Daniel (1970). *Anarchism: From Theory to Practice*. New York: Monthly Review Press.

Gurr, Ted R. (1971). *Why Men Rebel*. Princeton: Princeton University Press.

(1980). "On the Outcomes of Violent Conflict," in Gurr, ed., *Handbook of Political Conflict, Theory and Research*. New York: Free Press, pp. 238–94.

(1989). "Political Terrorism: Historical Antecedents and Contemporary Trends," in Gurr, ed., *Violence in America. vol. 2, Protest, Rebellion, Reform*. Newbury Park, Calif.: Sage, pp. 201–30.

Habermas, Jürgen (1981). "New Social Movements," *Telos* 49:33–37.

Hamilton, Charles (1986). "Social Policy and the Welfare of Black Americans: From Rights to Resources," *Political Science Quarterly* 101: 239–55.

Hanagan, Michael (1998). "Transnational Social Movements, Deterritorialized Migrants, and the State System: A Nineteenth-Century Case Study," in Marco Giugni, Doug McAdam, and Charles Tilly, eds., *How Movements Matter*. Minneapolis: University of Minnesota Press.

Hanagan, Michael, Leslie Page Moch, and Wayne te Brake, eds. (1998). *Challenging Authority: The Historical Study of Contentious Politics*. Minneapolis: University of Minnesota Press.

Hardin, Russell (1982). *Collective Action*. Baltimore: Johns Hopkins University Press.

(1995). *One for All: The Logic of Group Conflict*. Princeton: Princeton University Press.

Harrison, Carol (1996). "The Unsociable Frenchmen: Associations and Democracy in Historical Perspective," *Tocqueville Review* 17:37–56.

Heberle, Rudolf (1951). *Social Movements: An Introduction to Political Sociology*. New York: Appleton-Century-Crofts.

Hellman, Judith Adler (1987). *Journeys among Women: Feminism in Five Italian Cities*. New York: Oxford University Press.

Hellman, Stephen (1975). "The PCI's Alliance Strategy and the Case of the Middle Classes," in Donald L. M. Blackmer and Sidney Tarrow, eds., *Communism in Italy and France*. Princeton: Princeton University Press, pp. 372–419.

(1988). *Italian Communism in Transition: The Rise and Fall of the Historic Compromise in Turin, 1975–1980*. New York: Oxford University Press.

(1996). "Italian Communism in the First Republic," in Stephen Gundle and Simon Parker, eds., *The New Italian Republic*. London: Routledge, pp. 71–84.

Hill, Stuart, and Donald Rothchild (1992). "The Impact of Regime on the Diffusion of Political Conflict," in M. Midlarsky, ed., *The Internationalization of Communal Strife*. London: Routledge, pp. 189–206.

Hirschman, Albert (1982). *Shifting Involvements: Private Interest and Public Action*. Princeton: Princeton University Press.

Hobsbawm, Eric J. (1959). *Primitive Rebels: Studies in Archaic Forms of Social Movement in the 19th and 20th Centuries*. Manchester: Manchester University Press.

(1962). *The Age of Revolution: 1789–1848*. London: Weidenfeld and Nicolson.

(1964). *Labouring Men: Studies in the History of Labour*. London: Weidenfeld and Nicolson.

(1974). "Peasant Land Occupations," *Past and Present* 62: 120–52.

(1978). "The Left and the Crisis of Organization," *New York Review of Books*, March 23, pp. 3–5.

Hobsbawm, Eric J., and George Rudé (1975). *Captain Swing*. New York: Norton.

Hochschild, Arlie (1990). "Ideology and Emotion Management: A Perspective and Path for Future Research," in Theodore D. Kemper, ed., *Research Agendas in the Sociology of Emotions*. Albany: State University of New York Press, pp. 117–32.

Hoffer, Eric (1951). *The True Believer: Thoughts on the Nature of Mass Movements*. New York: Harper and Row.

Hoffmann, Stanley (1974). "The Ruled: Protest as a National Way of Life," in Hoffmann, *Decline or Renewal: France since the 1930s*. New York: Viking, pp. 111–44.

Hollis, Patricia (1970). *The Pauper Press: A Study in Working Class Radicalism of the 1830s*. London: Oxford University Press.

Horowitz, Irving Lewis, ed. (1964). *The Anarchists*. New York: Dell.

Hourwich, Isaac (1969). *Immigration and Labor: The Economic Aspects of European Immigration to the United States*. New York: Arno.

Hubrecht, Hubert G. (1990). "Le droit français de la manifestation," in P. Favre, ed., *La manifestation*. Paris: Presses de la Fondation Nationale des Sciences Politiques, pp. 181–206.

Hunt, Lynn (1984). *Politics, Culture, and Class in the French Revolution*. Berkeley: University of California Press.

(1992). *The Family Romance of the French Revolution*. Berkeley: University of California Press.

Imig, Doug, and Sidney Tarrow (1996). "The Europeanization of Movements? Contentious Politics and the European Union, October 1983–March 1995," Institute for European Studies Working Paper No. 96.3. Ithaca, N.Y.: Cornell University.

(1997). "From Strike to Eurostrike: The Europeanizaiton of Social Movements and the Development of a Euro-Polity," working paper, Harvard University, Center for International Affairs.

Inglehart, Ronald (1977). *The Silent Revolution: Changing Values and Political Styles among Western Publics*. Princeton: Princeton University Press.

(1990). *Culture Shift in Advanced Industrial Society*. Princeton: Princeton University Press.

Ion, Jacques (1997). *La fin des militants?* Paris: Editions Ouvrières.

Isserman, Maurice (1987). *If I Had a Hammer: The Decline of the Old Left and the Birth of the New Left.* New York: Basic Books.

Jenkins, J. Craig, and Craig Eckert (1986). "Channelling Black Insurgency: Elite Patronage and the Development of the Civil Rights Movement," *American Sociological Review* 51: 812–30.

Jenkins, J. Craig, and Charles Perrow (1977). "Insurgency of the Powerless: Farm Worker Movements (1946–1972)," *American Sociological Review* 42: 249–68.

Johnson, Chalmers (1962). *Peasant Nationalism and Communist Power: The Emergence of Revolutionary China, 1937–1945.* Stanford: Stanford University Press.

Johnson, Paul E. (1978). *A Shopkeeper's Millennium: Society and Revivals in Rochester, New York, 1815–1837.* New York: Hill and Wang.

Johnston, Hank (1995). "A Methodology for Frame Analysis: From Discourse to Cognitive Schemata," in Hank Johnston and Bert Klandermans, eds., *Social Movements and Culture.* Minneapolis: University of Minnesota Press, pp. 217–46.

Johnston, Hank, and Bert Klandermans, eds. (1995). *Social Movements and Culture.* Minneapolis: University of Minnesota Press.

Joll, James (1980). *The Anarchists.* 2nd ed. Cambridge, Mass.: Harvard University Press.

Kafka, Franz (1937). *Parables and Paradoxes.* Translated by Ernst Kaiser et al. New York: Schocken.

Kane, Ousmane (1997). "Muslim Missionaries and African States," in Susanne Rudolf and James Piscatori, eds., *Transnational Religion and Fading States.* Boulder, Colo.: Westview, pp. 47–62.

Kaplan, Steven L. (1982). *The Famine Plot Persuasion in Eighteenth Century France.* Transactions of the American Philosophical Society 72, Part 3. Philadelphia: American Philosophical Society.

(1984). *Provisioning Paris: Merchants and Millers in the Grain and Flour Trade during the Eighteenth Century.* Ithaca, N.Y.: Cornell University Press.

(1993). *Adieu 1789.* Paris: Seuil.

Katzenstein, Mary F. (1987). "Comparing the Feminist Movements of the United States and Western Europe: An Overview," in Mary F. Katzenstein and Carol McClurg Mueller, eds., *The Women's Movements of the United States and Western Europe: Consciousness, Political Opportunity and Public Policy.* Philadelphia: Temple University Press, pp. 3–20.

(1990). "Feminism within American Institutions: Unobtrusive Mobilization in the 1980s," *Signs* 16: 27–54.

(1993). "The Spectacle as Political Resistance. Feminist and Gay/Lesbian Politics in the Military," *Minerva: Quarterly Report on Women in the Military* 11: 1–16.

(1995). "Discursive Politics and Feminist Activism in the Catholic Church," in Myra Marx Ferree and Patricia Yancey Martin, eds., *Feminist Organization: Harvest of the New Women's Movement.* Philadelphia: Temple University Press, pp. 35–52.

(1998). *Faithful and Fearless: Moving Feminism into the Church and the Military.* Princeton: Princeton University Press.

Katzenstein, Mary F., and Carol McClurg Mueller, eds. (1987). *The Women's Movements of the United States and Western Europe: Consciousness, Political Opportunity and Public Policy*. Philadelphia: Temple University Press.

Katznelson, Ira (1981). *City Trenches: Urban Politics and the Patterning of Class in the United States*. New York: Pantheon Books.

Keck, Margaret E. (1995). "Social Equity and Environmental Politics in Brazil," *Comparative Politics* 27: 409–24.

Keck, Margaret E., and Kathryn Sikkink (1995). "Transnational Issue Networks in International Politics," presented to the Annual Conference of the American Political Science Association, Chicago.

(1998a). *Activists beyond Borders: Transnational Advocacy Networks in International Politics*. Ithaca, N.Y.: Cornell University Press.

(1998b). "Transnational Advocacy Networks in the Movement Society," in David Meyer and Sidney Tarrow, eds., *The Social Movement Society: Contentious Politics for a New Century*. Boulder, Colo.: Rowman and Littlefield, ch. 10.

Kennan, John (1986). "The Economics of Strikes," in Orley Ashenfelter and Richard Layard, eds., *Handbook of Labor Economics, vol. 2*. Amsterdam: Elsevier Science Publishers B.V., pp. 1091–1137.

Keniston, Kenneth (1968). *Young Radicals: Notes on Committed Youth*. New York: Harcourt, Brace and World.

Kertzer, David (1988). *Ritual, Politics and Power*. New Haven: Yale University Press.

Kielbowicz, Richard B., and Clifford Scherer (1986). "The Role of the Press in the Dynamics of Social Movements," in L. Kriesberg, ed., *Research in Social Movements, Conflicts and Change*. Greenwich, Conn.: JAI, pp. 71–96.

Kitschelt, Herbert (1986). "Political Opportunity Structures and Political Protest: Anti-Nuclear Movements in Four Democracies," *British Journal of Political Science* 16: 57–85.

Klandermans, Bert (1988). "The Formation and Mobilization of Consensus," in Bert Klandermans, Hanspeter Kriesi, and Sidney Tarrow, eds., *From Structure to Action: Comparing Social Movement Research across Cultures*. International Social Movement Research, vol. 1. Greenwich, Conn.: JAI, pp. 173–96.

(1989). "Social Movement Organizations and the Study of Social Movements," in B. Klandermans, ed., *Organizing for Change: Social Movement Organizations in Europe and the United States*. International Social Movement Research, vol. 2. Greenwich, Conn.: JAI, pp. 1–20.

(1997). *The Social Psychology of Protest*. Oxford: Blackwell.

ed. (1989). *Organizing for Change: Social Movement Organizations in Europe and the United States*. International Social Movement Research, Vol 2. Greenwich, Conn. JAI.

Klandermans, Bert, H. Kriesi, and S. Tarrow, eds. (1988). *From Structure to Action: Comparing Social Movement Research across Cultures*. International Social Movement Research, vol. 1. Greenwich, Conn.: JAI.

Klandermans, Bert, Marlene Roefs, and Johan Olivier (1998). "A Movement Takes Office," in David Meyer and Sidney Tarrow, eds., *The Social Movement Society: Contentious Politics for a New Century*. Boulder, Colo.: Rowman and Littlefield, ch. 8.

Klandermans, Bert, and Sidney Tarrow (1988). "Mobilization into Social Movements: Synthesizing European and American Approaches," in Bert Klandermans,

Hanspeter Kriesi, and Sidney Tarrow, eds., *From Structure to Action: Comparing Social Movement Research across Cultures. International Social Movement Research*, vol. 1. Greenwich, Conn.: JAI, pp. 1–38.

Kleidman, Robert (1992). "Organizations and Coalitions in the Cycles of the American Peace Movement," unpublished paper, Cleveland State University.

(1993). *Organizing for Peace: Neutrality, the Test Ban and the Freeze.* Syracuse: Syracuse University Press.

Klein, Ethel (1987). "The Diffusion of Consciousness in the United States and Western Europe," in M. F. Katzenstein and C. McClurg Mueller, eds., *The Women's Movements of the United States and Western Europe.* Philadelphia: Temple University Press, pp. 23–43.

Knapp, Vincent (1980). *Austrian Social Democracy, 1889–1914.* Washington, D.C.: University Press of America.

Kornhauser, William (1959). *The Politics of Mass Society.* Glencoe, Ill.: Free Press.

Kowalewski, David (1989). "Global Debt Crises in Structural-Cyclical Perspective," in W. P. Avery and D. P. Rapkin, eds., *Markets, Politics and Change in the Global Political Economy.* Boulder, Colo.: Lynne Reiner, pp. 357–84.

Kramnick, Isaac (1990). *Republicanism and Bourgeois Radicalism.* Ithaca, N.Y.: Cornell University Press.

Kriesi, Hanspeter (1985). *Bewegung in der Schweitzer Politik.* Frankfurt: Campus.

(1991). "The Political Opportunity Structure of New Social Movements: Its Impact on Their Mobilization," WZB Occasional Paper No. 91–103, Berlin: Wissenschaftszentrum.

(1996). "The Organizational Structure of New Social Movements in a Political Context," in D. McAdam, J. McCarthy, and M. Zald, eds., *Comparative Perspectives on Social Movements: Political Opportunities, Mobilizing Structures, and Cultural Framings.* Cambridge: Cambridge University Press, pp. 152–84.

Kriesi, Hanspeter, R. Koopmans, J. W. Duyvendak, and M. G. Giugni (1995). *The Politics of New Social Movements in Western Europe.* Minneapolis: University of Minnesota Press.

Kriesi, Hanspeter, and Dominique Wisler (1996). "Social Movements and Direct Democracy in Switzerland," *European Journal of Political Research* 30: 19–40.

Kubik, Jan (1994). *The Power of Symbols and the Symbols of Power.* University Park: Pennsylvania State University Press.

(1998). "Institutionalization of Protest during Democratic Consolidation in Central Europe," in David Meyer and Sidney Tarrow, eds., *The Social Movement Society: Contentious Politics for a New Century.* Boulder, Colo.: Rowman and Littlefield, ch. 6.

Kuran, Timur (1991). "Now Out of Never: The Element of Surprise in the East European Revolution of 1989," in Nancy Bermeo, ed., *Liberalization and Democratization: Change in the Soviet Union and Eastern Europe.* Baltimore: Johns Hopkins University Press, pp. 7–48.

Laba, Roman (1990). *The Roots of Solidarity: A Political Sociology of Poland's Working Class Democratization.* Princeton: Princeton University Press.

Laitin, David (1988). "Political Culture and Political Preferences," *American Political Science Review* 82: 589–97.

Lampe, John R. (1996). *Yugoslavia as History: Twice There Was a Country.* Cambridge: Cambridge University Press.

Lange, Peter, Cynthia Irvin, and Sidney Tarrow (1989). "Phases of Mobilization: Social Movements and the Italian Communist Party since the 1960s," *British Journal of Political Science* 22: 15–42.

Laraña, Enrique, Hank Johnston, and Joseph R. Gusfield, eds. (1994). *New Social Movements: From Ideology to Identity.* Philadelphia: Temple University Press.

Le Bon, Gustave (1977). *The Crowd: A Study of the Popular Mind.* New York: Penguin.

Lefebvre, Georges (1967). *The Coming of the French Revolution.* Princeton: Princeton University Press.

Lenin, V. I. (1929). *What Is to Be Done? Burning Questions of Our Movement.* New York: International Publishers.

Le Roy Ladourie, Emmanuel (1980). *Carnival in Romans.* New York: Brazilier.

Levine, Daniel H. (1990). "Popular Groups, Popular Culture, and Popular Religion," *Comparative Studies in Society and History* 32: 718–64.

Levine, Daniel H., and David Stoll (1997). "Bridging the Gap between Empowerment and Power," in Susanne Rudolf and James Piscatori, eds., *Transnational Religion and Fading States.* Boulder, Colo.: Westview, pp. 63–103.

Li, Lianjiang, and Kevin J. O'Brien (1996). "Villagers and Popular Resistance in Contemporary China," *Modern China* 22:28–61.

Lichbach, Marc (1995). *The Rebel's Dilemma.* Ann Arbor: University of Michigan Press.
    (1997). "Contentious Maps of Contentious Politics," *Mobilization* 1:87–98.

Lichterman, Paul (1996). *The Search for Political Community: American Activists Reinventing Commitment.* Cambridge: Cambridge University Press.

Linebaugh, Peter, and Marcus Rediker (1990). "The Many-Headed Hydra: Sailors, Slaves, and the Atlantic Working Class in the Eighteenth Century," *Journal of Historical Sociology* 3:225–52.

Lipsky, Michael (1968). "Protest as a Political Resource," *American Political Science Review* 62: 1144–58.

Lipsky, Michael, and David Olson (1976). "The Processing of Racial Crisis in America," *Politics and Society* 6:79–103.

Lockridge, Kenneth (1974). *Literacy in Colonial New England: An Enquiry into the Social Context of Literacy in the Early Modern West.* New York: Norton.

Lohmann, Susanne (1994). "The Dynamics of Information Cascades: The Monday Demonstrations in Leipzig, East Germany, 1989–1991," *World Politics* 47: 42–101.

Lumley, Robert (1990). *States of Emergency: Cultures of Revolt in Italy from 1968 to 1978.* London: Verso.

Lusebrink, Hans-Jürgen (1983). "L'imaginaire social et ses focalisations en France et en Allemagne à la fin du XVIII siècle," *Revue Roumaine d'Histoire* 22:371–83.

Maguire, Diarmuid (1990). "New Social Movements and Old Political Institutions: The Campaign for Nuclear Disarmament, 1979–1989." Ph.D. dissertation, Cornell University.

Maier, Pauline (1970). "Popular Uprisings and Civil Authority in Eighteenth Century America," *William and Mary Quarterly* 27:3–35.
    (1972). *From Resistance to Revolution: Colonial Radicals and the Development of American Opposition to Britain, 1765–1776.* New York: Knopf.

Mann, Patrice (1990). *L'activité tactique des manifestants et des forces mobiles lors des crises viticoles du midi, 1950–1990*. Paris: Institut des Hautes Etudes de la Sécurité Intérieure.

Mansbridge, Jane J. (1986). *Why We Lost the ERA*. Chicago: University of Chicago Press.

Margadant, Ted (1979). *French Peasants in Revolt: The Insurrection of 1851*. Princeton: Princeton University Press.

Markoff, John (1996). *Waves of Democracy*. Thousand Oaks, Calif.: Pine Forge Press.

(1997). *The Abolition of Feudalism: Peasants, Lords, and Legislators in the French Revolution*. University Park: Pennsylvania State University Press.

Marseille, Jacques, and Dominique Margairez (1989). *1790. Au jour le jour*. Paris: Albin Michel.

Marwell, Gerald, and Pam Oliver (1993). *The Critical Mass in Collective Action: A Micro-Social Theory*. Cambridge: Cambridge University Press.

Marx, Gary T., and Michael Useem (1971). "Majority Participation in Minority Movements: Civil Rights, Abolition, Untouchability," *Journal of Social Issues* 27:81–104.

Marx, Gary T., and James L. Wood (1975). "Strands of Theory and Research in Collective Behavior," *Annual Review of Sociology* 1:363–428.

Marx, Karl (1963a). *The Eighteenth Brumaire of Louis Bonaparte*. New York: International Publishers.

(1963b). *The Poverty of Philosophy*. New York: International Publishers.

(1967). "Towards the Critique of Hegel's Philosophy of Law: Introduction," in Loyd D. Easton and Kurt H. Guddat, eds., *Writings of the Young Marx on Philosophy and Society*. New York: Doubleday, pp. 249–64.

Mathews, Donald G. (1969). "The Second Great Awakening as an Organizing Process, 1780–1830," *American Quarterly* 21: 23–43.

Maza, Sarah (1993). *Private Lives and Public Affairs: The Causes Célèbres of Prerevolutionary France*. Berkeley: University of California Press.

Mazey, Sonia, and Jeremy Richardson (1993). *Lobbying in the European Community*. Oxford: Oxford University Press.

McAdam, Doug (1982). *The Political Process and the Development of Black Insurgency*. Chicago: University of Chicago Press.

(1983). "Tactical Innovation and the Pace of Insurgency," *American Sociological Review* 48:735–54.

(1986). "Recruitment to High Risk Activism: The Case of Freedom Summer," *American Journal of Sociology* 92:64–90.

(1988). *Freedom Summer*. New York: Oxford University Press.

(1995). "'Initiator' and 'Spin-off' Movements: Diffusion Processes in Protest Cycles," in Mark Traugott, ed., *Repertoires and Cycles of Collective Action*. Durham, N.C.: Duke University Press, pp. 217–40.

(1996). "Conceptual Origins, Current Problems, Future Directions," in Doug McAdam, John D. McCarthy, and Mayer N. Zald, eds., *Comparative Perspectives on Social Movements: Political Opportunities, Mobilizing Structures, and Cultural Framings*. Cambridge: Cambridge University Press, pp. 23–40.

(1998). "On the International Origins of Domestic Political Opportunities," in Anne N. Costain and Andrew McFarland, eds., *Social Movements and American Political Institutions*. Boulder, Colo.: Rowman and Littlefield, ch. 14.

McAdam, Doug, John D. McCarthy, and Mayer N. Zald, eds. (1996). *Comparative Perspectives on Social Movements: Political Opportunities, Mobilizing Structures, and Cultural Framings*. Cambridge: Cambridge University Press.

McAdam, Doug, and Dieter Rucht (1993). "The Cross-National Diffusion of Movement Ideas," *Annals of the American Academy of Political and Social Science* 528: 56–74.

McAdam, Doug, Sidney Tarrow, and Charles Tilly (1996). "To Map Contentious Politics," *Mobilization* 1:17–34.

McAdam, Doug, Sidney Tarrow, and Charles Tilly (1997). "Towards an Integrated Perspective on Social Movements and Revolution," in Marc Irving Lichbach and Alan Zuckerman, eds., *Ideals, Interests, and Institutions: Advancing Theory in Comparative Politics*. Cambridge: Cambridge University Press.

McCarthy, John D. (1987). "Pro-Life and Pro-Choice Mobilization: Infrastructure Deficits and New Technologies," in Mayer N. Zald and John D. McCarthy, eds., *Social Movements in an Organizational Society*. New Brunswick, N.J.: Transaction, pp. 49–66.

(1997). "The Globalization of Social Movement Theory," in J. Smith, C. Chatfield, and R. Pagnucco, eds., *Transnational Social Movements and World Politics: Solidarity beyond the State*. Syracuse: Syracuse University Press, ch. 14.

McCarthy, John D., and Jim Castelli (1994). *Working for Justice: The Campaign for Human Development and Poor Empowerment Groups*. Report prepared for the Aspen Institute Nonprofit Sector Research Fund, Aspen, Colo.

McCarthy, John D., and Clark McPhail (1998). "The Institutionalization of Protest in the USA," in David Meyer and Sidney Tarrow, eds., *The Social Movement Society: Contentious Politics for a New Century*. Boulder, Colo.: Rowman and Littlefield, ch. 4.

McCarthy, John D., Clark McPhail, and David Schweinberger (1997). "Policing Protest in the United States," in Donatella della Porta and Herbert Rieter, eds., *Policing Protest: The Control of Mass Demonstrations in Contemporary Democracies*. Minneapolis: University of Minnesota Press.

McCarthy, John D., and Mark Wolfson (1992). "Consensus Movements, Conflict Movements and the Cooptation of Civic and State Infrastructures," in Aldon Morris and Carol McClurg Mueller, eds., *Frontiers in Social Movement Theory*. New Haven: Yale University Press, pp. 273–97.

McCarthy, John D., and Mayer N. Zald (1973). "The Trends of Social Movements in America: Professionalization and Resource Mobilization," monograph. Morristown, N.J.: General Learning Press. Also in Mayer N. Zald and John D. McCarthy, eds., *Social Movements in an Organizational Society*. New Brunswick, N.J.: Transaction, 1987, pp. 337–92.

(1977). "Resource Mobilization and Social Movements: A Partial Theory," *American Journal of Sociology* 82: 1212–41. Also in Mayer N. Zald and John D. McCarthy, eds., *Social Movements in an Organizational Society*. New Brunswick, N.J.: Transaction, 1987, pp. 15–48.

McPhail, Clark (1991). *The Myth of the Madding Crowd*. New York: Aldine De Gruyter.

Melucci, Alberto (1988). "Getting Involved: Identity and Mobilization in Social Movements," in Bert Klandermans, Hanspeter Kriesi, and Sidney Tarrow, eds., *From Structure to Action: Comparing Social Movement Research across Cul-*

tures. International Social Movement Research, vol. 1. Greenwich, Conn.: JAI, pp. 329–48.

(1996). *Challenging Codes: Collective Action in the Information Age.* Cambridge: Cambridge University Press.

Mershon, Carol A. (1990). "Generazioni di leader sindicali in fabbrica. L'eredità dell'autunno caldo," *Polis* 2:277–323.

Meyer, David (1990). *A Winter of Discontent: The Nuclear Freeze and American Politics.* New York: Praeger.

Meyer, David, and Josh Gamson (1995). "The Challenge of Cultural Elites: Celebrities and Social Movements," *Sociological Inquiry* 65: 181–206.

Meyer, David, and Tom Rochon (1997). "Towards a Coalitional Theory of Social and Political Movements," in T. Rochon and D. Meyer, eds., *Coalitions and Political Movements: The Lessons of the Nuclear Freeze.* Boulder, Colo.: Lynne Rienner, pp. 237–51.

Meyer, David, and Suzanne Staggenborg (1996). "Movements, Countermovements, and the Structure of Political Opportunity," *American Journal of Sociology* 101:1628–60.

Meyer, David, and Sidney Tarrow, eds. (1998). *The Social Movement Society: Contentious Politics for a New Century.* Boulder, Colo.: Rowman and Littlefield.

Meyer, David, and Nancy Whittier (1994). "Social Movement Spillover," *Social Problems* 41:277–98.

Meyer, John W., John Boli, George M. Thomas, and Francisco O. Ramirez (1996). "World Societies and the Nation-State," unpublished paper, Stanford University Department of Sociology.

Meyer, John W., David John Frank, Ann Hironaka, Evan Shofer, and Nancy Brandon Tuma (1997). "The Structuring of a World Environmental Regime, 1870–1990." *International Organization* 51:623–51.

Michels, Robert (1962). *Political Parties. A Sociological Study of the Oligarchical Tendencies of Modern Democracy.* New York: Collier Books.

Mikkelsen, Flemming (1996). "Contention and Social Movements in Denmark in a Transnational Perspective," presented at the Second European Conference on Social Movements, University of the Basque Country, Bilbao, July.

Miller, James (1987). *Democracy Is in the Streets: From Port Huron to the Siege of Chicago.* New York: Simon and Schuster.

Minkoff, Debra C. (1994). "From Service Provision to Institutional Advocacy: The Shifting Legitimacy of Organizational Forms," *Social Forces* 72:943–69.

(1997). "Producing Social Capital: National Social Movements and Civil Society," *American Behavioral Scientist* 40: 606–19.

Mitchell, J. Clyde (1973). "Networks, Norms, and Institutions," in Jeremy Boissevain and J. Clyde Mitchell, eds., *Network Analysis: Studies in Human Interaction.* The Hague: Mouton, pp. 15–36.

Molotch, Harvey (1979). "Media and Movements," in Mayer N. Zald and John D. McCarthy, eds., *Dynamics of Social Movements.* Cambridge, Mass.: Winthrop, pp. 71–93.

Moore, Barrington, Jr. (1978). *Injustice: The Social Bases of Obedience and Revolt.* White Plains, N.Y.: M. E. Sharpe.

Moore, R. Lawrence (1994). *Selling God: American Religion in the Marketplace of Culture.* New York: Oxford University Press.

Morgan, Jane (1987). *Conflict and Order: The Police and Labor Disputes in England and Wales, 1900–1939.* Oxford: Oxford University Press.

Morris, Aldon (1984). *The Origins of the Civil Rights Movement: Black Communities Organizing for Change.* New York: Free Press.

Morris, Aldon, and Carol McClurg Mueller, eds. (1992). *Frontiers in Social Movement Theory.* New Haven: Yale University Press.

Morris, R. J. (1983). "Voluntary Societies and British Urban Elites, 1780–1850: An Analysis," *Historical Journal* 26:95–118.

Mosse, George (1975). *The Nationalization of the Masses: Political Symbolism and Mass Movements in Germany from the Napoleonic Wars through the Third Reich.* New York: H. Fertig.

Mouriaux, René, ed. (1992). *1968. Exploration du Mai français.* 2 vols. Paris: Harmattan.

Nelkin, Dorothy (1975). "The Political Impact of Technical Expertise," *Social Studies of Science* 5:35–54.

Oberschall, Anthony (1996). "Opportunities and Framing in the Eastern European Revolts of 1989," in Doug McAdam, John D. McCarthy, and Mayer N. Zald, eds., *Comparative Perspectives on Social Movements.* Cambridge: Cambridge University Press, pp. 93–121.

O'Donnell, Guillermo, and Philippe Schmitter (1986). *Transition from Authoritarian Rule: Tentative Conclusions about Uncertain Democracies.* Baltimore: Johns Hopkins University Press.

Offe, Claus (1990). "Reflections on the Institutional Self-Transformation of Movement Politics: A Tentative Stage Model," in Russell Dalton and Manfred Kuechler, eds., *Challenging the Political Order.* Oxford: Oxford University Press, pp. 232–50.

Oliver, Pam (1989). "Bringing the Crowd Back In: The Nonorganizational Elements of Social Movements," in Louis Kriesberg, ed., *Research in Social Movements, Conflict and Change* 11. Greenwich, Conn.: JAI, pp. 1–30.

Olson, Mancur (1965). *The Logic of Collective Action.* Cambridge, Mass.: Harvard University Press.

O'Neil, Michael (1993). *The Roar of the Crowd: How Television and People Power Are Changing the World.* New York: Times Books.

Open University (1976). *Music and Revolution: Verdi.* London: Open University.

Ortoleva, Peppino (1988). *Saggio sui movimenti del 1968 in Europa e in America.* Rome: Riuniti.

Osa, Maryjane (1995). "Ecclesiastical Reorganization and Political Culture: Geopolitical and Institutional Effects on Religion in Poland," *Polish Sociological Review* 3:193–209.

    (1998). "Contention and Democracy: Labor Protest in Poland, 1989–1993," *Communist and Post-Communist Studies*, March.

Ozouf, Mona (1988). *Festivals and the French Revolution.* Translated by Alan Sheridan. Cambridge, Mass.: Harvard University Press.

Pagnucco, Ron (1996). "Social Movement Dynamics during Democratic Transitions: A Synthesis of Political Process and Political Interactionist Theories," *Research on Democracy and Society* 3:3–38.

Pagnucco, Ron, and David Atwood (1994). "Global Strategies for Peace and Justice," *Peace Review* 6:411–18.

Paige, Jeffrey M. (1975). *Agrarian Revolutions: Social Movements and Export Agriculture in the Underdeveloped World*. New York: Free Press.

Paine, Thomas (1989). *Political Writings*. Edited by Bruce Kuklick. Cambridge: Cambridge University Press.

Percheron, Annick (1991). "La mémoire des générations: La guerre d'Algérie – Mai 68," in Olivier Duhamel and Jérôme Jaffré, eds., *SOFRES: L'état de l'opinion, 1991*. Paris: Seuil, pp. 39–57.

Perry, Elizabeth (1993). *Shanghai on Strike: The Politics of Chinese Labor*. Stanford, Calif.: Stanford University Press.

Pitt-Rivers, Julian (1971). *The People of the Sierra*. 2nd ed. Chicago: University of Chicago Press.

Piven, Frances Fox, and Richard Cloward (1977). *Poor People's Movements: Why They Succeed, How They Fail*. New York: Vintage Books.

  (1993). *Regulating the Poor: The Functions of Public Welfare*. 2nd ed. New York: Vintage.

Pizzorno, Alessandro (1978). "Political Exchange and Collective Identity in Industrial Conflict," in Colin Crouch and Alessandro Pizzorno, eds., *The Resurgence of Class Conflict in Western Europe since 1968*, vol. 2. London: Macmillan, pp. 277–98.

Plamenatz, John (1954). *German Marxism and Russian Communism*. London: Longmans, Green.

Popkin, Jeremy D. (1989). "Journals: The New Face of News," in Robert Darnton and Daniel Roche, eds., *Revolution in Print: The Press in France, 1775–1800*. Berkeley: University of California Press, pp. 141–64.

Popkin, Sam (1979). *The Rational Peasant: The Political Economy of Rural Society in Vietnam*. Berkeley: University of California Press.

Postgate, Raymond (1955). *The Story of a Year: 1848*. London: Cassell.

Price, Richard (1997). "Reversing the Gunsights: Transnational Civil Society Takes Aim at Landmines," unpublished paper, University of Minnesota, Department of Political Science.

Price, Roger (1989). *The Revolutions of 1848*. Atlantic Highlands, N.J.: Humanities Press International.

Putnam, Robert (1995). "Bowling Alone: America's Declining Social Capital," *Journal of Democracy* 6:65–78.

Putnam, Robert, Robert Leonardi, and Raffaella Nanetti (1993). *Making Democracy Work: Civic Traditions in Modern Italy*. Princeton: Princeton University Press.

Quattrone, George A., and Amos Tversky (1988). "Contrasting Rational and Psychological Analysis of Political Choice," *American Political Science Review* 82: 719–36.

Ramet, Sabrina (1987). *The Soviet Rock Scene*. Washington, D.C.: Kennan Institute for Advanced Russian Studies.

Read, Donald (1964). *The English Provinces, c. 1760–1960: A Study in Influence*. New York: St. Martin's.

Rihoux, Benoît (1997). "Mobilisations de parents de victimes et comités blancs," in N. Bornay, P. Lannoy, and L. Panafit, eds., in *La société indicible*. Brussels; Luc Pire, pp. 65–80.

Risse, Thomas (1995). *Bringing Transnational Politics Back In: Non-State Actors, Domestic Structures and International Institutions*. Ithaca, N.Y.: Cornell University Press.

Risse, Thomas, and Hans Peter Schmitz (1995). "Principled Ideas, International Institutions, and Domestic Political Change in the Human Rights Area: Insights from African Cases," presented to the Annual Meetings of the American Political Science Association, Chicago, September.

Risse, Thomas, and Kathryn Sikkink (1997). Introduction to T. Risse and K. Sikkink, eds., *The Socialization of Human Rights Norms into Domestic Practices.*

Robins, Kevin (1995). "Globalization," in Adam Kuper and Jessica Kuper (eds.), *Social Science Encyclopedia.* London: Routledge, pp. 345–6.

Rochon, Thomas R. (1988). *Mobilizing for Peace: The Antinuclear Movements in Western Europe.* Princeton: Princeton University Press.

(1998). *Culture Moves: Ideas, Activism, and Changing Values.* Princeton: Princeton University Press.

Rochon, Thomas R., and Daniel Mazmanian (1993). "Social Movements and the Policy Process," *Annals of the American Academy of Political and Social Science* 528:75–87.

Rochon, Thomas R., and David Meyer (1997). *Coalitions and Political Movements: The Lessons of the Nuclear Freeze.* Boulder, Colo.: Lynne Rienner.

Rogers, Kim Lacy (1993). *Righteous Lives: Narratives of the New Orleans Civil Rights Movement.* New York: New York University Press.

Rosenau, James (1990). *Turbulence in World Politics: A Theory of Change and Continuity.* Princeton: Princeton University Press.

Rosenthal, Naomi B., and Michael Schwartz (1990). "Spontaneity and Democracy in Social Movements," in Bert Klandermans, ed., *Organizing for Change: Social Movement Organizations in Europe and the United States.* International Social Movement Research, vol. 2. Greenwich, Conn.: JAI, pp. 33–59.

Ross, Marc Howard (1997). "Culture and Identity in Comparative Political Analysis," in Marc Irving Lichbach and Alan S. Zuckerman, eds., *Comparative Politics: Rationality, Culture, and Structure.* Cambridge: Cambridge University Press, ch. 4.

Roth, Guenther (1963). *The Social Democrats in Imperial Germany: A Study on Working-Class Isolation and National Integration.* Totowa, N.J.: Bedminster.

Rotondi, Clementina (1951). *Bibliografia dei periodici toscani, 1847–1852.* Florence: L. S. Olschki.

Rucht, Dieter (1990). "Campaigns, Skirmishes and Battles: Anti-Nuclear Movements in the USA, France and West Germany," *Industrial Crisis Quarterly* 4:193–222.

(1991). "The Study of Social Movements in West Germany: Between Activism and Professionalism," in Dieter Rucht, ed., *Research in Social Movements: The State of the Art in Western Europe and the United States.* Frankfurt: Campus; Boulder, Colo.: Westview.

(1993). "The Impact of National Contexts on Social Movement Structures: A Cross-Movement and Cross-National Comparison," unpublished paper, Berlin Wissenschaftszentrum.

(1997). "Limits to Mobilization: Environmental Policy for the European Union," in J. Smith, C. Chatfield, and R. Pagnucco, eds., *Transnational Social Movements and World Politics: Solidarity beyond the State.* Syracuse: Syracuse University Press, ch. 11.

(1998a) "Mobilizing for Distant Issues," in John Guidry. Michael Kennedy, and

Mayer N. Zald, eds. *Globalizations and Social Movements,* in preparation.

(1998b). "The Structure and Culture of Collective Protest in Germany since 1950," in David Meyer and Sidney Tarrow, eds., *The Social Movement Society: Contentious Politics for a New Century.* Boulder, Colo.: Rowman and Little-field, ch. 2.

ed. (1991). *Research on Social Movements: The State of the Art in Western Europe and the USA.* Boulder, Colo.: Westview.

Rucht, Dieter, Ruud Koopmans, and Friedhelm Neidhardt, eds. (1988). *Acts of Dissent: The Study of Protest in Contemporary Democracies.* Berlin: Sigma.

Rudolf, Susanne Hoeber (1997). "Religion, States, and Transnational Civil Society," in Susanne Rudolf and James Piscatori, eds., *Transnational Religion and Fading States.* Boulder, Colo.: Westview, pp. 1–26.

Rudolf, Susanne Hoeber, and James Piscatori, eds. (1997). *Transnational Religion and Fading States.* Boulder, Colo.: Westview.

Rule, James (1988). *Theories of Civil Violence.* Berkeley: University of California Press.

Rupp, Leila J. (1980). " 'Imagine My Surprise': Women's Relationships in Historical Perspective," *Frontiers*: 5:61–70.

Rupp, Leila J., and Verta A. Taylor (1987). *Survival in the Doldrums: The American Women's Rights Movement, 1945 to the 1960s.* New York: Oxford University Press.

Ryan, Barbara (1992). *Feminism and the Women's Movement.* New York: Routledge.

Ryerson, Richard A. (1978). *The Revolution Is Now Begun: The Radical Committees of Philadelphia, 1765–1776.* Philadelphia: University of Pennsylvania Press.

Salvati, Michele (1981). "May 1968 and the Hot Autumn of 1969: The Responses of Two Ruling Classes," in Suzanne Berger, ed., *Organizing Interests in Western Europe.* Cambridge: Cambridge University Press, pp. 329–63.

Schama, Simon (1989). *Citizens: A Chronicle of the French Revolution.* New York: Knopf.

Scheler, Max (1972). *Ressentiment.* New York: Schocken.

Schelling, Thomas C. (1960). *The Strategy of Conflict.* Cambridge, Mass.: Harvard University Press.

Schennink, Ben (1988). "From Peace Week to Peace Work: Dynamics of the Peace Movement in the Netherlands," in Bert Klandermans, Hanspeter Kriesi, and Sidney Tarrow, eds., *From Structure to Action: Comparing Social Movement Research across Cultures.* International Social Movement Research, vol. 1. Greenwich: JAI Press, pp. 247–79.

Schlesinger, Arthur M., Jr. (1986). *The Cycles of American History.* Boston: Houghton Mifflin.

Schnapp, Alain, and Pierre Vidal-Naquet (1988). *Journal de la commune étudiante: Textes et documents, novembre 1967–juin 1968.* 2nd ed. Paris: Seuil.

Schneider, Cathy (1995). *Shantytown Protest in Pinochet's Chile.* Philadelphia: Temple University Press.

Schumaker, Paul D. (1975). "Policy Responsiveness to Protest-Group Demands," *Journal of Politics* 37: 488–521.

Scott, James C. (1976). *The Moral Economy of the Peasant: Rebellion and Subsistence in Southeast Asia.* New Haven: Yale University Press.

(1985). *Weapons of the Weak: Everyday Forms of Peasant Resistance.* New Haven: Yale University Press.

(1990). *Domination and the Arts of Resistance: Hidden Transcripts.* New Haven: Yale University Press.

Selbin, Eric (1993). *Modern Latin American Revolutions.* Boulder, Colo.: Westview.

(1997). "Contentious Cartography," *Mobilization* 2:99–106.

Sewell, William, Jr. (1980). *Work and Revolution in France: The Language of Labor from the Old Regime to 1848.* Cambridge: Cambridge University Press.

(1986). "Artisans, Factory Workers, and the Formation of the French Working Class, 1789–1848," in Ira Katznelson and Aristide R. Zolberg, eds., *Working Class Formation: Nineteenth Century Patterns in Western Europe and the United States.* Princeton: Princeton University Press, pp. 45–70.

(1990). "Collective Violence and Collective Loyalties in France: Why the French Revolution Made a Difference," *Politics and Society* 18: 527–52.

(1996). "Historical Events as Transformations of Structures: Inventing Revolution at the Bastille," *Theory and Society* 25:841–81.

Sharp, Gene (1973). *The Politics of Nonviolent Action.* Boston: Porter Sargent.

Sherkat, Darren E., and T. Jean Blocker (1997). "Explaining the Political and Personal Consequences of Protest," *Social Forces* 75:1049–76.

Shorter, Edward, and Charles Tilly (1971). *Strikes in France, 1830–1968.* Cambridge: Cambridge University Press.

Sigmann, Jean (1973). *1848: The Romantic and Democratic Revolutions in Europe.* New York: Harper and Row.

Silver, Beverly (1992a). "Class Struggle and Kondratieff Waves, 1870 to the Present," in Alfred Kleinknecht, Ernest Mandel, and Immanuel Wallerstein, eds., *New Findings in Long Wave Research.* New York: St. Martin's, pp. 279–95.

(1992b). "Labor Unrest and Capital Accumulation on a World Scale." Ph.D. dissertation, State University of New York at Binghamton.

Skocpol, Theda (1979). *States and Social Revolutions: A Comparative Analysis of France, Russia, and China.* Princeton: Princeton University Press.

Skowronek, Steven (1982). *Building a New American State: The Expansion of National Administrative Capacities, 1877–1920.* Cambridge: Cambridge University Press.

Smelser, Neil (1962). *Theory of Collective Behavior.* London: Routledge and Kegan Paul.

Smith, Christian, ed. (1996). *Disruptive Religion: The Force of Faith in Social Movement Activism.* New York: Routledge.

Smith, Jackie (1994). "Organizing Global Action," *Peace Review* 6:419–26.

(1997). "Characteristics of the Modern Transnational Social Movement Sector," in J. Smith, C. Chatfield, and R. Pagnucco, eds., *Transnational Social Movements and World Politics: Solidarity beyond the State.* Syracuse: Syracuse University Press, ch. 3.

Smith, Jackie, Charles Chatfield, and Ron Pagnucco, eds. (1997). *Transnational Social Movements and World Politics: Solidarity beyond the State.* Syracuse: Syracuse University Press.

Snow, David E., and Robert Benford (1988). "Ideology, Frame Resonance, and Participant Mobilization," in Bert Klandermans, Hanspeter Kriesi, and Sidney Tarrow, eds., *From Structure to Action: Comparing Social Movement Research across Cultures.* International Social Movement Research, vol 1. 1988, Greenwich, Conn.: JAI Press, pp. 197–217.

(1992). "Master Frames and Cycles of Protest," in Aldon Morris and Carol McClurg Mueller, eds., *Frontiers in Social Movement Theory*. New Haven: Yale University Press, pp. 133–55.

Snow, David, E. Burke Rochford, Steven Worden, and Robert Benford (1986). "Frame Alignment Processes, Micromobilization, and Movement Participation," *American Sociological Review* 51:464–81.

Snyder, David, and William R. Kelly (1976). "Industrial Violence in Italy, 1878–1903," *American Journal of Sociology* 82:131–62.

Snyder, David, and Charles Tilly (1972). "Hardship and Collective Violence in France: 1830–1960," *American Sociological Review* 37:520–32.

Soboul, Albert (1964). *The Parisian Sans-culottes and the French Revolution*. Oxford: Oxford University Press.

Soskice, David (1978). "Strike Waves and Wage Explosions, 1968–1970: An Economic Interpretation," in Colin Crouch and Alessandro Pizzorno, eds., *The Resurgence of Class Conflict in Western Europe since 1968*, vol. 2. London: Macmillan, pp. 221–46.

Soule, Sarah, and Sidney Tarrow (1991). "Acting Collectively, 1847–1849: How the Repertoire of Collective Action Changed and Where It Happened," presented to the annual conference of the Social Science History Association, New Orleans, October.

Spriano, Paolo (1975). *The Occupation of the Factories: Italy, 1920*. London: Pluto.

Staggenborg, Suzanne (1991). *The Pro-Choice Movement: Organization and Activism in the Abortion Conflict*. New York: Oxford University Press.

Steedly, Homer R., and John W. Foley (1979). "The Success of Protest Groups: Multivariate Analyses," *Social Science Research* 8:1–15.

Stinchecombe, Arthur (1987). Review of *The Contentious French* by Charles Tilly. *American Journal of Sociology* 93:1248.

Stone, Lawrence (1969). "Literacy and Education in England, 1640–1900," *Past and Present*, no. 42:69–139.

Strang, David, and John W. Meyer (1993). "Institutional Conditions for Diffusion," *Theory and Society* 47:242–3.

Swarts, Heidi (1997). "Comparative Models of Community Organizing in American Cities," unpublished paper, Cornell University, Department of Government.

Szymanski, Ann-Marie (1997). "Think Globally; Act Gradually." Ph.D. dissertation, Cornell University.

Taft, Philip, and Philip Ross (1969). "American Labor Violence: Its Causes, Character, and Outcome," in Ted R. Gurr, ed., *Violence in America: Historical and Comparative Perspectives*. New York: Praeger, pp. 281–395.

Tamason, Charles (1980). "From Mortuary to Cemetery: Funeral Riots and Funeral Demonstrations in Lille, 1779–1870," *Social Science History* 4:15–31.

Tarde, Gabriel de (1989). *L'opinion et la foule*. Paris: Presses Universitaires de France.

Tarrow, Sidney (1967). *Peasant Communism in Southern Italy*. New Haven: Yale University Press.

(1988). "Old Movements in New Cycles of Protest: The Career of an Italian Religious Community," in Bert Klandermans, Hanspeter Kriesi, and Sidney Tarrow, eds., *From Structure to Action: Comparing Social Movements across Cul-*

tures. International Social Movement Research, vol. 1. Greenwich, Conn.: JAI, pp. 281–304.

(1989a). *Democracy and Disorder: Protest and Politics in Italy, 1965–1975.* Oxford: Oxford University Press.

(1989b). *Struggle, Politics and Reform: Collective Action, Social Movements and Cycles of Protest.* Western Societies Paper No. 21. Ithaca, N.Y.: Cornell University.

(1992). "Mentalities, Political Cultures and Collective Action Frames: Constructing Meaning through Action," in Aldon Morris and Carol McClurg Mueller, eds., *Frontiers in Social Movement Research.* New Haven: Yale University Press, pp. 174–202.

(1993a). "Modular Collective Action and the Rise of the Social Movement: Why the French Revolution Was Not Enough," *Politics and Society* 21:69–90.

(1993b). "Social Protest and Policy Reform: May 1968 and the Loi d'Orientation in France," in *Comparative Political Studies* 25:579–607.

(1995a). "Cycles of Collective Action: Between Moments of Madness and the Repertoire of Contention," in Marc Traugott, ed., *Repertoires and Cycles of Collective Action.* Durham, N.C.: Duke University Press, pp. 89–116.

(1995b). "The Europeanization of Conflict: Reflections from a Social Movement Perspective," *West European Politics* 18:223–51.

(1995c). "Mass Mobilization and Elite Exchange: Democratization Episodes in Italy and Spain," *Democratization* 2:221–45.

(1996a). "The People's Two Rhythms: Charles Tilly and the Study of Contentious Politics," *Comparative Studies in Society and History* 38:586–600.

(1996b). "States and Opportunities: The Political Structuring of Social Movements," in Doug McAdam, John D. McCarthy, and Mayer N. Zald, eds., *Comparative Perspectives on Social Movements: Political Opportunities, Mobilizing Structures, and Cultural Framings.* Cambridge: Cambridge University Press, pp. 62–92.

(1998a). "Fishnets, Internets, and Catnets: Globalization and Transnational Collective Action," in Michael Hanagan, Leslie Page Moch, and Wayne te Brake, eds., *Challenging Authority: The Historical Study of Contentious Politics.* Minneapolis: University of Minnesota Press, ch. 15.

(1998b). "Studying Contentious Politics: From Event-ful History to Movement Cycles," in Dieter Rucht, Ruud Koopmans, and Friedhelm Neidhardt, eds., *Acts of Dissent: The Study of Protest in Contemporary Democracies.* Berlin: Sigma, ch. 2.

(1998c). " 'The Very Excess of Democracy': State Building and Contentious Politics in America," in Anne Costain and Andrew McFarland, eds., *Social Movements and American Political Institutions.* Boulder, Colo.: Rowman and Littlefield, ch. 2.

Tartakowsky, Danielle (1996). *Le front populaire: La vie est à nous.* Paris: Découverte/ Gallimard.

(1997). "1919–1968: Des barricades?," in Alain Corbin, ed., *La barricade.* Paris: Presses de la Sorbonne.

Taylor, Verta (1995). "Watching for Vibes: Bringing Emotions into the Study of Feminist Organizations," in Myra Marx Ferree and Particia Yancey Martin, eds., *Feminist Organizations: Harvest of the New Women's Movement.* Philadelphia: Temple University Press, pp. 223–33.

Taylor, Verta, and Marieke Van Willigen (1996). "Women's Self-Help and the Reconstruction of Gender: The Postpartum Support and Breast Cancer Movements," *Mobilization* 1:123–42.

te Brake, Wayne (1997). "Popular Politics and the Divergent Paths of Political Change in Europe," unpublished paper, Purchase College, State University of New York.

    (1998). *Shaping History: Ordinary People in European Politics, 1500–1700.* Berkeley: University of California Press.

Thomas, Daniel (1997). "Norms and Change in World Politics: The Helsinki Accords, Human Rights and the Demise of Communism, 1975–1990." Ph.D. dissertation, Cornell University.

Thomis, Malcolm I., and Peter Holt (1977). *Threats of Revolution in Britain, 1789–1848.* Hamden, Conn.: Archon Books.

Thompson, Dorothy (1984). *The Chartists: Popular Politics in the Industrial Revolution.* New York: Pantheon.

Thompson, E. P. (1966). *The Making of the English Working Class.* New York: Vintage.

    (1971). "The Moral Economy of the English Crowd in the Eighteenth Century," *Past and Present*, no. 50:76–136.

Tilly, Charles (1964). *The Vendée.* Cambridge, Mass.: Harvard University Press.

    (1975a). "Food Supply and Public Order in Modern Europe," in Charles Tilly, ed., *The Formation of National States in Western Europe.* Princeton: Princeton University Press, pp. 380–455.

    (1975b). "Reflections on the History of European State-Making," in Charles Tilly, ed., *The Formation of National States in Western Europe.* Princeton: Princeton University Press, pp. 3–83.

    (1978). *From Mobilization to Revolution.* Reading, Mass.: Addison-Wesley.

    (1982). "Britain Creates the Social Movement," in James Cronin and Jonathan Schneer, eds., *Social Conflict and the Political Order in Modern Britain.* New Brunswick, N.J.: Rutgers University Press, pp. 21–51.

    (1983). "Speaking Your Mind without Elections, Surveys, or Social Movements," *Public Opinion Quarterly* 47:461–78.

    (1984a). *Big Structures, Large Processes, Huge Comparisons.* New York: Russell Sage.

    (1984b). "Social Movements and National Politics," in C. Bright and S. Harding, eds., *Statemaking and Social Movements: Essays in History and Theory.* Ann Arbor: University of Michigan Press, pp. 297–317.

    (1986). *The Contentious French.* Cambridge, Mass.: Harvard University Press.

    (1990). *Coercion, Capital, and European States, 990–1990.* Cambridge, Mass.: Blackwell.

    (1991). "Prisoners of the State," Center for Studies of Social Change Working Paper No. 129. New York: New School for Social Research.

    (1992). "How to Detect, Describe, and Explain Repertoires of Contention," unpublished paper, New School for Social Research.

    (1993). *European Revolutions, 1492–1992.* Oxford: Blackwell.

    (1995a). "Contentious Repertoires in Britain, 1758–1834," in Mark Traugott, ed., *Repertoires and Cycles of Collective Action.* Durham, N.C.: Duke University Press, pp. 15–42.

    (1995b). *Popular Contention in Great Britain, 1758–1834.* Cambridge, Mass.: Harvard University Press.

(1997a). *Durable Inequality*. Berkeley: University of California Press.

(1997b). "Kings in Beggar's Raiment," *Mobilization* 2:107–11.

Tilly, Charles, Louise Tilly, and Richard Tilly (1975). *The Rebellious Century, 1830–1930*. Cambridge, Mass.: Harvard University Press.

Tocqueville, Alexis de (1954). *Democracy in America*. 2 vols. New York: Vintage.

(1955). *The Old Regime and the French Revolution*. Translated by Stuart Gilbert. Garden City, N.Y.: Doubleday Anchor.

(1987). *Recollections: The French Revolution of 1848*. New Brunswick, N.J.: Transaction Books.

Touraine, Alain (1988). *Return of the Actor: Social Theory in Postindustural Society*. Minneapolis: University of Minnesota Press.

Traugott, Marc (1990). "Neighborhoods in Insurrection: The Parisian Quartier in the February Revolution of 1848," unpublished paper.

(1995a). "Barricades as Repertoire: Continuities and Discontinuities in the History of French Contention" in Traugott, ed., *Repertoires and Cycles of Collective Action*. Durham, N.C.: Duke University Press, pp. 43–56.

ed. (1995b). *Repertoires and Cycles of Collective Action*. Durham, N.C.: Duke University Press.

Tucker, Robert C., ed. (1978). *The Marx-Engels Reader*. 2nd ed. New York: Norton.

Turner, Lowell (1996). "The Europeanization of Labour: Structure before Action," *European Journal of Industrial Relations* 2:325–44.

Turner, Ralph T., and L. M. Killian (1972). *Collective Behavior*. 2nd ed. Englewood Cliffs, N.J.: Prentice Hall.

Tyrrell, Ian R. (1979). *Sobering Up: From Temperance to Prohibition in Antebellum America, 1800–1860*. Westport Conn.: Greenwood Press.

Usher, Douglas (1997). "Republican Rules and Religious Right Takeovers," presented at the Midwest Political Science Association Annual Meeting, Chicago, April 18–20.

Valelly, Richard M. (1993). "Party, Coercion and Inclusion: The Two Reconstructions of the South's Electoral Politics," *Politics and Society* 21:37–68.

van Praag, Philip, Jr. (1992). "The Velvet Revolution: The Role of the Students, Political Opportunities and Informal Networks in an Authoritarian Regime," presented to the First European Conference on Social Movements, Berlin Wissenschaftszentrum, June.

van Zoonen, Liesbet (1992). " 'A Dance of Death'? New Social Movements and the Media," unpublished paper, University of Amsterdam.

Vernus, Michel (1989). "A Provincial Perspective," in Robert Darnton and Daniel Roche, eds., *Revolution in Print: The Press in France, 1775–1800*. Berkeley: University of California Press, pp. 124–38.

Vejvoda, Ivan (1997). "Cogito Ergo Ambulo; First Steps in Belgrade," *Bulletin of the East and Central Europe Program*, New School for Social Research, 2:1–2.

Wade, Robert (1996). "Globalization and Its Limits: Reports of the Death of the National Economy Are Greatly Exaggerated," in Suzanne Berger and Ronald Dore, eds., *National Diversity and Global Capitalism*. Ithaca, N.Y.: Cornell University Press, pp. 60–88.

Walker, Jack (1991). *Mobilizing Interest Groups in America: Patrons, Professions, and Social Movements*. Ann Arbor: University of Michigan Press.

Walsh, Richard W. (1959). *Charleston's Sons of Liberty: A Study of the Artisans, 1763–1787.* New York: Columbia University Press.

Walters, Ronald G. (1976). *The Antislavery Appeal: American Abolitionism after 1830.* Baltimore: Johns Hopkins University Press.

(1978). *American Reformers, 1815–1860.* New York: Hill and Wang.

Walton, John (1989). "Debt, Protest and the State in Latin America," in Susan Eckstein, ed., *Power and Popular Protest: Latin American Social Movements.* Berkeley: University of California Press, pp. 299–328.

Walzer, Michael (1971). *The Revolution of the Saints: A Study in the Origins of Radical Politics.* New York: Atheneum.

Wapner, Paul (1995). "Bringing Society Back In: Environmental Activism and World Civic Politics," *World Politics* 47:311–40.

(1996). *Environmental Activism and World Civic Politics.* Albany: State University of New York Press.

Webster, Richard (1960). *The Cross and the Fasces Christian Democracy and Fascism in Italy.* Stanford: Stanford University Press.

Wellman, Barry, and Milena Gulia (1998). "Net Surfers Don't Ride Alone: Virtual Communities as Communities," in Peter Kollock and Marc Smith, eds., *Communities in Cyberspace.* London: Routledge.

Whittier, Nancy (1995). *Feminist Generation.* Philadelphia: Temple University Press.

Wickham-Crowley, Timothy (1992). *Guerillas and Revolution in Latin America.* Princeton: Princeton University Press.

Wilentz, Sean (1984). *Chants Democratic: New York City and the Rise of the American Working Class, 1788–1850.* New York: Oxford University Press.

Wisler, Dominique, and Marco G. Giugni (1996). "Social Movements and Institutional Selectivity," *Sociological Perspectives* 39:85–109.

Wood, Gordon S. (1991). *The Radicalism of the American Revolution.* New York: Vintage.

Yashar, Deborah J. (1996). "Indigenous Protest and Democracy in Latin America," in Jorge I. Dominguez and Abraham Lowenthal, eds., *Constructing Democratic Governance: Latin America and the Caribbean in the 1990s.* Baltimore: Johns Hopkins University Press, pp. 87–105.

Zald, Mayer N. (1970). *Organizational Change: The Political Economy of the YMCA.* Chicago: University of Chicago Press.

Zald, Mayer N., and Roberta Ash (1966). "Social Movement Organizations: Growth, Decay and Change," *Social Forces* 44:327–41. Also in Mayer N. Zald and John D. McCarthy, eds., *Social Movements in an Organizational Society.* New Brunswick, N.J.: Transaction, 1987, pp. 121–41.

Zald, Mayer N., and Michael A. Berger (1978). "Social Movements in Organizations: Coup d'Etat, Bureaucratic Insurgency, and Mass Movement," *American Journal of Sociology* 83: 823–61. Also in Mayer N. Zald and John D. McCarthy, eds., *Social Movements in an Organizational Society.* New Brunswick, N.J.: Transaction Books, 1987, pp. 185–222.

Zald, Mayer N., and John D. McCarthy, eds. (1987). *Social Movements in an Organizational Society.* New Brunswick, N.J.: Transaction Books.

Zdravomyslova, Elena (1996). "Opportunities and Framing in the Transition to Democracy: The Case of Russia," in Doug McAdam, John D. McCarthy, and

Mayer N. Zald, eds., *Comparative Perspectives on Social Movements.* Cambridge: Cambridge University Press, pp. 122–37.

Zolberg, Aristide R. (1972). "Moments of Madness," *Politics and Society* 2:183–207.

(1978). "Belgium," in Raymond Grew, ed., *Crises of Political Development in Europe and the United States.* Princeton: Princeton University Press, pp. 99–138.

INDEX

CAMBRIDGE STUDIES IN COMPARATIVE POLITICS